M000170322

AUTOCRACY RISING

AUTOCRACY RISING

How Venezuela Transitioned to Authoritarianism

JAVIER CORRALES

BROOKINGS INSTITUTION PRESS
Washington, D.C.

Copyright © 2022
THE BROOKINGS INSTITUTION
1775 Massachusetts Avenue, N.W.
Washington, D.C. 20036
www.brookings.edu

All rights reserved. No part of this publication may be reproduced or transmitted in any form or by any means without permission in writing from the Brookings Institution Press.

The Brookings Institution is a private nonprofit organization devoted to research, education, and publication on important issues of domestic and foreign policy. Its principal purpose is to bring the highest quality independent research and analysis to bear on current and emerging policy problems. Interpretations or conclusions in Brookings publications should be understood to be solely those of the authors.

Library of Congress Control Number: 2022931974
ISBN 9780815738077 (pbk)
ISBN 9780815738084 (ebook)

9 8 7 6 5 4 3 2 1

Typeset in Adobe Garamond Pro

Composition by Elliott Beard

To all victims of autocratization

Contents

Preface

In 2015, when Michael Penfold and I published the second edition of *Dragon in the Tropics*, our study of Venezuela's transition to semi-authoritarianism in the 2000s, we could foresee that the regime was turning increasingly autocratic over time. Back then, we were unsure about what would become of this turn, but we did venture a guess about what was prompting it. We argued that the ruling party transferred by President Hugo Chávez to his successor, Nicolás Maduro, was losing electoral ground. Venezuela's famous competitive-authoritarian regime was becoming less competitive electorally, and therefore was turning more authoritarian.

Two things changed significantly since the early 2010s, one at the level of the case, and the other, at the level of theory. At the level of the case, the opposition to *Chavismo* would actually manage to gain renewed strength, and the economy would plunge to record lows. The ruling party lost even more competitiveness than we had imagined. Defying this context, the regime still managed to stay the course in its path toward deeper authoritarianism. By almost every measure used by political scientists, Venezuela under Nicolás Maduro became one of the most autocratic nations on earth. Also, one of the poorest.

Second, at the level of theory, the study of democratic backsliding and autocratization experienced a boom in the field of political science. By the mid-2010s, scholars were noticing that not just Venezuela, but many other democracies were turning less democratic, and many semi-authoritarian regimes were turning more autocratic. Attention to backsliding and autocratization expanded.

As a result of this scholarly boom, theories proliferated. Scholars began to offer increasingly more powerful and nuanced theories to explain different aspects of democratic backsliding. In 2015, Ellen Lust and David Waldner issued their famous white paper "Unwelcome Change: Understanding, Evaluating, and Extending Theories of Democratic Backsliding," listing no less than six families of theories, each with different subcomponents, to explain backsliding. These families of theories covered every angle: political leadership, political culture, political institutions, political economy, political coalitions, and international factors. Scholars had their work cut out for them: the challenge was no longer just to describe and analyze democratic backsliding and autocratization but also to offer and test theories about them.

This book addresses these two developments since the mid-2010s. It is first an effort to bring the study of the political regime in Venezuela up to date, that is, to document and explain the rise of a brutal autocracy in the 2010s. It is also an effort to connect the study of regime dynamics in Venezuela with more recent theories of democratic backsliding worldwide.

Any reader familiar with *Dragon in the Tropics* will recognize that this book, *Autocracy Rising*, revisits many themes and events from the Chávez era, but is in reality more focused on what has happened since Chávez. In addition, readers will notice that *Autocracy Rising* is perhaps more theoretical-minded in that it tries to advance one particular theory of democratic backsliding. It is also a bit more comparative, with some sections offering implicit or explicit references to trends elsewhere in the region. One full chapter is devoted to comparisons with Nicaragua, Colombia, and Ecuador.

The theory proposed here refines the concept of declining competitiveness among semi-authoritarian regimes. It seeks to explain autocratization by drawing from theories on party systems and state capacity. Specifically, I take further the concept of power asymmetry that I develop in my 2018 book, *Fixing Democracy*; this time I pay more attention to degrees of fragmentation of the opposition. I also develop further the concept of autocratic legalism and its links to theories of state capturing.

My hope is that political scientists find my theoretical propositions compelling. And for all other readers who care less about political science debates, my hope is that they not be too put off by this book's overt attempt at theory development. I also hope that readers notice that, despite covering the grim subject of a rising dictatorship, this book is also an account of how the forces of democratic resistance in Venezuela continue to fight and refuse to die.

Acknowledgments

In writing *Autocracy Rising*, I have acquired a long list of debts. I would like to express my heartfelt gratitude to all the people and institutions who have inspired and shaped the ideas for this book.

First, I would like to express my gratitude to a large community of scholars on Latin American politics and democratic backsliding, whose work has been enormously influential to my own thinking. For the past decade, I have been privileged to receive a number of invitations from colleagues at other universities to give talks, participate in panels, attend workshops, and read their papers. The aim of these invitations was to discuss and debate populism, democratic backsliding, and autocratization in Venezuela, Latin America, or elsewhere. These invitations have been too numerous to list in this preface, but I want to acknowledge that every single one of them left a lasting imprint on my thinking. They offered me opportunities to hear new questions, clarify and refine my own arguments, and sometimes even rethink my conclusions.

Much of this book was written during the pandemic. And while the pandemic gave us many travails, it gave us the gift of Zoom. Zoom was a godsend for this book.

One of the ways in which Zoom helped this book is that it gave me the chance to interact more closely and frequently with the community of scholars who write actively on contemporary Venezuela. One example was a series of monthly meetings organized by Cindy Arnson and Michael Penfold at the Woodrow Wilson Center in Washington, D.C. These meetings gathered top Venezuelanists, including Paul Angelo, Guillermo Aveledo, Bram Ebus, Philip Gunson, Marihen Jiménez, Miriam Kornblith, Margarita López-Maya, Abe Lowenthal, Jennifer McCoy, Keith Mines, Francisco Monaldi, Asdrúbal Olivares, Joy Olson, John Polga-Hecimovich, Francisco Rodríguez, Rocío San Miguel, David Smilde, Harold Trinkunas, Leonardo Vera,

Verónica Zubillaga, among others. I am most grateful to Miguel Ángel Santos, at Harvard University's Growth Lab, Gerardo González, at IESA (Caracas), and Jeremy McDermott, at Insight Crime, for sharing data.

There were many other Zoom meetings. All of them allowed me to listen and talk to many brilliant colleagues. So yes, thank you, Zoom.

Thank you also to various academic journals that gave me the opportunity to publish earlier versions of arguments about democratic backsliding in general and Venezuela's descent into autocracy in particular. Specifically, the *Journal of Democracy* published a piece on autocratic legalism (Corrales 2015) and another on Maduro's survival (Corrales 2020a); the *European Review of Latin American and Caribbean Studies* published a piece on backsliding and electoral irregularities (Corrales 2020b); the *Journal of Energy Policy* published a piece on executive aggrandizement over the oil sector (Corrales et al. 2020); and *Tribuna: Revista de Asuntos Públicos* published a piece on Venezuela's economic crisis (Corrales 2017). I am also grateful to the *New York Times, Foreign Policy,* and *Americas Quarterly* for publishing various op-eds discussing democratic backsliding topics throughout the Americas. All these publishing opportunities gave me the chance to rehearse ideas and receive important feedback from editors and reviewers, all of which directly or indirectly influenced this book.

I am especially grateful to my home institution, Amherst College, and my colleagues in the Department of Political Science for supporting my research. Theresa and Steve Laizer, thank you for all your support while I was chairing. Thank you also, Barbara Hogenboom, and the entire faculty and staff of the Center for Latin American Research and Documentation (CEDLA), at the University of Amsterdam, for always inviting me as a visiting fellow. CEDLA is a great place to do some writing, and Amsterdam is a great city for biking, which helps me with my writing.

I would also like to thank several people who provided valuable comments on earlier drafts of this project. Scott Morgenstern and Aníbal Pérez-Liñán in particular have been intellectual partners. In the spring of 2021, we started collaborating on ways to expand some of the theories in this book into a larger study. Interacting with them has been transformative.

In addition, Angus Berwick, Benedicte Bull, Katrina Burgess, Larry Diamond, Gonzalo Hernández Jiménez, Barbara Hogenboom, Bob Kaufman, Mariana Llanos, Leiv Marsteintredet, Francisco Monaldi, Michael Penfold, John Polga-Hecimovich, Antulio Rosales, Franz von Bergen, and Julienne Weegels have offered comments on various parts of this manuscript. I am most grateful to Miguel Ángel Santos, at Harvard University's Growth Lab, Gerardo González, at IESA (Caracas), and Jeremy McDermott, at Insight Crime, for sharing data with me. Thank you, Bill Finan, at Brookings

Institution Press, for believing in this project from the start, for your support during the writing process, and for getting me fantastic reviewers for my first manuscript.

Finally, I am absolutely grateful to my undergraduate students at Amherst College. They are the biggest gift of my profession. At Amherst, I teach various courses that address questions of democracy in general and in Latin America more specifically. In those courses, I try to give students the opportunity to write on many of the subjects covered in this book. These undergraduates turned out to be unofficial research assistants. My work draws significantly from the many analytical essays, literature reviews, research papers, senior theses, and research notes that many of these undergraduates produced over the years. I truly mean it when I say that I too learn from my students. These students are Dayla R. Ackerman, Jordan Aucoin, Viraj Ayar, Brian Behen, Robert L. Casey, Philip Corbo, Vivian Cordon, Bayard T. DeMallie, Lance Duncan, Jack P. Elvekrog, Caroline L. Fischer, Conner Glynn, Telmo D. Gonzalez, Alex Hartwich, Ian Herel, Alexandre Jabor, Blue S. Kirkpatrick, Kendall Kurlander, Griffin Lessell, Ellie K. Lundberg, Erin McClave, Sarah C. Montoya, Grayson A. Mugford, Jack M. Patton, Gordon Powers, Chris Rivera, Pedro M. Sánchez, Logan Seymour, Jack Siegel, Emmy H. Sohn, Carolyn Thomas, Jack B. Vander Vort, Stefan Walzer-Goldfeld, and Matthew Walsh.

Five undergraduates in particular deserve special recognition: Scott Brasesco, Alexander Jabor, Gordon Powers, Guillermo Rodríguez, and Martin Wilkinson. Through the financial generosity of Amherst College, my home institution, I was able to hire them as research assistants for this book. They each worked on different parts of this manuscript on a number of tasks, always with the best disposition. They are brilliant; devoted; imaginative; and, thankfully for me, graciously tolerant of my quirks. They always delivered far more than I could hope for. They are real intellectual partners.

I also want to thank my enormously talented nieces, Viviana Vela and Valeria Vela, for their help with references and data, and my sister Mabel and her husband René, for letting them take time out of their busy school schedules to help me. My mother, Mirta Corrales, is always an inspiration. Despite having no training in political science, she can talk and think like a political scientist. Finally, I want to thank my partner, Bob Hemmer, for all his advice over the years. Bob never minds when I talk about my work incessantly, or when I prefer "not to go there."

Being exposed to criticisms is one way we can get better at what we do. I therefore want to thank everyone who has challenged me to be better at my work. However, I also want to thank anyone who has said positive things to me or about me. All those words helped.

1

Introduction

PARTY SYSTEMS, INSTITUTIONAL CAPTURING, AND AUTOCRATIZATION

In this book, I present a theory on the origins and evolution of what political scientists call "democratic backsliding," the process whereby an existing democracy, through actions of a democratically elected executive branch, experiences decline in its democratic institutions (Haggard and Kaufman 2021:1). I focus on Venezuela since the 1990s, as a stand-alone case and in comparison.

Venezuela's process of democratic backsliding between 1999 and 2013 was typical of processes of democratic backsliding worldwide: a popularly elected president manages to undermine the system of checks and balances, concentrate powers, limit the ability of the opposition to compete electorally, and restrict pluralism within and outside the ruling party. But thereafter, the process of democratic backsliding became a bit more exceptional. Under President Nicolás Maduro, from 2013 to the present, backsliding reached further than is typical in other cases of democratic backsliding: the regime became a full-fledged autocracy.

Because not all semi-authoritarian regimes descend into full-blown authoritarianism, the Venezuelan case emerges as a puzzle worth explaining. Why is it that some semi-authoritarian regimes become fully autocratic while others stabilize in that hybrid state, or even transition to democracy? This book seeks to answer this question of regime dynamics after semi-authoritarianism.

To explain Venezuela's democratic backsliding, including its transition to full autocracy, this book privileges two key variables: the evolution of the party system and institutional reservoirs at the disposal of the executive branch. Although these are not the only factors that shape democratic backsliding and autocratization, they deserve a bit more scholarly attention than they have received.

The first part of my argument is that in democracies where the party system explodes or implodes, democratic backsliding is more likely. Specifically, if the party system acquires the characteristics of asymmetrical party fragmentation, in which the ruling party becomes strong and united while the opposition splinters into multiple and disorganized factions, then a president intent on concentrating power has the advantage. Asymmetrical party system fragmentation (APSF) is a permissive condition of democratic backsliding.

But halfway through this process of backsliding, the party system in Venezuela became, somewhat unpredictably, less asymmetrical. The opposition regained electoral strength starting in 2007. I not only explain this unexpected rerise of the opposition but also theorize about its effects. More specifically, I argue that a rerise of the opposition, essentially an easing of APSF, brings semi-authoritarian regimes to a critical juncture: either negotiate some form of liberalization, or turn more autocratic. The Venezuelan regime chose to turn more autocratic.

Turning more autocratic, of course, did not mean that the regime would necessarily prevail. Other cases of autocratic response to rising opposition end badly for the incumbent, with the opposition sometimes toppling the president, if not the regime. But in Venezuela by 2021, the regime seems to have been able to survive the challenge posed by the opposition. This survival demands an explanation too.

Here is where I introduce my second variable of interest: institutional reservoirs. Semi-authoritarian regimes with a specific institutional reservoir are more likely to survive rising opposition pressure. This reservoir consists of having full control of the traditional tools of autocratic legalism, especially the courts and the electoral authorities, as well as the coercive apparatus (Corrales 2015). Because the regime needs to bring repression to new levels, only those semi-authoritarian regimes that already enjoy this institutional reservoir will survive the new threats posed by a rising opposition.

In the case of Venezuela, Maduro in fact inherited this formidable reservoir from his predecessor, Hugo Chávez. Maduro's challenge was to redeploy (rather than invent) this reservoir. And so he did. Because it was not necessary to invent the reservoir, the regime found it less costly and less difficult to autocratize. The available reservoir made the transition to authoritarianism less costly and, therefore, more likely.

At the same time, the Venezuelan regime also engaged in autocratic innovation, not just autocratic redeployment. One of this book's contributions is to discuss one particular autocratic innovation, which I call "function fusion": granting governing institutions or key government allies a multitude of functions in the act of repressing and co-opting.

I thus offer an explanation for a double puzzle: When should we expect a semi-authoritarian regime to turn autocratic? The answer: when the ruling party experiences a serious decline in electoral competitiveness. When does this authoritarian response succeed, meaning the regime prevails politically, survives in office, and contains the opposition? The answer: when the ruling party enjoys sufficient forms of control over the courts, the electoral bodies, and the coercive apparatus. A semi-authoritarian regime's chances of survival increase if it also engages in some degree of institutional adaptation and innovation.

The Main Case: Venezuela

Two presidents, two legislatures, two oil companies, two diplomatic corps, one country. This was the state of politics in Venezuela in 2020.

On the one hand, Venezuela had an actual president, Nicolás Maduro, a dictator. Although unrecognized by the opposition, Maduro had control of the government. He also controlled an extra-official legislative body, the Constituent National Assembly (Asamblea Nacional Constituyente, CNA), a body technically elected to draft a constitution, but which became the de facto legislature. This assembly rubber-stamped most of the regime's decisions. The government was engaged in heavy-handed repression of political leaders, protesters, and military officials who had defied Maduro. His brutality and criminal ties provoked sanctions from the United States and other countries, and prompted the largest migration in the Americas since the 1980s. Maduro also controlled Venezuela's state-owned oil company, Petróleos de Venezuela, S.A. (PDVSA), and had full support from strong autocratic states such as Cuba, China, Russia, Iran, and Turkey, among others.

On the other hand, operating under this dictatorship, Venezuela in 2020 had a powerful opposition force. The opposition was able to rise politically since its low point in 2005, and by 2015 managed to gain control of the official legislature, the National Assembly (Asamblea Nacional). The National Assembly refused to recognize Maduro's 2018 fraudulent reelection, and in 2019 appointed its new president, Juan Guaidó, as the country's interim president. The opposition also obtained control of part of the oil company, CITGO, and deployed a fairly active foreign policy, which earned it significant international allies, such as the United States, Canada, most of Latin America, and the European Union.

To be sure, these two Venezuelas were never politically equal. Maduro's Venezuela consisted of a political regime *entrenched in power* for more than two decades; Guaidó's Venezuela was a movement *hoping to seize power.* Maduro had control of many more institutions than just a quasi-legislature and an oil company. Guaidó had trouble controlling the one and only institution under his control, the legislature, and in fact, lost that control in 2020. Maduro had a disciplined ruling party whose leadership didn't publicly question his presidency. He also had the support of numerous business interests—some legal, others illicit. Guaidó, in contrast, presided over a coalition of parties in permanent danger of splitting and often producing open defections. Given the country's economic deterioration, Guaidó's Venezuela faced increasing difficulty accessing financial resources. In short, Maduro's Venezuela represented a formidable power; Guaidó's Venezuela, an aspiring power.

Despite the differences, these two Venezuelas represent a political phenomenon worth explaining: the rise of a dictatorship coexisting with an opposition that, despite shortcomings, posed serious challenges to the dictatorship. Autocratization happened in the context of resistance, and perhaps because of it.

Since its start in 2013, the Maduro regime has faced one political crisis after another, mostly the result of resistance from the opposition. Maduro barely won the presidential election of 2013. His regime lost control of the National Assembly in 2015, and it faced increasing protests before and after this election. Maduro's 2018 reelection was so fraught with irregularities that it was rejected by more than fifty countries. By the end of 2019, Maduro's approval ratings were in the low 20 percent. These setbacks are nothing if not signs of a vigorous opposition.

Yet, how has Maduro's regime been able to hang on to power? The most obvious answer is that Maduro has survived because he has turned more authoritarian. That is true. But to make this point analytically useful, we need to specify the authoritarian practices that have allowed Maduro to survive as long as he has. This book does that.

Two Puzzles and Several Comparisons

Interrupted Presidencies in Latin America and the Maduro Exception

A useful way to start examining Maduro's remarkable survival in office in the context of economic crisis and political opposition is to compare Venezuela under Maduro to cases in Latin America of interrupted presidencies (Valenzuela 2004). We know that presidents in presidential systems tend to enjoy what is known as an incumbent's advantage: when they seek reelection, they tend to win (Cuzán 2015). In Latin America, this advantage is huge. All things being equal, most presidents who run for reelection get reelected, often easily and by large margins. Only when they face deep economic crises do they struggle to get reelected.[1] Many presidents in Latin America since the 1990s have managed to change the constitution to obtain the right to reelection (Corrales 2018a), another sign of the incumbent's advantage.

However, not all presidents in Latin America since the start of the Third Democratic Wave (mid-1970s to late 1990s) have managed to complete their mandates. Scholars studying these presidential interruptions have essentially argued that they are often the result of extraordinary crises, often more than one crisis at a time (Pérez-Liñán 2005, Negretto 2006, Morgenstern et al. 2008, Llanos and Marsteintredet 2010, Marsteintredet 2014). These crises can include the following:

- *Economic crisis:* Unusually high inflation, unemployment rates, and negative growth rates for a period of time.

- *Minority status in congress:* A majority control of congress is lost following a midterm election.

- *Expanding protests:* Massive and sustained street protests take place.

- *Ruling party defections:* A significant number of party leaders, including cabinet members, withdraw their support for the government, quit their government posts, or join the opposition in congress to censure the president.

- *Constitutional crisis:* The judiciary declares that the president is acting unconstitutionally, and the president refuses to comply.

- *Military crisis:* An increasing number of high-ranking officers begin to disobey or publicly criticize the president, plot to replace the president on their own or in combination with civilian opposition forces.

- *Electoral crisis:* The ruling party suffers a serious and unexpected setback in an election, which could include winning by a smaller margin than expected, leading to internal questioning of the president within the ruling party.

- *International pressure:* Foreign actors pressure the president to cease and desist from certain policies, encourage the opposition to rebel, and refuse to provide economic aid.

Table 1-1 shows all of the presidents in Latin America who left office—or rather, were "pushed" out of office—before completing their mandates, between 1985 and 2021 (n = 23). These are cases of nonsurvival. The table shows the kind of crises associated with these early terminations. Several important observations can be made from this table.

In general, it is not easy for presidents to fall. It takes more than one type of crisis to make that happen. Except in the case of Pedro Pablo Kuczynski and perhaps that of Fernando Lugo, interrupted presidencies seem to require three or more types of crises simultaneously. Second, four types of crises tend to be more common than the others: economic crisis, losing majority-status in Congress, street protests, and ruling party splits. In combination, these crises tend to be fairly lethal.

The remarkable aspect about the Maduro regime is that by 2016 it was experiencing or was close to experiencing every one of the crises in table 1-1. And yet, the regime survived. It did so, not by turning more democratic, that is, by making concessions to the opposition, but by taking the opposite approach. The Maduro case stands as an unusual case of regime survival in a region where equally challenged regimes tend to fall.

Regime Dynamics in Latin America and Worldwide

Maduro's decision not to liberalize raises yet another puzzle: Why choose this autocratic path? Maduro inherited a semi-authoritarian regime from his predecessor (Corrales and Penfold 2015). As he began to confront resistance and thus one political crisis after another, one possible scenario would have been to negotiate with the opposition and offer some concessions, as a way to placate tensions. Such a scenario would have led to a transition to democracy, or at least, would have maintained the regime as a semi-authoritarian state. Instead, Maduro transitioned to full-fledged autocracy.

This transition to autocracy was not preordained. While autocratic consolidation is the next step after democratic backsliding (Lührmann and Lindberg 2019), not all cases of democratic backsliding in the world end up as full-fledged autocracies. In contemporary Latin America, the turn to autocracy has been especially rare.

This is clear from table 1-2, which shows regime dynamics in Latin America between 2000 and 2020. It uses V-Dem's Liberal Democracy Index and Freedom House to list countries according to regime type (democracy, hybrid, autocracy). It also shows the duration of these regimes. Only two hybrid cases experienced full transition to autocracy: Nicaragua and Venezuela. The table also shows that two semi-authoritarian regimes since the 2010s actually moved in the opposite direction, that is, became more democratic: Colombia and Ecuador. In other words, although many countries in Latin America exhibit regime durability, others show regime movement, especially hybrid regimes (Corrales and Hidalgo 2013). In addition, it is not the case that the only path after semi-authoritarianism is to plunge further into autocracy. Chapter 6 of this book is devoted entirely to explaining this variation in regime dynamics among hybrid regimes by comparing Venezuela to Nicaragua, Colombia, and Ecuador.

In fact, Venezuela's backsliding has been profound not just by Latin American standards but also by global standards. The process of democratic backsliding under *Chavismo* was, by almost any quantitative and qualitative measure, unusually steep. Figure 1-1 shows all of the democratic and semi-authoritarian regimes in the world that have experienced backsliding since the 1990s (with a starting point of 0.4 or higher in V-Dem's Liberal Democracy Index). The chart shows that only a minority of them decline to the same depth as Venezuela (below the 0.1 mark), measured in terms of distance traveled from starting point to end point. The only comparable case is Turkey under Recep Tayyip Erdoğan. Nicaragua under Daniel Ortega drops even lower than Venezuela, but it started out with weaker democracy. In other words, measured in terms of size of the drop, Venezuela is even more significant than Nicaragua. Furthermore, while there are many wealthy democracies that have experienced democratic backsliding, including the United States, very few wealthy democracies have declined as much as Venezuela.

Venezuela's autocracy also seems to defy the playbooks of conventional autocratic politics (see Smilde 2021). Linz (1964) famously argued that modern authoritarian regimes display three characteristics: (1) mentalities instead of ideology, (2) limited pluralism, and (3) limited or even predictable police and coercive powers. In Venezuela's autocracy, there certainly is an erosion of ideology, if there ever was any; however, rather than mentalities, what prevails is entitlement. The leadership of the ruling party justifies hanging on to power with no argument other than that it has the power and that it, and nobody else, deserves it. Rather than limited pluralism, the regime systematically attacks the security, and often freedoms, of nearly every nongovernment-affiliated organization. And rather than limited and predictable coercive force, there is actually an expansion of free rein and impunity for these actors.

Philip (1984), discussing South American authoritarian regimes of the 1960s and 1970s, has already argued that the region had long violated Linz's notion of limited police power. But Venezuela, as I will argue, goes further. The executive branch gives enormous latitude to not just coercive state actors but also non-state armed actors.

The one element that is still classic about Venezuela's autocracy is of course

Table 1-1. Interrupted Mandates of Elected Presidents in Latin America and Underlying Conditions, 1985–2021

President (country, year)	Type[a]	Economic crisis	Minority in Congress	Street protests	Ruling party/ Cabinet/ Coalition splits	Constitutional crisis	Military crisis	Electoral crisis	International pressure	Number of factors
1. Siles Zuazo (Bol 85)	ST	Yes	Yes	Yes	Defects	...	...	...	...	4.0
2. Alfonsín (Arg 89)	R	Yes	Senate Yes	Yes	Yes	...	Yes	...	...	4.5
3. Aristide (Hai 91)	C	Yes	Yes	Yes	Yes	...	Yes	...	...	4.0
4. Collor (Bra 92)	IT	Yes	Yes	Yes	Yes	Yes	...	...	...	5.0
5. Pérez (Ven 93)	IT	Yes	Yes	Some	Yes	...	Yes	Yes	...	5.5
6. Serrano (Gua 93)	R	Yes	Yes	Yes	Yes	Yes	...	...	Yes	6.0
7. Balaguer (DR 94-96)	ST	...	Yes	Yes	...	Yes	...	Yes	Yes	5.0
8. Bucaram (Ecu 96)	IT	Yes	Yes	Yes	Yes	...	...	...	...	4.0
9. Cubas (Par 99)	IT	...		Yes	Yes	Yes	Yes	...	...	4.0
10. Mahuad (Ecu 00)	C	Yes	Yes	Yes	Yes	...	Yes	...	...	5.0
11. Fujimori (Per 00)	R	Yes	Yes	Yes	...	Yes	Yes	Yes	...	5.0
12. de la Rúa (Arg 01)	R	Yes	Yes	Yes	Yes	...	...	Yes	Yes	6.0
13. Chávez (Ven 02)[b]	R/C	Yes	...	Yes	...	Yes	Yes	...	...	4.0
14. Sánchez de Lozada (Bol 03)[c]	R	Yes	Yes	Yes	Yes	...	...	...	...	4.0
15. Aristide (Hai 04)	C	Yes	...	Yes	Yes	...	...	...	...	3.0
16. Gutiérrez (Ecu 05)	IT	Yes	Yes	Yes	Yes	...	...	...	...	4.0
17. Zelaya (Hon 09)	IT/C	...	Yes	...	Yes	Yes	Yes	Yes	...	5.0

18. Lugo (Par 12)	IT	...	Yes	Some	Yes	...	...	2.5
19. Pérez Molina (Gua 15)	IT	...	Yes	Yes	Apparently	...	Yes	4.0
20. Rousseff (Bra 16)	IT	Yes	Yes	Yes	Partial	...	...	3.5
21. Kuczynski (Per 19)	IT	...	Yes	...	...	...	...	1.0
22. Morales (Bol 19)	C	...	...	Yes	...	Yes	Yes	4.0
23. Moïse (Hai 21)	A	Yes	Yes	Yes	...	Yes	?[d]	6.0

Notes: Bol = Bolivia; Arg = Argentina; Hai = Haiti; Bra = Brazil; Ven = Venezuela; Gua = Guatemala; DR = Dominican Republic; Ecu = Ecuador; Par = Paraguay; Per = Peru; Hon = Honduras; . . . (three periods) = not applicable.

a. Types include ST = Shortening of term (i.e., the president was pressured to); R = Resignations; C = Coups or heavy military pressure; IT = Impeachment or impeachment threat; A = Assassination.

b. Chávez is the only president on this list who was restored to power.

c. Sánchez de Lozada's successor, Carlos Mesa, also resigned prematurely, but he is not listed here because he was not democratically elected.

d. Although Moïse was assassinated by paramilitary forces (mostly foreign mercenaries), the level of official military involvement remains unclear.

Sources: Valenzuela (2004); Marsteintredet (2014); Llanos and Marsteintredet (2010); Pérez-Liñán (2007); Negretto (2006).

Table 1-2. Political Regime Changes in Latin America and the Caribbean, 2000–2020

Stable democracies (more than 15 years in which r > 0.5)	Democracies that declined (changed from r > 0.5 to 0.1< r < 0.5)	Hybrid regimes that improved (changed from 0.1 < r < 0.5 to r > 0.5)	Stable hybrid regimes (more than 15 years in which 0.1 < r < 0.5)	Hybrid regimes that transition to autocracy (changed from: 0.1 < r < 0.5 to r < 0.1)	Autocracies that improved (changed from r < 0.1 to 0.1 < r < 0.5)	Stable autocracies (more than 15 years in which r < 0.1)
Antigua and Barbuda	Bolivia (2006–)	Colombia (2012–)	Dominican Republic	Nicaragua (2018–)	Haiti (2006–)	Cuba
Argentina	Ecuador (2007–2018)	Ecuador (2019–)	El Salvador	Venezuela (2017–)		
Bahamas	Mexico (2007–)	Mexico (2001–2007)	Guatemala			
Barbados	Paraguay (2013–)	Paraguay (2011–2012)	Honduras			
Belize						
Brazil						
Chile						
Costa Rica						
Dominica						
Grenada						
Jamaica						
Panama						
Peru (2002–)						
St. Kitts and Nevis						
St. Lucia						
St. Vincent and the Grenadines						
Suriname						
Trinidad and Tobago						
Uruguay						

Notes:

r = range

Democracies: Countries scoring 0.5 or higher.

Hybrid regimes: Countries scoring between 0.5 and 0.1.

Authoritarian regimes: Countries scoring below 0.1.

Sources: V-Dem Liberal Democracy Index (2021), with Caribbean nations not covered by V-Dem scored using Freedom House (2021).

Figure 1-1. Democratic Backsliding: Countries Experiencing Continuous Declines in Liberal Democracy Scores, 1990–2019

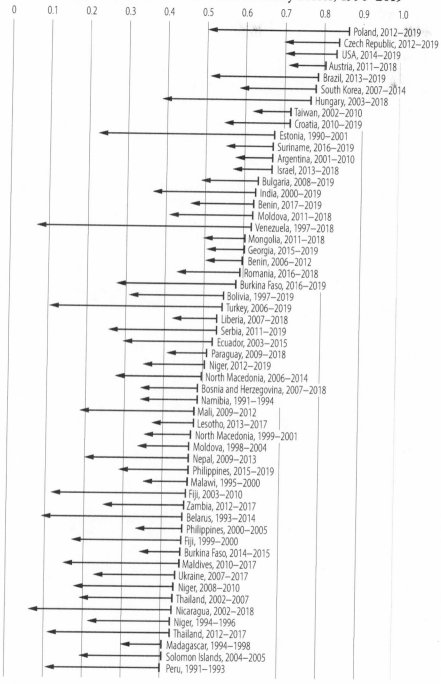

Source: V-Dem Liberal Democracy Index 2020, www.v-dem.net/en/online-graphing.

Note: Figure includes all countries that experienced a 10 percent decline or more uninterruptedly. Each line indicates the year the decline started, the starting level in terms of liberal democracy, and how far the country backslid.

the arbitrariness of power and its ability to constantly adapt to political challenges, more so than to economic challenges. It survives political challenges by always innovating the way it both co-opts and represses potential rivals (Frantz and Mogenbesser 2017, Frantz 2018). This book discusses the origins and effects of these survival-driven toolkit innovations.

The Argument

To explain backsliding, autocratization, and regime survival, this book invokes two types of variables: party system features and executive-driven institutional capturing (figure 1-2).

Figure 1-2. The Argument

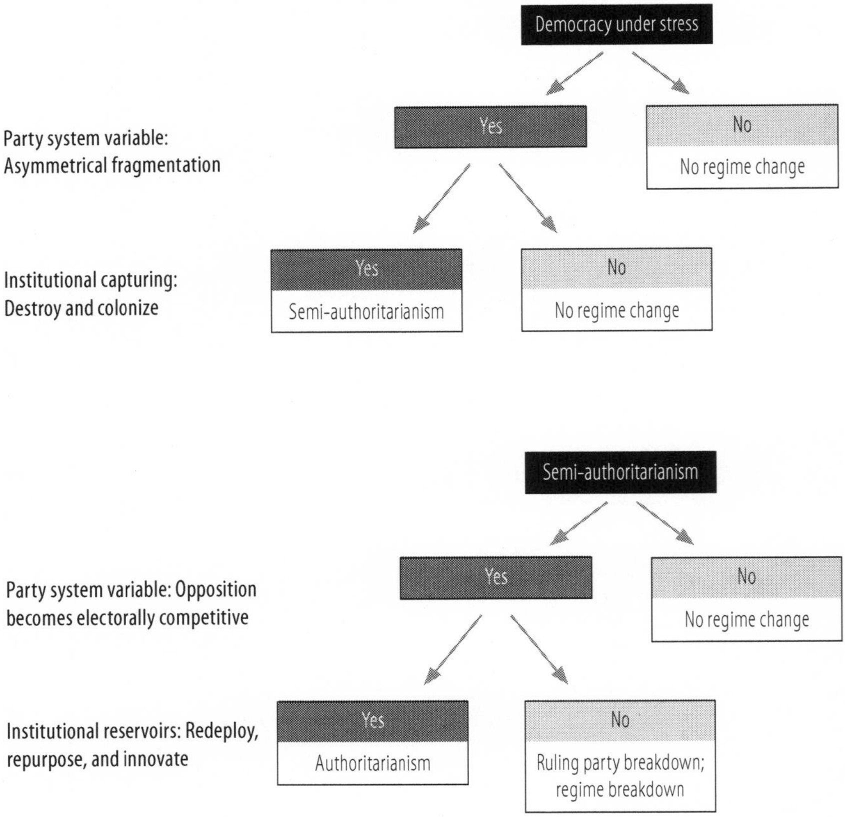

Party system variable:
Asymmetrical fragmentation

Democracy under stress

Yes / No — No regime change

Institutional capturing:
Destroy and colonize

Yes — Semi-authoritarianism / No — No regime change

Semi-authoritarianism

Party system variable: Opposition
becomes electorally competitive

Yes / No — No regime change

Institutional reservoirs: Redeploy,
repurpose, and innovate

Yes — Authoritarianism / No — Ruling party breakdown;
regime breakdown

Source: Author.

The first part of the argument is that democratic backsliding is more likely under conditions of APSF. By this I mean the emergence of a ruling party that is electorally strong and unified with an opposition that is fragmented or uncompetitive. An illiberal president who comes to power under conditions of APSF will have an easier time engaging in democratic backsliding.

One mechanism of backsliding is what is known as "executive aggrandizement" (Bermeo 2016), whereby the executive branch undermines the system of checks and the rule of law. Another mechanism is called "executive degradation of rights" (Diamond 2015), whereby the executive branch places restrictions on the opposition, hampering its ability to compete for office. When executive aggrandizement and political rights degradation are achieved, and the ruling party maintains electoral appeal, the regime is typically known as semi-authoritarian or competitive authoritarian (Levitsky and Way 2002). A mixture of democratic institutions (e.g., elections, some press freedoms, some freedom of association) coexist with an executive branch and a ruling party that often act with impunity, and thus, with quasi-dictatorial powers. The opposition, in contrast, experiences diminishing legal recourse. Democratic backsliding dominated Venezuelan politics under President Hugo Chávez (1999–2013).

Democratic backsliding is induced by APSF. Under this type of party system, the ruling party enjoys all the power advantage to enact regime change. Before backsliding, fragmented party systems create opportunities for new parties to rise to the top (Mainwring et al. 2017). Many times, these new parties tend to be "anti-establishment" (Casal Bértoa and Rama 2020), and are therefore potential candidates to engage in backsliding. If they win office and if the party system fragmentation becomes asymmetrical, that is, affecting only the opposition, then backsliding is likely because the ruling party has a higher chance of asserting itself (Jones 2010). When the opposition is either "feeble" because it is too small, or it is too large but in "disarray" because it is too divided, the president prevails (Morgenstern et al. 2008). In addition, fragmentation of the opposition hampers two of the mechanisms through which backsliding can be stopped: a united front at the legislature to block the executive's agenda and a united front at election time (Bernhard et al. 2020). And even though most processes of democratic backsliding lead to polarization (a huge ideological divide between government and the opposition), often this polarization is not enough to counteract APSF. Divisions in the opposition regarding best strategy to pursue and candidates to present can persist even if different factions/groups within the opposition share an animosity toward the government. In other words, even in polarized systems, the opposition can still be divided, which may explain why polarization is often associated with the ability of the executive to engage in democratic backsliding rather than with the ability of the opposition to stop it (Corrales 2005, 2011, Enyedi 2016).

The next question is what does the state do with the power advantage conferred by APSF. For democratic backsliding to occur, the president must destroy or colonize the liberal democratic institutions his regime has inherited (Freeman 2020). This is the second part of the argument. Destroying institutions consists of abolishing them, of course, but can also include other less drastic steps such as turning institutions inoperative or inconsequential. Colonization refers to populating institutions designed to be independent with loyal partisans aligned with the president (Müller 2016). Important targets of this process of institutional colonization, I argue, are the courts and the electoral authorities. Control of courts is essential for the regime to engage in autocratic legalism, defined as the use, abuse, and lack of use of the law to extend presidential powers (Corrales 2015, Scheppele 2018). Control of electoral authorities is essential in engaging in electoral irregularities to maintain an uneven playing field during elections (Levitsky and Way 2006).

If one of these variables—APSF or capturing of key state and coercive institutions—is missing, the regime is less likely to experience democratic backsliding. It might remain a flawed democracy, maybe even a gridlocked or perhaps unstable democracy, but it is unlikely to transition to semi-authoritarianism.

During the last part of the Chávez administration (2010–2013) and the first Maduro administration (2013–2018), Venezuela experienced the deeper stage of autocratization, a transition from semi-authoritarianism to full-fledged autocracy. The regime eliminated the few democratic spaces that were still available. Between 2015 and 2016, a threshold was crossed when the regime effectively illegalized the democratically elected Congress held by the opposition and blocked a widespread citizen's movement calling for a constitutionally allowable recall referendum.

This process of deep autocratization also depended on party variables and institutional capturing, but the causal mechanisms differ from what was the case under the earlier stages of democratic backsliding. Autocratization is more likely if the ruling party loses electoral competitiveness and the opposition rises. At this point, the bargaining leverage changes to favor the opposition. This does not necessarily mean that the ruling party experiences a breakdown. Losing electoral competitiveness is not the same as party breakdown, if breakdown is defined as "a massive electoral defeat for an established party in a single electoral cycle" (Lupu 2016:5). In Venezuela, the ruling party has not experienced a massive defeat. It has instead lost competitiveness to the opposition.

By definition, a party system characterized by declining ruling party competitiveness does not give the ruling party the *power* to prevail, at least electorally. What this new party system gives the ruling party is an *incentive* to take desperate measures. This party system makes the ruling party realize it faces an existential threat. It knows it can no longer prevail electorally, even with basic electoral irregularities. One way the ruling party can hang on to power is to become more autocratic.

But becoming more autocratic is only possible if two additional conditions are met: (1) sufficient autocratic institutional reservoirs at the regime's disposal, and (2) the ability to redeploy those reservoirs to confront the specific crises that might arrive. In other words, institutional reservoirs must be adapted to incoming challenges. And the adaptation has to be specific. Responses have to be tailor-made to address the variety of challenges the regime confronts. If this form of adaptation does not occur, the more likely scenario is ruling party breakdown (huge electoral loss in an election cycle) or even regime collapse (e.g., pacted transition to democracy, interrupted presidency).

Figure 1-2 presents a diagram of the argument, and table 1-3 summarizes the causal mechanisms. Whereas transitions to semi-authoritarianism are more likely under APSF, transitions to autocracy are more likely when the asymmetry flips in favor of the opposition. In the former, the party system provides the ruling party the power to act; in the latter, the party system provides the ruling party the urgency to act autocratically. For autocracy to occur, the state must count on institutional capturing and engage in innovation, of sorts. These two variables help us understand Venezuela's regime dynamics from democracy in 1999 to full-fledged authoritarianism two decades later.

What are the key institutions that the executive branch must control to be able to autocratize? The first is the courts, since that allows the state to engage in autocratic legalism. During the early backsliding stage, autocratic legalism is used mostly to expand the powers of the executive branch. During the autocratic stage, it is used mostly to justify repression and the disbanding of organizations, such as parties and even the legislature. The second institution is the electoral authorities. This reservoir is essential since it allows the regime to commit flagrant electoral irregularities, which are needed when the ruling party loses electoral competitiveness. Finally, the state must have full control of the coercive apparatus, which is needed to deal with the expansion of protest.

In the case of Maduro, these institutional reservoirs were in place when he came to power. And thus when APSF changed and the opposition posed an existential threat to the regime, the regime had the right tools to respond autocratically. And it did. Maduro used the regime's inherited control of the courts to disarm the legislature (2016–2017), to legally justify the repression of protests (in 2014 and 2017), and to arrest high-profile political leaders. He also used his control of electoral authorities and electoral regulations, also inherited from the past regime, to block an election (recall referendum), to rig an election (for a new Constituent National Assembly), to prevent a credible electoral audit of elections (the 2018 presidential elections), and to ban or behead political parties (especially for the 2021 legislative election). And, finally, Maduro used the regime's control of the coercive apparatus, including non-state armed actors, to bring repression of dissent—within and outside the ruling party—to depths not seen in Latin America since the era of military juntas in the late 1970s.

The rest of the book builds on this argument, by parts. The first three chapters explain the change in party systems starting in the 1990s, and then the rise of the opposition starting in 2007 (chapters 2–4). Here, party system change will become the dependent variable. The book then turns to how the regime made use of institutional reservoirs to survive party-system challenges.

Plan of the Book

Chapter 2 discusses democratic backsliding theoretically and in the context of Venezuela and how changes in the party system shaped this process. It begins by reviewing politics before Chavismo, and in particular the debate about whether Venezuela was experiencing democratic decay or not. It then examines the concept of democratic backsliding to show that it is conceptually different than democratic decay because it is executive-driven, and encompasses assaults on all three fundamental pillars of democracy (minimal, liberal, and participatory institutions), rather than just a few institutions. Backsliding also makes more use of autocratic legalism. Carrión (2021) describes the whole process as a "tsunami moment" (the rise of a powerful ruling party) that morphs into a "Hobbesian moment," in which the ruling party engages in blatant power grabs. Chapter 2 then shows the aspects of backsliding that make it hard to discern at first: not every institution is attacked at the same time or with the same level of intensity, and all is justified with a discourse of liberation (from previous political maladies). This leads to polarization, with some groups actually supporting the new regime. The chapter then shows how APSF explains backsliding in Venezuela. The chapter concludes with a discussion of the aspects of backsliding that seem to be less universal and more case-specific; in the case of Chavismo, these sui generis features included leftist populism, militarism, consumption boom, social spending, and attacks on the private sector.

Because backsliding can adopt different characteristics, and because APSF can evolve during the process of backsliding, the politics of what happens

Table 1-3. Explaining Autocratization: Parties and Institutional Capturing

Starting regime	Dependent variable 1 and causal mechanism: Party system	Dependent variable 2 and causal mechanism: Institutional capturing	Regime outcome
	Democratic backsliding (Hugo Chávez, 1999–2007)		
Liberal democracy under stress	**Variable:** Pro-incumbent, asymmetrical party system fragmentation	**Variable:** (1) destroy or (2) colonize liberal democratic institutions	Semi-authoritarianism
	Causal mechanism: Grants the executive branch the power to carry out an ambitious agenda of regime change; opposition lacks bargaining leverage to block the president	**Causal mechanism:** Diminish the ability of organized opposition to compete or hold the president accountable	
	Transition to Authoritarianism (Hugo Chávez and Nicolás Maduro, 2007–2019)		
Semi-authoritarian	**Variable:** Rising opposition: The opposition becomes more electorally competitive than the ruling party.	**Variable:** Institutional reservoir: (1) Redeploy and repurpose, custom-tailor, and (2) innovate (e.g., function fusion)	Autocracy
	Causal mechanism: Executive branch incentivized to take desperate measures to survive in office	**Causal mechanism:** Repress dissent and reward the selectorate	

Source: Author.

after backsliding can vary from case to case. In Venezuela, APSF started to ease during the last years of Hugo Chávez and the first years of Nicolás Maduro. López-Maya (2016) called this moment—when *Chavistas* begin to lose competitiveness and nonetheless persist with their top-heavy approach to governance—"the twilight of Chavismo." This turning point in APSF gave rise to tougher forms of autocratization. However, my point is not that one regime died and a new and different one emerged. As I will show, the rise of autocracy was a natural evolution from what came before—the new regime used the institutional inheritance of autocratic tools that existed in the previous hybrid regime.

Because variations in APSF are posited to affect the evolution of democratic backsliding, it is important to explain the change in party system in the last part of the Chávez administration and throughout the Maduro administration. I offer two causes: economic deterioration and opposition strategies.

Chapter 3 focuses on the first cause: Venezuela's world-historic economic crash. By 2010, Venezuela started to experience what soon became the most dramatic economic collapse outside of war. Between 2013 and 2019, the economy contracted by 65 percent (Werner 2020). By all accounts, this is one of the most spectacular economic contractions in history. This chapter describes the different dimensions of this implosion: how it unfolded, its severity compared to other such crises, and its impact on society. This contraction, eventually, produced a decline in electoral support for the ruling party. This is not surprising. What is surprising is why the regime did little to reverse the crisis. To understand this, one needs to understand how the regime actually gained politically from the model in place. I describe the model as an imbalance of controls in relation to states and markets.[2] Venezuela under Hugo Chávez adopted a model of development predicated on few controls, if any, on the state, juxtaposed with excessive and stifling controls on the market. This asymmetry of controls typically leads to a number of failures in both the public and private sectors—so-called state and market failures (Kaufman and Stallings 1991, Edwards 2012, Kingstone 2018)—and Venezuela was no exception. Despite these failures, the model was nonetheless favorable to state office-holders: it allowed the state to reward loyalists, divide the private sector through the use of rewards and punishments, and transfer costs to potential challengers. This explains why Maduro has done little to introduce corrective measures.

Chapter 4 turns to the second and perhaps more important explanation for the rise of the opposition: specific party-building strategies to solve electoral decline and international isolation (Levitsky et al. 2016). The opposition's rise was not just the result of capitalizing on bad economics or government mistakes. The rise was due mostly to moves made to achieve coalition-building, electoral unity, mobilization, links with social movements and different income groups, institutional guardianship, and relations with international allies (Álvarez and Hidalgo 2020) These moves allowed the Venezuelan opposition to flip the APSF in its favor. The opposition acquired electoral dominance in relation to the ruling party and was able to place the regime in a number of serious political crises.

But Maduro did not fall, and the opposition under Maduro, after rising, started to stagnate. What explains this stagnation, or conversely, what explains Maduro's remarkable ability to survive. The argument for Maduro's survival, like the argument for the opposition's rise, is made in two parts: first, the regime deployed the traditional tools of autocracy (chapters 5 and 6); and, second, the regime invented new tools (chapter 7).

Chapter 5 discusses how Maduro survived by redeploying traditional autocratic reservoirs inherited from Chávez. Maduro updated these reservoirs and retargeted them to address new crises. By 2016, Maduro was facing, or was close to facing, all of the previously discussed threats that can lead to an interrupted presidency. As crises multiplied, Maduro made the decision to respond to each with institutions or policies that violate principles of democracy. Table 1-4 offers a summary of these crises and the state's response. These responses (except the one pertaining to international ties) are simply unavailable to democratic administrations—they would either be illegal or completely repudiated by veto players in democracies. A conventional democracy, therefore, would have experienced collapse or negotiated some resolution with the opposition. But in Venezuela, the state enjoyed a formidable capacity to respond autocratically because of its reservoirs. Specifically, the state had (1) an authoritarian-institutional inheritance: preexisting authoritarian practices and laws that could be adapted to deal with the new challenges; and (2) an authoritarian intention: to prevent at all costs the return of the opposition to power. These reservoirs allowed Maduro to contain the crises or, at least, to protect his regime from succumbing to them. In the process, the expansion in levels and reach of these responses transformed the semi-authoritarian regime into a full authoritarian regime.

Chapter 6 turns to other cases to show the applicability of this book's argument. Arguments are more credible when they can explain more than just one case. For that reason, chapter 6 looks at three cases of democratic backsliding, each with different outcomes: Nicaragua under Daniel Ortega, Colombia under Álvaro Uribe and then Juan Manuel Santos, and Ecuador under Rafael Correa and then Lenín Moreno. Initially, all three cases move into, or stay comfortably within, semi-authoritarian conditions. However, they vary in terms of what follows. Autocratization became severe under Ortega, as in Venezuela. This is the case that resembles the Venezuelan case the

**Table 1-4. Autocracy Rising: Governance Crisis and the
State's Institutional Response, 2010–2021**

Type of crisis (actual or imminent) 2013–2021	Institutional response	Democratic principle violated
Constitutional	Judicial shield (packing the courts; provisional judges)	Separation of power; judicial independence
Minority in Congress	Skirt Congress; establish parallel body (Constituent Assembly)	No self-coups
Electoral decline	Increase electoral irregularities	Free and fair elections; electoral integrity
Economic crisis; collapse of oil industry	Heightened cronyism; conditional welfare assistance; reliance on criminal syndicates	Participatory democracy; impartiality of state institutions
Street protests	Repress by using the military and paramilitaries	Basic human rights; freedom of association and speech; subordination of armed forces to the rule of law
Military defections	Militarization of the economy; coup-proofing; internal espionage	No nonelected tutelary actors; professionalism of the armed forces
Ruling party defections	Impunity for party loyalists	Equal treatment of political parties; separation of state and party
International pressure	Strengthen ties with autocracies, illicit traders, and drug dealers	Adherence to norms of transparency and the rule of law in foreign policy; congressional oversight of foreign relations

Source: Author.

most. In contrast to Venezuela, however, autocratization after Uribe and Correa actually reversed under their successors. Chapter 6 shows how changes in APSF and authoritarian-institutional reservoirs explain this variation in transitions into and from semi-autocracy.

Although I make the case that Venezuela's starting conditions (semi-authoritarianism) resemble those of Nicaragua, Colombia, Ecuador, and many others, I also recognize that there is one aspect of the politics of Venezuela's transition from semi-authoritarianism that was a bit more distinct: the role of external economic sanctions. Starting in 2017, and especially after 2019, the United States, with support from Canada, the European Union, and many Latin American countries, began to impose severe sanctions on Venezuela's financial transactions and oil trade. This significantly aggravated the economic contraction, to a point unmatched by any of the cases in chapter 6. Nicaragua also experienced sanctions, but not as severely as Venezuela. How did the regime in Venezuela manage to survive the added economic pressure stemming from sanctions?

Chapter 7 argues that the state not only updated, repurposed, and escalated classic autocratic tools (as argued in chapter 5) but also engaged in institutional innovation. Specifically, the regime engaged in what I call "function fusion." This is the second important tool used by Maduro to survive. Function fusion consists of granting existing institutions the ability to perform a variety of functions typically reserved for other institutions and at times even outside the law. This innovation actually originated in Cuba, which is not surprising, since Cuba is the one case of autocratic survival in the Americas in the context of external economic sanctions. Venezuela took Cuba's concept of function fusion to new levels. In particular, function fusion under Maduro involved the following:

- The military acquired civilian and business functions.

- Organized civilian groups acquired quasi-military and criminal functions.

- The Constituent National Assembly acquired the combined function of legislature and ruling party.

- Judges were allowed to become state contractors.

- Party officials in subnational offices were allowed to become mini-dictators.

- The state shared sovereignty with foreign armies.

Function fusion means that the regime is adapting the concept of multitasking in the service of twenty-first-century authoritarianism. Whereas traditional autocratic practices essentially exist to repress dissent, function fusion is deployed to repress but also to keep the governing coalition content with the status quo. In thinking about the governing coalition, I follow Bueno de Mesquita and Smith's (2011) idea of the winning coalition or the "influentials": those few actors from within and outside the state that keep a ruler in power. With each new task, function fusion grants greater powers and reach to existing members of the winning coalition.

Function fusion is one way that the regime uses institutions to signal that it is committed to "power-sharing" to use Svolik's (2021) concept. The difference is that, instead of relying on transparent and clear rules, function fusion works precisely by erasing the line between what is allowable and what is not. This is no doubt a risky strategy—it faces the risk of the Frankenstein effect—but under Maduro, it has allowed the regime to maintain its repressive rule and keep its coalition fairly aligned behind the regime.

Svolik (2012) has argued that every authoritarian regime faces the double challenge of resistance from the people it governs, and demands from the domestic allies it needs for governance. While repression and co-optation are the traditional tools that authoritarian regimes employ to deal with these challenges, these regimes still need to find creative ways to co-opt. This in turn depends on the kind of resistance the opposition poses, the type of demands coalition allies place, and the structure of the economy over which regimes govern. This book discusses this resistance, these demands, and these economic structures, and how the regime adapted its institutional reservoirs to deal with each.

2

Rethinking Democratic Backsliding
POLITICS BEFORE MADURO

This chapter's first objective is to describe regime change under *Chavismo*, specifically, the process of democratic backsliding prior to the Nicolás Maduro administration. "Democratic backsliding" is the term used to describe erosions in democratic institutions driven mostly by the executive branch. This chapter identifies both common and sui generis features of democratic backsliding, and how Chavismo as a case of backsliding met these features. A second objective is to show how this type of regime change is the result of shifts in the features of the party system, namely variations in party system fragmentation, along with changes in the way the state both destroyed and colonized governance institutions.

Although scholars have emphasized a number of variables to explain democratic backsliding (Lust and Waldner 2015), the role of party system variables is not always stressed enough. In the case of Venezuela, I argue this variable was crucial.

The focus on party variables does not mean that it is the only driving force behind, or even sufficient condition for, democratic backsliding. An indispensable contributor to democratic backsliding is, of course, an executive interested in moving in this direction, and more fundamentally, some initial opportunities to gain control of key institutions of liberal democracy, namely, those affecting the system of checks and balances (Diamond 2019). In the case of Venezuela, the Hugo Chávez administration, since its inception, acted "intentionally" on this front (Kneuer 2021). In fewer than five years, the presidency achieved control of a Constituent Assembly and thus a new constitution, a newly elected legislature, the judiciary, the electoral council, the military, and most governorships. The key message of this chapter is therefore that asymmetrical party fragmentation along with institutional capturing caused democratic backsliding under Chávez.

Another objective of this chapter is to describe the ways in which the process of democratic backsliding in Venezuela displayed both typical and atypical features of democratic backsliding more generally. The typical characteristics of democratic backsliding under Hugo Chávez included frontal attacks on liberal democracy with the aim of producing executive aggrandizement, more ambiguous and hard-to-discern attacks on minimal and participatory democracy, and a significant reliance on polarization and confrontation, what Carrión (2021) calls the "Hobbesian moment." The more case-specific features that appear in some but not all cases of backsliding included a radical leftist-populist orientation; a heavy dose of militarism; and, for a while at least, enormous social spending and a state-directed consumption boom that lifted people's incomes across all sectors, including those of economic elites.

Finally, this chapter provides the essential background on the causes of autocratic solidification post-Chávez. While Venezuela's asymmetrical party fragmentation did not endure under Chávez, his institutional capturing did survive into the Maduro era. This inheritance conferred upon Maduro the essential incentive and arsenal to turn the regime more autocratic.

Politics before Chavismo: Democratic Degradation or Renovation?

Scholars agree that Venezuela in the 1960s had a strong, early-rising democracy. It was strong in that Venezuela managed to establish most institutions typically associated with liberal democracy: separation of powers, including an independent judiciary and a bicameral Congress, commitment to the rule of law, and civic liberties. The system was not perfect, but by Latin American standards and in fact global South standards of the 1960s, Venezuela's liberal democracy was remarkable and deep. According to some indexes, Venezuela's liberal democracy in the 1960s came close to matching the same scores as those of the United States (figure 2-1). It was early-rising in that these liberal democratic institutions became self-sustaining by the mid 1960s, long before the start of the Third Democratic Wave in the late 1970s (Levine 1973, Karl 1987, Myers 2004, Kornblith 2007). Until the 1990s, there were no coup attempts and power was transferred peacefully from one term to the next.

Figure 2-1. Liberal Democracy Index: Venezuela,
the United States, and Latin America, 1940–2018

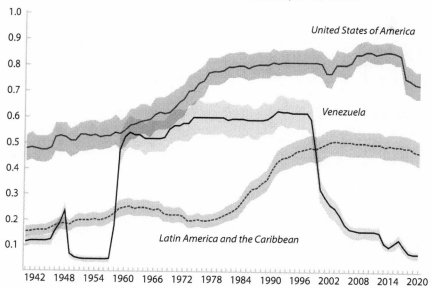

Source: V-Dem Liberal Democracy Index (2020), www.v-dem.net/en/online-graphing.

Scholars disagree, however, regarding the course of democracy in the 1980s and 1990s. For some, democracy decayed. For others, signs of democratic renewal—amid obvious turmoil—were visible.

To understand this debate, it is important to start with the economic context of the period. Venezuela has been an oil-dominated economy since the 1920s, and a petro-state since the 1970s, the latter meaning that the state held control of the oil industry.[1] In the 1980s, Venezuela experienced two severe external economic shocks: the onset of the Latin American debt crisis in 1982 and the drastic drop in oil prices between 1981 and 1983. The debate on the evolution of Venezuela's democracy during this period hinges on different views on how institutions responded to these shocks.

For most of the twentieth century, and especially in the 1970s, the price of oil was high enough to sustain healthy fiscal revenues, leading to rising incomes and expanding consumption standards. But in the early 1980s, oil prices dropped precipitously and stayed low for two decades, plunging Venezuela into a profound economic crisis. Budget deficits, high inflation, rising debt, exchange rate instability, declining investments, banking crises, and, of course, rising poverty were commonplace in the 1980s and 1990s (Naim 1993).

In my coauthored book with Michael Penfold, *Dragon in the Tropics*, we argued that the rise of populist leaders willing to assault liberal democracy is more likely in the context of what we could call the five Is: Inequality (low-income groups failing to make progress or even falling behind economically), Instability (rapid changes in the party system and political institutions), Insecurity (the rise of threats such as crime or economic anxiety), Incapacity (the perception that governments and politicians are unable to turn things around for the better), and Intolerance (rising resentment against prominent actors in politics). Venezuela's two long lost decades created or exacerbated these five Is.

While no scholar disagrees that these external shocks took a disproportionately large toll on the economy and society (Karl 1997, Coppedge 2005, Dunning 2008, Hausmann and Rodríguez 2013), there is a debate on the impact of the shock on democratic institutions (Corrales 2014).

For some scholars, democratic institutions decayed. Evidence of democratic decay focuses on several institutions. Many scholars rightly focus on parties, arguing that they became unresponsive and more corrupt (Ellner 2003, Molina 2004, McCoy 2004, Coppedge 2005, Myers 2007). Instead of renovating their leadership, they hung on to old-timers. Instead of introducing necessary political and economic reforms, they adhered to old rules and policies (Rey 1991, Kornblith 1997, López-Maya 2002, Hellinger 2003, Kelly and Palma 2004). By failing to address corruption, update their programs, and renew their leadership, Venezuelan parties lost their "linkage" with their constituencies (Morgan 2011, Seawright 2012). Other scholars focus on the executive branch: presidents became less, rather than more, consultative of civil society (Crisp 2000). Critics from the left denounced presidents (and ruling parties) for embracing too uncritically dictates from the International Monetary Fund (IMF) and for trying to implement economic adjustments that protected economic elites to the detriment of the poor (Buxton 2003). Critics from the right denounced presidents and parties for refusing to let go of all the corruption associated with an overextended state (Naim and Piñango 1984, Naim 1993).

For these declinists, institutional atrophy of the 1980s and 1990s explains the rise and victory in the 1998 presidential election of political maverick Hugo Chávez—who prevailed by capitalizing on the discontent toward democratic institutions, especially political parties, and promised a complete overhaul of Venezuela's democratic institutions. They point to the fact that Chávez's core (and prototypical) support came from the 23 de Enero neighborhood, a once-thriving example of modern urbanism built in the 1950s, that in the 1980s became the center of poverty, crime, violence, and repression (Velasco 2015). Support also came from a number of new parties and social movements that were not part of the Punto Fijo Pact (an agreement signed in 1958 by Venezuela's largest parties that set the stage for power-sharing and democracy), and had little, if any, parliamentary representation (López Maya and Lander 2004, Kornblith 2007).[2] Had democratic and economic institutions been more responsive—and the state less exclusionary—the electoral demand for a radical leader like Chávez would have been weaker (Ellner 2008).

Other scholars, without denying these crises, see signs of democratic renewal or at least resilience. As Coppedge states, the fact that an institution (such as parties) might decline does not mean necessarily that democracy failed: Venezuela was experiencing symptoms of "weakened institutionalization, not of less democracy" (Coppedge 2005:309). And in fact, some democratic institutions might have become stronger.

For instance, following a complex self-study (by the Presidential Commission for State Reform [Comisión Presidencial para la Reforma del Estado, COPRE]), the state introduced greater transparency in the public sector and nationwide decentralization for the first time ever, including elections for governors and mayors (Levine 1998, Penfold-Becerra 2004, Monaldi and Penfold 2014). The state terminated a major corruption scheme based on a currency exchange control program (Régimen de Cambio Diferencial, RECADI), and Congress peacefully impeached a president, Carlos Andrés Pérez, for acts of corruption in the early 1990s. Congress also approved a new Labor Law (Ley Orgánica del Trabajo, 1990), which, contrary to the neoliberal trends of the time, provided more labor protection (Bernardoni de Govea 2011). Also in the 1990s, the stranglehold of the two traditional parties (Acción Democrática and Copei) came to an end, and formerly fringe parties (Movement to Socialism [Movimiento al Socialismo, MAS] and Radical Cause [Causa-R]) rose politically. This volatility in the party system, which peaked in 1998 (Kronick et al. 2021), was not just the result of voter discontent but also of democratizing electoral reforms (Morgenstern and Vázquez-D'Elía 2007): Venezuela scrapped its proportional representation (PR) system of medium-size districts in favor of a two-level system where voters choose half of their deputies in single-member districts and the rest from multiple state-level closed lists (Kulisheck and Crisp 2003). The system changed again in 1997 to increase the number of PR seats.

The instability of the party system in the 1990s can be seen as positive for democracy because it permitted the rise of new forms of party representation (Wills-Otero 2020). This opening of the party system, in turn, was accompanied by a boom in civil society and new forms of democratic protests (López Maya and Lander 2004). According to one study, civil associations went from

10,000 in the early 1990s to as many as 54,000 by the 2000s (Salamanca 2004). While there was serious regime-threatening political instability (the Caracazo riots in 1989; two coup attempts in 1992), by the late 1990s, instability declined and political competition was being channeled, again, through peaceful electoral contests rather than extraconstitutional avenues. One could argue that the electoral success of Hugo Chávez was a sign of democratic rejuvenation: a newcomer decides to run for office rather than continue armed insurrection, to create a new party mobilizing discontented sectors, and to establish alliances with established parties and social movements.

For this school of thought, therefore, without some democratic opening in the 1990s, or at least, democratic resilience, it would have been impossible for Hugo Chávez to rise electorally. The system would have produced a perpetuation of old elites, or even worse, a sudden democratic collapse at the hands of an outright dictatorship. These two outcomes were avoided in Venezuela. The old parties lost their stranglehold, and a would-be coup-plotter was compelled to take a democratic route to power, promising institutional reform through the Constitution (rather than revolutionary change) (Kronick et al. 2021). Radical leftist leaders, community organizers, Afro-Indigenous voices, and new movements therefore found increasing opportunities to expand their influence in politics, leading some to argue that these movements created the Chávez phenomenon (Ciccariello-Maher 2013). But the promise for change made by Chávez was palatable enough that it was acceptable not just to fringe, discontented voters but to many voters from all social classes.

Either way, few dispute that Venezuela's democracy was under serious stress in the 1990s, besieged by economic crisis, policy paralysis, episodic instability, party volatility, and rising new movements. In some areas, democracy was faltering; in other areas, it was regenerating. There was an opening of the party system—and this opening allowed new parties to come in. Paradoxically, this opening for new parties would also create an opening, in the 2000s, for democratic backsliding.

Democratic Backsliding and Autocratic Legalism

Prior to Chávez, the debate among scholars centered on how far democracy decayed (or reinvented itself). Under Chávez, the debate centered on the concept of democratic backsliding, which is related but different from democratic decay (Diamond and Morlino 2004; Gerschewski 2021).

Under democratic backsliding, the executive branch is the major offender. In addition, the president attacks not just one aspect of democracy, but all three fundamental pillars: elections (minimal democracy), checks and balances (liberal democracy), and institutions of representation (participatory democracy). This frontal attack against all three types of democratic institutions is the sine qua non of democratic backsliding. For the most part, the executive's attacks focus on liberal democracy, and some of the biggest declines happen in that realm. But with time, the other two types of democratic institutions (elections and institutions of representation) will erode as well.

I have argued that autocratic legalism is the preferred tool of governance in processes of democratic backsliding. Autocratic legalism is the use, abuse, and lack of use of the law and norms to advance the president's agenda and hurt opponents (Corrales 2015, Scheppele 2018). De Sa e Silva (2021) has argued correctly that autocratic legalism is also used in other regimes, not just with democratic backsliding. It is important therefore to distinguish how autocratic legalism operates differently across regime types.

Following de Sa e Silva's work, table 2-1 shows key differences in terms of three areas: (1) aim or target of autocratic legalism, (2) frequency and mode of use, and (3) whether the opposition or victims of autocratic legalism have any legal recourse.

In a democracy, the executive branch will use autocratic legalism for two main aims: to create states of exception and to engage in corruption. However, the use is infrequent (in the former instances) and covert (in the latter instances). Furthermore, opposition actors and victims of autocratic legalism in a democracy typically enjoy full, professional, and independent legal recourse.

In processes of backsliding, in contrast, the executive branch deploys autocratic legalism with an additional, more-threatening aim: to produce executive aggrandizement and to create legal complications for opposition groups, such as parties, business actors, NGOs, and the press. Autocratic legalism in

Table 2-1. Autocratic Legalism across Regime Type

Regime type	Main aim	Frequency or mode of use	Opposition's legal recourse?
Liberal democracies	Create and sustain states of exception; legal manipulation to engage in corruption	Infrequent (for states of exception) or in hiding (for corruption)	Substantial
Backsliding democracies	Executive aggrandizement; creation of obstacles for opponents (e.g., uneven playing field)	Constant and open	Declining
Autocracies	Justify repression; dismantling institutions of minimal democracy	Sporadic	None

Source: Author's adaptation of de Sa e Silva (2021).

backsliding contexts occurs promiscuously and openly. The legal recourses available for the opposition decline gradually.

In authoritarian settings, autocratic legalism occurs in a more punitive fashion and a bit more selectively: to justify blatant repression by coercive actors, and even the full dismantling of minimal democracy (Ermakoff 2020). The state might for example use the law to cancel a legal election or to supersede an independent branch of government. Victims of autocratic legalism enjoy virtually no legal recourse.

In the early stages of backsliding, when the regime is transitioning from democracy to semi-authoritarianism, a salient characteristic of autocratic legalism is frequency. Presidents are constantly changing constitutions, legal codes, norms, and regulations. There is enormous legal, regulatory, and norm instability; in contrast, legal changes in democracies and authoritarian regimes tend to occur less frequently. This density of legal, regulatory, and norm change in backsliding processes in and of itself creates confusion for the opposition, which has trouble keeping up and adapting to every new regulation. In contrast, supporters of the regime see this legal hyperactivity as a sign that, finally, things are changing—that the policy gridlock and paralysis of the past are finally being addressed. In other words, supporters of the incumbent see autocratic legalism as progress.

Autocratic legalism, of course, is not the only way democracies can decline or die. Since ancient times, scholars have known that democratic declines can be driven by societal forces, either powerful elites with concentrated and oligarchic power, or opposition-based, nonelite forces (sometimes even just mobs) seeking to topple governments. Sometimes the process of democratic decay is driven by exogenous forces (foreign actors, global market forces) or even by dynamics where no one actor is necessarily guiltier than another (e.g., in polarized contexts). Sometimes the process of decline can occur not by commission but by omission, when, for instance, government leaders fail to take action to ameliorate systematic exclusion of sectors of the population. Other times, democratic decline can occur due to institutional decay: a given institution fails to adapt, or to receive sufficient incentives to do its job, or is captured by societal agents wishing to colonize it (Diamond and Morlino 2004, Gerschewski 2021).

Throughout this book, I don't deny that these alternative paths to democratic decline exist and, in fact, might have played a role in Venezuela's or in other countries' democratic decline. But I strongly believe that, since the early 2000s, the Venezuelan case conforms with the classic component of democratic backsliding—the executive acts as the "change agent," to use the term by Mahoney and Thelen (2010), leading the process. Opposition groups, of course, also incurred undemocratic excesses (Tomini 2017), but in my estimation, the executive in the Venezuelan story committed the most sweeping forms of democratic infractions, often unprompted and exaggeratedly.

Why Democratic Backsliding Is Ambiguous, at First

With time, as argued, the process of backsliding affects the three main pillars of democratic life: elections (minimal democracy), institutions of checks and balances and the system of political rights (liberal democracy), and institutions of representation and inclusion (participatory democracy). Eventually, most observers will notice the damage. But in the early stages, the signs are not that clear.[3] It is not easy for many actors to notice backsliding. Why is backsliding so difficult to discern for so many actors at first?

The ambiguity stems not just from the fact that backsliding presidents employ a disguising discourse[4] but also because not all dimensions of democracy are attacked simultaneously. Even as one key aspect of democracy declines, other aspects may not decline as fast or at all. In other words, the process begins with leaders engaging in "trade-offs between distinct democratic values" (Cianetti and Hanley 2021).

In addition, although the literature on democratic regression tends to distinguish between two temporalities of democratic regression—gradual versus rapid forms of backsliding (see Gerschewski 2021)—most often, democratic backsliding shows both temporalities occurring *simultaneously*, with some institutions declining fast and others more slowly, if at all.

In the specific case of Venezuela, it was the institutions of liberal democracy that declined rapidly. These are institutions that govern the powers of the executive branch. The aspects of democracy that did not decline rapidly at first had to do with participatory features (Ellner and Hellinger 2003, Brown 2018, Hellinger 2011).[5] Figure 2-2 compares these two temporalities, where V-Dem's participatory index shows that participatory elements actually improved (briefly) and stayed relatively strong before they began to decline by the end of the 2000s. In other words, while the president was concentrating powers and imposing restrictions on the opposition in the early part of his regime, he was also expanding or preserving opportunities for many Venezuelans to participate in politics.

Another reason that many actors don't notice backsliding is that backsliding, even in the areas where it is occurring fast, is never abrupt. Unlike the case of Nazi Germany, where a parliamentary democracy created a one-party dictatorship in a matter of a few weeks, in contemporary backsliding processes the regime attacks aspects of democracy gradually, sometimes one at a time (Ermakoff 2020). Rather than a blitzkrieg, it is regime change drop by drop.

Figure 2-2. Venezuela: Different Rates of Democratic
Backsliding According to Institution Type

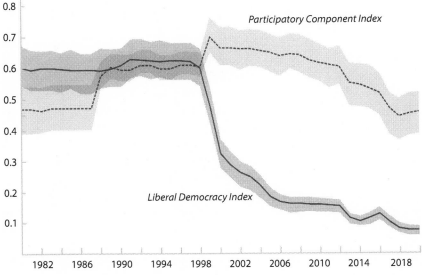

Source: V-Dem Liberal Democracy Index (2020), www.v-dem.net/en/online-graphing.

This mixed temporality (different rates of decline in different aspects of democracy) causes another commonality in processes of democratic back-sliding: an intense cleavage across the political system, including polariza-tion (Corrales 2005, Haggard and Kaufman 2021, McCoy et al. 2018, Svolik 2019, Vachudova 2019). On the one hand, leaders of the opposition will, more than any other actors, notice the decline in liberal democracy—those changes leading to executive aggrandizement, degradation of rights, and an uneven playing field—in part because they are the most direct cost-bearers of this type of decline. But for the rest of the electorate, the panorama is not that clear-cut. In Venezuela, the ruling party not only offered followers opportunities to participate in politics but also spent copious amounts on social services. The part of the electorate that cared more about the aspects of democracy that are less in decline (in the case of Venezuela, participation of new groups or access to social services) may end up ignoring or forgiving other declines in democracy—as they see plenty of hope in the other indica-tors they value most.

In other words, the mixed process of democratic backsliding, at least in the beginning, creates an electorate that is very divided about the actual democratic trajectory of the regime. For some, democracy is crashing; for others, democracy is rising. Initially, at first, the split in the electorate often goes beyond conventional cleavages: democrats versus authoritarians, high-income versus low-income groups, elites versus common folks, defenders of the status quo versus change-seekers (Roberts 1998, Brown 2018). Often, the most salient cleavage is based on voters disagreeing on which aspect of democracy they value more, regardless of class.

A final commonality is the rise of a group in the electorate that is turned off by this polarization. These voters see little difference between—or little to admire about—the extremist positions adopted by either side. In Venezuela, this group was called the *ni/nis* (Spanish for the "neither/nors"), meaning that they sided with neither group. Their tendency is to abstain politically. An important part of the battle between both poles is to try to capture this group.

The only actors for whom the process never seems gradual, ambiguous, or undetectable is the organized opposition. The issue for the opposition is not that the process of democratic backsliding is unnoticeable. Rather, the issue is that the process is uneven (some aspects remain democratic) and asymmetrical (impacting the opposition severely). They will disagree about the right response. The two other groups are not part of the opposition: supporters of the president and the so-called ni/nis may not be alarmed at all. Whether the process gets stopped or not therefore depends on the organizational attributes and electoral force of the opposition.

The Chávez Record

Between 1999 and 2013, Venezuela's process of democratic backsliding advanced significantly. By the end of Chávez's life, all three fundamental pillars of democracy were wounded or distorted. He left Nicolás Maduro a regime that (1) systematically violated minimal democracy with electoral irregularities, (2) had few surviving elements of liberal democratic institutions, and (3) promoted distortions of participatory democratic institutions.

Minimal Democracy: Becoming Less Free and Fair

Minimal democracy refers to the rules guaranteeing that state offices be determined by elections. It is the idea that democracy requires, at a minimum, electoral competition to determine who governs and who represents whom. This is achieved when several conditions are met: (1) elections must be held for the executive branch and the legislature; (2) civil and political rights must exist for the vast majority of political groups to compete; and (3) elections must be free (no costs or rewards must be imposed on voters based on how they vote) and fair (the system cannot be biased in favor of the incumbent).

Under Chávez, Venezuela experienced a gradual erosion of mostly rules 2 and 3 (Corrales 2020b). Table 2-2 shows all of the irregularities for each election until 2018. Each irregularity is classified according to type of violation and effect. Types are drawn from international conventions, regional conventions, and think tanks (e.g., OSCE 2005; United Nations 2005; OAS 2007; Freedom House, various years; Sabatini n.d.). Two kinds of effects exist: legacy and election specific. Legacy irregularities are those that, once introduced, tend to have lasting effects, tarnishing the electoral arena into the future, or at least until a new reform is introduced to make amends. Examples include eroding the impartiality of electoral authorities, biased state-run media, and inexplicable and uncorrected changes in voter registration patterns. The other type of irregularity is election specific. It refers to practices or regulations introduced for the conduct of a particular election. Examples include voting day disruption in the infrastructure, mishandling claims of fraud, restrictions on who gets to compete, manipulation of the timing of the election, and poor or impartial observation of elections on voting day.

Several empirical observations can be made based on table 2-2: (1) almost every electoral process has featured at least one irregularity; (2) with time, irregularities have multiplied; (3) at the end of the Chávez administration, the cumulus of irregularities was substantial; (4) large sectors of the opposition boycotted several electoral moments, including the 2005 legislative election and all elections starting in 2017.

The overall point is that the country saw a steady decrease in the freedom and fairness of elections in Venezuela. But it is also worth noting that at first the evidence was mixed. Chávez conducted a constitutional reform in 1999–2000 that involved various electoral contests, giving the impression of being highly committed to electoral politics. And while elections for president, the legislature, and subnational office took place, severe restrictions were gradually introduced during almost every contest, which ended up undermining two of the conditions to achieve a minimal democracy: the existence of civil and political rights for the vast majority of political groups to compete and free and fair elections.

Liberal Democracy: Near Extinction

Maduro also inherited a system in which most liberal democratic institutions were near extinction. Liberal democracy is generally understood as the set of institutions intended to create limits on the power of the executive branch and to protect the rights of citizens from state encroachments. In presidential systems, those limits come from the constitution and the law, and the separation of powers among the different branches of government (the legislature; the judiciary; and subnational governments, in federal systems).

Under Chávez, liberal democracy institutions were the first to suffer the most significant erosions (Corrales and Penfold 2015). Again, initially, the steps were mixed. The 1999 Constitution gave the impression of creating newer checks on the power of the president by creating new offices intended to hold the president accountable, while at the same time significantly expanding presidential powers and reducing the power of other branches of government. By 2004, the mixed record became less mixed. The president essentially eliminated or reformed most laws restricting his own discretionary power in the use of oil money and the autonomy of the Central Bank; packed the courts and fired many judges who were not aligned with the ruling party; began to restrict the operation of the independent media by imposing fines, denying them resources, refusing to allow them to import paper, banning journalists from covering certain stories, and so forth; and curtailed the autonomy of the ruling party.

The erosion included all the standard avenues identified in the literature: (1) autocratic legalism: applying the law harshly against enemies but softly or not at all toward loyalists (Corrales 2015, Scheppele 2018, Ermakoff 2020); (2) constitutional tinkering: amending or revamping the Constitution to give the executive more powers vis-à-vis other actors (Huq and Ginsburg 2018); (3) legislative dodging: sidestepping the legislature in enacting policy or lowering the degree to which members of the executive branch become accountable to legislators (Pérez-Liñán et al. 2019); (4) judicial co-optation: ending the independence of the judicial branch (Gibler and Randazzo 2011, International Commission of Jurists 2014, Taylor 2014, Bennaim 2020); and (5) centralization of power: lessening the autonomy of subnational actors (Dickovick 2011), or transferring subnational powers to subnational actors who were more aligned with the president.

Participatory Democracy: Biases

With time, even participatory democracy began to backslide under Chávez. Chávez infused partisanship, sectarianism, and antipluralism into most institutions of representation. Participatory democracy is generally understood as institutions and policies designed to empower groups that have been traditionally nondominant. It includes, of course, ideological groups (e.g., the opposition), but it can also include socioeconomic actors, such as ethnic and religious groups, women, sexual minorities, immigrants, low-income people, certain professions, and so forth.

Table 2-2. Electoral Irregularities: Violations to Principles of Electoral Integrity 1999–2018

Date (Month.Day.Year) and electoral event		Total	Freedom from coercion (IS1)	Impartiality of electoral authorities (IS7)	Voting registration normalcy (IS12)	Impartiality of electoral laws (IS8)	Impartial access to public resources (IS2)	Equal access to state media (IS3)
Chávez era								
4.25.99	Referendum to create a Constituent Assembly	1						
6.25.99	Constituent Assembly	1				1		
12.15.99	Referendum on new Constitution	3	1					
6.30.00	Mega-elections for all public posts	2		1				
12.2.00	Municipal councils, civil parishes	0						
9.12.03	First recall referendum request	7	1	2	1	1		
8.15.04	Presidential recall referendum	7			1	1	1	
10.30.04	Governors, state legislature, mayors	1						
8.7.05	Municipal councils, civil parishes	2		1		1		
12.4.05	National Assembly, Andean & LAC Parliament	2		1				
12.3.06	Presidential	3	2			1		
12.2.07	Constitutional referendum	5						1
11.23.08	Governors, mayors	6	1			1	1	
2.15.09	Referendum to abolish term limits	3				2		
9.26.10	National Assembly	4		1		2	1	
10.7.12	Presidential	8			1	1	1	2
12.16.12	Governors and mayors	1						
	Total	56	5	6	4	8	5	4
Maduro era (until 2018)								
17.4.13	Presidential	7	1		1			
8.12.13	Municipal	1						
6.12.15	Legislative	12	1			2		1
2016	Presidential recall referendum (Disallowed)	11	1			2		
7.30.17	Constituent Assembly	7	1			2		
10.15.17	State governors	14				1		
12.10.17	Municipal	4			1	1		
5.20.18	Presidential	5				3		
Total Maduro era		61	4	0	2	11	0	1
Total Chavista era, 1999–2018		*117*	*9*	*6*	*6*	*19*	*5*	*5*

Notes: See overleaf.

Freedom to compete (IS10)	Timing or scheduling regularity (T)	Respect for elected post (IS13)	Compliance with constitutional law (L)	Voting Day normalcy (VD)	Secrecy of vote (IS5)	Transparency of voting process (IS6)	Recognition of results (IS9)	Reliable fraud investigation (IS11)	Boycotted by major parties
			1						
			2						
	1								
	1				1				
					1	2		1	
	1								
								1	Yes
			2			1		1	
1		1					1		
			1						
	1				1	1			
								1	
1	4	1	6	0	3	4	1	4	
			2	1	1			1	
	1								
4	1		2			1			
	3		1			2		2	
1			1			1		1	Yes
1	1	2	2	1	1	3	1	1	
	1					1			Yes
	1		1						Partial
6	8	2	9	2	2	8	1	5	
7	12	3	15	2	5	12	2	9	

Table 2-2 Notes:

The table provides the number of violations of electoral principles introduced at each electoral event.

Dark grey = Legacy Irregularity: A change that compromised the electoral system into the future.

Light grey = Election-specific irregularity: A violation of electoral principles that affected that particular election.

Charcoal = Opposition boycott.

LAC = Latin American and Caribbean

Type of electoral irregularity:

1. Violation of constitutional law = L.

2. Manipulation of timing (and scheduling) for self-serving purposes = T.

3. Voting day irregularity, including major disruption of infrastructure needed for voting to happen smoothly (e.g., broken machines, power outages) or disorder and lack of transparency at voting booths = VD.

4. Violation of international standards for clean elections = IS.

IS1. Freedom from coercion: Voting authorities are supposed to ensure that voters are not coerced or bribed to participate in the elections or cast their vote for a specific side.

IS2. Impartial access to public resources: Avoid gross, overt use of state resources—funds, state offices, armed forces, other public officials, materials, social welfare programs—for partisan or campaign purposes.

IS3. Relatively equal access to public media and general information in terms of content, air or paper space, and coverage in public media during the campaign.

IS4. Voter access to information: All major candidates should be able to distribute materials and information without intimidation or efforts to block them by opponents.

IS5. Secrecy of the vote: Voters should be assured that their vote is secret and that their participation on Election Day will not be used against them.

IS6. Transparency of the voting process: To ensure confidence in the voting process, credible, nonpartisan groups should be allowed to observe voter lists (through a sample), the processes for establishing voting locations, the voting process (with due respect for secrecy), and the process or algorithms for tabulating votes.

IS7. Impartiality of electoral authorities: Officials regulating an election must act in a nonbiased, effective, transparent, and accountable manner.

IS8. Impartiality of electoral laws: Electoral laws must be approved with the consent of and input from leading opposition forces, must be enforced impartially, and should not be changed unilaterally or ad hoc (close to Election Day).

IS9. Recognition of results: Elected officials must recognize the results of the election and allow for a smooth transfer of full powers to winners.

IS10. Freedom to compete: Opposition figures should not face unreasonable restrictions on their right to compete for office.

IS11. Reliable fraud investigation: Serious allegations of fraud must be investigated following principles of impartiality and with the consent of the parties involved.

IS12. Voter registration normalcy: No systematic impediment to voter registration; anomalous changes in the growth rate of registry must be adequately explained and accounted for.

IS13. Respect for the powers of the elected office: Government should not arbitrarily change the powers of elected posts after an election, especially if the post went to the opposition.

Source: Corrales (2020b).

Chávez gained a significant following at home and abroad because he initially took steps to expand participatory democracy (López-Maya 2003, Burbach and Piñeiro 2007, Wilpert 2007, Ellner 2008, Fernandes 2010). Over time, however, Chávez distorted participatory democracy by making it sectarian. New groups were incorporated, and even given new and expanded powers, provided they were demonstrably loyalist. For instance, members of the ruling party were given priority in hiring decisions in state-owned corporations. These were appealing jobs because they offered incomparable labor security. New labor unions, civic organizations, neighborhood committees, and schools and universities were created—all of which incorporated people and sectors that were traditionally underprivileged and underrepresented, but with the expectation that they needed to show support. Chavista groups ended up dominating these institutions, and they themselves became increasingly nonpluralistic. In the end, participation tended to include mostly "a group of dedicated activists" who were strongly colored by partisanship (Hawkins 2010b:54–55). Being discovered to be in the opposition carried huge risks: unemployment, disqualification from access to state services, public ostracism.

In short, the erosion of participatory democracy in Venezuela under Chávez also followed almost every conventional recipe: (1) political discrimination: offering state privileges mostly to loyalists and denying them to everyone else (Collier 2001, Weyland 2001, Corrales and Penfold 2015, Pappas 2019); (2) demonization and exclusion of the opposition, often described as elite or antipeople (Weyland 2001, Müller 2016, Hawkins and Kaltwasser 2017, Mudde and Kaltwasser 2017, Mounk 2018); (3) expropriation of the property and assets of dissident groups (North et al. 2000); and (4) declining pluralism: populating the civic space with new organizations that were semi-associated with the state and highly partisan (Naim 2009, Galston et al. 2018, Diamond 2019).

The Role of Asymmetrical Party System Fragmentation

One reason Chávez was able to achieve executive aggrandizement so quickly had to do with asymmetrical party system fragmentation (APSF). From the start, the ruling party became electorally competitive and fairly unified behind the president, while the opposition splintered into small and declining parties.

Chávez's original party, the Revolutionary Bolivarian Movement-200 (Movimiento Bolivariano Revolucionario-200, MBR-200), absorbed most of the parties of the left, forming the Movement of the Fifth Republic (Movimiento V [Quinta] República, MVR) and then the United Socialist Party of

Venezuela (Partido Socialista Unido de Venezuela, PSUV), and its leadership during this process remained united behind the president and able to compete in elections. Some leaders, along with small leftist parties, did defect periodically, especially before 2003, but none was able to grow electorally. At no point during all the decisions made by Chávez did the ruling party stop supporting the president. Furthermore, the president used his allies not just to endorse controversial power grabs but also to quickly colonize institutions and turn them into rubber stamps for the ruling party.

In contrast, the opposition emerged fragmented from the 1998 election and stayed that way until about 2006. Opposition parties—new and old—eschewed cooperation with each other. Often, new political leaders wanted no association with parties. In the 1990s, the party system experienced volatility. After Chávez, only two parties from the pre-Chávez era managed to survive, Acción Democrática and to a lesser degree Copei (Crisp et al. 2003). Neither ever managed to grow electorally. New electorally competitive parties emerged with time (Un Nuevo Tiempo, Primero Justicia, Voluntad Popular), but they only added to the opposition's fragmentation. Together with former Chavista-allied parties, these opposition parties faced enormous divisions. Every democracy-defying decision made by Chávez produced significant divisions about how best to respond. The opposition had to spend significant resources working out those divisions. Oftentimes consensus was difficult to establish. When consensus was achieved, decisions inevitably displeased some constituents. Whereas the government could focus on institutional power grabs, the opposition had to solve collective action problems: building consensus, keeping the herd together, and then trying to stop Chávez. The opposition had the numbers (widespread support), but lacked coordination capacity. The proliferation of parties impeded coordination. As the sole united actor in this context, the ruling party was able to assert itself in almost every arena of government-opposition competition: at the polls, in the legislature, and on the airwaves.

The opposition, in desperation, also committed some democratic infractions, mostly in the initial years. It supported extreme measures: massive protests in 2001 calling for early resignation, followed by a coup led by a business leader in 2002, then a crippling strike of the oil industry in 2002–2003. The opposition fell into the hands of extremists, who started calling for election boycotts and abstentionism.

APSF is not the only route to democratic backsliding. But when it occurs, backsliding is likelier. Some of the most important cases of democratic backsliding occurred with prior party system volatility and subsequent asymmetrical party fragmentation (e.g., Peru under Alberto Fujimori, Ecuador under Rafael Correa, Turkey under Recep Tayyip Erdoğan, Russia under Vladimir

Putin, Nicaragua under Daniel Ortega, India under Narendra Modi, Hungary under Viktor Orbán). This makes sense. Under this institutional condition, the government has a strong political machine from and through which it can attack institutions, and the opposition lacks a strong armor to repel those attacks and, moreover, is distracted by its own disagreements and the complications associated with achieving unity.

The one force encouraging the opposition to unite, though never fully or consistently, was the polarization of politics. Venezuela's process of democratic backsliding, as is typical of most cases, featured a rise in political polarization (Haggard and Kaufman 2011, Corrales 2005). Never in Venezuela's history of party politics did parties stand further apart in terms of ideology and willingness to cooperate than during the process of democratic backsliding.

All scholars who study Venezuela agree that Chavismo, from the start, polarized government-opposition relations. The debate centers on whether the polarization was preexisting and class-driven, with the state taking on a preexisting class divide between the have-less and the have-more (Ellner and Hellinger 2003, García-Guadilla 2007), or instead, intentionally pursued by party leaders, so-called intentional polarization (see Moraes 2015, Vachudova 2019).

I have argued that the latter case became more dominant (Corrales 2005, 2011). Chávez discovered, perhaps accidentally, that exacerbating polarization could reward him politically. The logic is that all forms of power grabs, which are, by definition, inherent to democratic backsliding, generate outrage among the opposition (Carrión 2021). The opposition feels tempted to respond with radical acts: intensify radical discourse; mobilize street protests; and call for extreme measures such as massive strikes, impeachments, noncooperation, and so forth. This radicalization of the opposition is no doubt risky for the government—it increases the incentives for the opposition to overcome some differences and unite. And in terms of electoral contests between 2005 and 2015, the opposition tended to unite far more than it divided. However, polarization offers the state another asset: it rallies its base. Ambiguous supporters join ranks with hard-core supporters, united against what both sides perceive to be unacceptably extreme and out-of-control opposition behavior. And if the other pole is electorally weak and organizationally in disarray, that is, if APSF conditions prevail, the prospects that the ruling party will triumph are even stronger.

This notion of executive-driven intentional polarization explains why the state pursued incremental radicalization of discourse toward the opposition as well as of economic policies. This radicalization made little economic sense, but it provided political benefits by rallying the base and even attracting some support from the center-left.

Chavista Backsliding: Sui Generis Characteristics

While APSF helps explain some of the most important features of democratic backsliding, it cannot explain the sui generis features of the Chavista version of democratic backsliding. All forms of backsliding come with case-specific elements that may or may not be present in other cases. In the case of Chávez, these case-specific elements included: (1) a heavy dose of leftist populism; (2) reliance on militarism; (3) massive state spending (at least until 2010), which generated a huge economic boom; (4) heavy income distributionism; (5) attacks on the private sector; and (6) significant presence of foreign actors, especially Cuba and China.

Chávez's assault on democracy was justified through a left-wing-populist discourse (Hawkins 2003, Ellner 2008, Cannon 2009, Hawkins 2010, Gill 2018, Pappas 2019). A major study of speeches by forty world leaders placed Hugo Chávez and Nicolás Maduro as the top two most intense users of populist rhetoric (Lewis et al. 2019). Chávez used the same rhetorical device for every assault: he represented the best interests of the (poor, underrepresented) majorities against the biased interests of institutions and groups in the opposition, all dominated by enemies of the people, described as economic elites, oligarchs, capitalist, and pro-American (Sagarzazu and Thies 2019). Not all forms of democratic backsliding adopt leftist-populist discourse. Noting that Chávez used this leftist variation helps explain why he remained popular for many leftist international observers, and it also explains his model of economic development, which placed so much emphasis on the state over the market, as the next chapter will discuss.

Second, the process of democratic backsliding involved a heavy dose of militarism, at a time when the influence of the military in Latin America was perhaps at an all-time low (Corrales 2014). Since the very beginning, by his own admission, Chávez was intent on creating a civil-military alliance (Chávez et al. 2005). He imposed this alliance in a country that had essentially achieved civil domination of the military since the early 1960s and where the military was not such a dominant actor (Trinkunas 2005).[6] Chávez offered the Armed Forces the opportunity to change from being mere guardians of stability to partners in institutional overhaul (Olivar 2020). While Chavista apologists claim that the Venezuelan military was more progressive and less elitist than the military elsewhere in South America, no one denies that the military became central to governance under Chavismo (Strønen 2016). Chávez unilaterally and openly interfered in military affairs, appointed military and former military officers to his cabinet, encouraged them to run for office, and consulted with them more frequently than with members of Parliament. He maintained support from the military throughout. Even during his most serious political crisis, when several of his generals refused to cooperate with Chávez's instructions to repress protests and briefly took him out of power in 2002, the vast majority of soldiers sided with Chávez: only 200 of 8,000 officials supported this coup; the vast majority of soldiers stayed loyal (Kozloff 2007). This loyalty to Chávez would become stronger with time, and in return, Chávez always treated the military as priority, protecting its budgets, its privileges, and its influence.

Third, between 2004 and 2010, the state created one of the largest, broadest consumption booms in the history of Venezuela and even Latin America. All classes benefitted, generating political loyalties across all sectors that would outlive Chávez, and defying theories that predict that economic growth is an antidote to democratic regression. In Venezuela, as in many other cases of backsliding, economic growth helped democratic backsliding by winning important allies for the state across different economic classes.

Fourth, the process involved a heavy dose of social spending, possibly even more on a per capita basis than in other petro-states. Large sections of low-income households (and not a small portion of elites) did profit from social spending. That said, the return on these massive social investments, in terms of poverty alleviation, left much to be desired (Rodríguez 2008, Maingon 2016). A significant portion of the spending remains unaccounted for, and was probably diverted by corrupt officials. A synthetic control analysis by Grier and Maynard (2016) found no evidence that Chávez had a significant impact on the poverty rate in Venezuela. Improvements such as poverty alleviation and life expectancy increases were not found to be "any different [under Chávez] than they would have been with another national leader" (Grier and Maynard 2016:14). Grier and Maynard imply that other factors, such as the oil boom, bear greater responsibility for poverty alleviation. Grier and Maynard do credit Chávez for inequality reduction at a faster rate than would otherwise have occurred.

Fifth, in addition to heavy distributionism, the model also created conditions that were significantly adverse to the private sector. One indicator of conditions for the private sector is the Economic Freedom Index, which ranks nations according to twelve factors that affect the freedom of citizens and firms to engage in free market activities. Venezuela under Chávez experienced a significant decline. No other country in Latin America or petro-state in the world (except Libya) experienced a comparable drop. Private firms that were not politically aligned with the ruling party were treated with a heavy dose of regulation, price controls, heavy taxation, and selective auditing. Under these adverse conditions, firms faced two choices: either engage in rent-seeking (which generated closer alignment with the state) or discontinue production of some or all its output (which generated unemployment). If the latter outcome was chosen by the private firm, the state would often use that as an excuse to take over the firm through expropriation. Workers at times welcomed the expropriation as a way to preserve employment. In essence, the state's policy of harassing the private sector contained a mechanism for generating demand for more and more statism, on the part of both firms and workers (Corrales 2010).

Finally, the process involved the direct intervention of foreign actors, especially Cuba. Many autocratizing presidents receive (or seek out) support from external authoritarian actors. Venezuela was no different. What is unique about Venezuela is the degree to which it opened its territory to the direct presence of actual foreigners. Cuba and Venezuela not only signed a number of trade, oil, military, and technical cooperation agreements (Romero 2012, Romero and Pedraza 2013), but Venezuela also invited a disproportionately large number of Cubans (as of 2011, there were 51,000 Cuban *colaboradores* working in Venezuela, including 31,315 in the health sector and 5,000 political workers training revolutionary cadres). While Cuba has become known as an exporter of labor-for-dollars, no other country has received as many Cubans as Venezuela. This partnership, often referred to as "Cubazuela," became so strong under Chávez that it is difficult to find another case of democratic backsliding in the Americas and Europe with this much direct, physical presence of foreign actors (Demarest 2018). Venezuela became one of Cuba's most important economic subsidizers, and Cuba became one of Venezuela's most important suppliers of technical assistance. Each country was supplying the other with plenty of what it had in abundance: substantial oil subsidies and dollars-for-labor in the case of Venezuela and plenty of doctors and security experts in the case of Cuba (Corrales 2006).

Conclusion

This chapter made a few contributions to the study of democratic backsliding. It identified aspects that are common across cases as well as sui generis. Some of the common elements are as follows: The executive branch launches intentional assaults on institutions of minimal, liberal, and participatory democracy. The primary target is liberal democracy, but with time, minimal and participatory democracy also erode. In addition, democratic backsliding is initially hard to recognize by observers. While some institutions of democracy decline rapidly at first, other forms of democracy do not decline as fast and may even show signs of improvement at first. Sectors of the opposition are the first to see the signs of backsliding, but many other actors, and especially supporters of the incumbent, hardly notice any decline, and may even become convinced that democracy is actually expanding. Consequently, democratic backsliding polarizes the electorate: the government and the opposition enter into an intense conflict, and each side can achieve significant support from voters.

This chapter also discussed variations. In assaulting institutions of democracy, presidents can vary in terms of the scale of the assault and institutions targeted. In addition, they can engage in ancillary policies. In the case of Chávez, democratic backsliding was supplemented with an embrace of a leftist-populist, anti-American discourse, a heavy reliance on the military, a consumption boom, a boost in social spending, an assault on the private sector, and a willingness to grant foreign actors significant sovereignty in the national territory. Not all backsliders engage in these policies, and, thus, not all backsliders produce the same kind of institutional changes. In many ways, what happens after semi-authoritarianism depends precisely on these variations.

Finally, this chapter emphasized two variables that were crucial in explaining the extent of democratic backsliding: APSF and institutional destruction and colonization. Venezuela's process of democratic backsliding started, arguably, with two external economic shocks: declining oil prices and increasing debt (1980s). These shocks led to an opening of the party system, from a strict bipartisan to a multiparty and unstable party system (1990s). Traditional parties declined (Acción Democrática) or split (Copei). Traditionally small parties became large (MAS and Causa-R), and new parties emerged (MVR). New democratic alternatives emerged in the electoral menu as well.

Among the new parties, the one with the lowest commitment to liberal democracy, led by Hugo Chávez, managed to win the 1998 presidential elections, in coalition with other smaller parties. Soon, Chávez's party absorbed its minor coalition partners, while the other parties continued their electoral decline and splintering between 1999 and 2000. The result was asymmetrical party system fragmentation: the ruling party became the most cohesive party in a system where most other parties were too weak or small, or in decline.

APSF allowed Chávez to overhaul or colonize a good number of liberal democratic institutions. At first, Chávez's record was mixed, introducing some democratic innovations along with some democratic reversals. But by 2004, the democratic innovations had slowed down and the reversals acquired speed and scope. The opposition and many civic organizations managed to remain independent, but they were unable to stop the process of democratic backsliding: the state, the ruling party, and the restrictions imposed on independent organizations, including parties, were too strong for anyone to resist.

The process of deepening autocratization (2010 to the present) was also the result of changes in the party system, as well as in institutional capacity. This is the argument developed in subsequent chapters. As a preview, the ruling party lost electoral competitiveness (2010–2015). This was the result of two forces: discontent resulting from Venezuela's spectacular economic crash and party adaptation by the opposition, discussed in chapters 3 and 4, respectively. Opposition parties learned how to adapt to semi-authoritarian rules and instituted changes in strategy that paid off electorally. As the ruling party declined in electoral competitiveness, the only chance to survive in office was to impose greater restrictions on party competition and turn more autocratic against opponents. The ruling party was able to achieve these objectives because it was able to redeploy and update many of its autocratic practices and institutions.

The key takeaway is that when Maduro came to office in 2013, the regime had a number of institutional reservoirs: a unified ruling party in a party system prone to divisions; an executive branch that had colonized the most important institutions of the state; a leftist-populist approach to politics that allowed the regime to garner international support from leftist and anti-capitalist political forces and opinion-makers; and a track record of support from both low- and high-income Venezuelans—that is, a strong network of clientelism and cronyism. These reservoirs played an important role in explaining the regime's economic collapse, the ruling party's electoral decline, and the hardening of autocratization between 2013 and 2020.

3

The Worst Economic Crisis outside of War

THE POLITICAL ECONOMY OF COLLAPSE

One of this book's central questions is: Why did the party system change so significantly in favor of the opposition in the midst of semi-authoritarian conditions? Toward the end of the Chávez administration, the ruling party started losing electoral competitiveness, and under Nicolás Maduro, it became fully uncompetitive. I offer two explanations for this: economic crisis and the opposition's party-building strategies. This chapter focuses on the first explanation; the next chapter, on the second explanation.

One reason *Chavismo* lost electoral competitiveness was Venezuela's epochal economic crisis, rightly called "the worst outside of war in decades" (Kurmanaev 2019). In the last years of the Chávez administration, Venezuela's economy started to deteriorate palpably. Under Maduro, the economy collapsed entirely. As the political science literature suggests, economic crises do not necessarily hurt incumbents electorally when the crisis is mild, the ruling party has a strong brand name and links to voters, and the party system is polarized. But when economic crises and corruption become severe, economic crises can produce massive voter detachment (Remmer 1991, Morgan 2007, Morgan 2011, Seawright 2012, Lupu 2016, Morgan and Meléndez 2016, Wills-Otero 2020). By the mid-2010s, this voter flight happened to the United Socialist Party of Venezuela (Partido Socialista Unido de Venezuela, PSUV), leading to declining electoral strength.

This chapter describes how Venezuela's boom turned to bust and the toll this bust took across society. The chapter then turns its attention to a different question: Why did the government do little to remedy the crisis as it unfolded? One way the ruling party could have attempted to survive politically would have been to fix the economy. Many leftist and populist parties in the 1980s and 1990s switched policy preferences in order to address economic crises (Haggard and Kaufman 1995, Roberts 1995, Corrales 2002, Weyland 2002). However, as of 2021, the PSUV did not take this route—a conscious choice to avoid "policy-switching," to borrow Stokes's (2001) famous phrase. To understand this choice, it helps to understand how the ruling party profited politically from the existing model.

The crisis has an economic and an institutional explanation. The economic explanation focuses on the collapse of the oil industry under Maduro, leading to a sharp drop in both oil export revenues and overall imports (Rodríguez 2021). The institutional explanation is that Venezuela's economic institutions, including the oil industry, were in dire straits, mostly because the economic model adopted by Chavismo was faulty. That model could be summarized as follows: an overexpanded state that placed minimal controls on the executive branch while simultaneously placing excessive controls on the private sector. In other words, the crisis was the result of institutions, not just external or structural shocks. And this institutional arrangement, while ruinous for the economy, allowed the government to insulate most state office-holders from the costs of the crisis, and to co-opt a few actors in the private sector by allowing them to make huge profits during the crisis.

The Contours of Immiseration

After staggering between 2010 and 2013, Venezuela's economy experienced one of the deepest contractions in history starting in 2014. Venezuela became one of the few countries in the world to experience negative growth rates consecutively from 2014 to 2018 (table 3-1). The accumulated effect was a spectacular shrinking of the economy.

In May 2019, the Venezuelan Central Bank, which had stopped publishing data on Venezuela's economic performance in 2015, surprised everyone by finally publishing data, and the picture was shocking: Between 2013 and 2018, the Venezuelan economy per capita shrank by 52 percent. This makes the Venezuelan crisis the ninth-worst economic crisis since 1980 (table 3-2). By the first quarter of 2020, before the arrival of COVID-19, the shrinkage continued (Abuelafia and Saboin 2020).

Table 3-1. Venezuela Real GDP Growth Indicators, Global Rankings, 2013–2018

	2013	2014	2015	2016	2017	2018
Number of countries with positive growth rates	164	172	171	169	173	177
Number of countries with negative growth rates	27	20	21	24	19	15
Number of countries with growth rate of zero	2	1	1	0	1	1
Countries with no data reported	1	1	1	1	1	1
Total countries	194	194	194	194	194	194
Venezuela growth rate	1.3	−3.9	−6.2	−17	−15.7	−18
Venezuela's ranking	148th of 164 countries with positive rates.	3rd lowest of 20 countries with negative rates.	7th lowest of 21 countries with negative rates.	Lowest of 24 countries with negative rates.	Lowest of 19 countries with negative rates.	Lowest of 15 countries with negative rates.

Source: IMF (2019).

Note: Annual percentage growth rate of GDP at market prices based on constant local currency. Aggregates are based on constant 2010 U.S. dollars. GDP is the sum of gross value added by all resident producers in the economy plus any product taxes and minus any subsidies not included in the value of the products. It is calculated without making deductions for depreciation of fabricated assets or for depletion and degradation of natural resources.

To get an idea of its magnitude, the financial crisis in the United States between 2006 and 2011, considered by many analysts to be one of the most painful in the country since the Great Depression, entailed a contraction of −1.6 percent. In Venezuela, every sector shrank, but the most affected sectors were industrial activity (−76.2 percent), construction (−95.0 percent), and retail (−79.4 percent).

Table 3-2 also shows that the majority of the world's worst crises occur in autocracies, and Venezuela is no exception. However, among autocracies at peace, Venezuela's crisis by 2019 was probably at the top of the list. Venezuela's economic shrinkage was comparable to the contraction experienced by war-torn nations. Most of the descriptive statistics discussed in this chapter refer to the crisis prior to the pandemic.

What made this crisis especially devastating is that it was accompanied by prolonged levels of very high inflation. Latin America overcame hyperinflation in the 1990s. In fact, the world as a whole virtually eliminated inflation in the 1990s, with one famous economist declaring inflation in 1996 to be "an extinct volcano" unlikely to "rise from the dead" (Thurow 1996:185, 191). However, Hugo Chávez brought high inflation back. Inflation during the Chávez era became the eighth highest in the world starting in 2006 (Puente and Rodríguez 2015). In 2017, Venezuela's high inflation became hyperinflation, and was the single highest in the world. Hyperinflation means

Table 3-2. Worst Economic Crises, War Conditions, and Regime Type, 1980–2018

	Percentage change in GDP per capita	War?	Authoritarian
Liberia (1988–1993)	-85.49426	Yes	Yes
Georgia (1989–1994)	-76.81451	Yes	Yes
Tajikistan (1991–1996)	-68.52847	Yes	Yes
Yemen, Rep. (2011–2016)	-61.12866	Partial (began in 2015)	Yes
Azerbaijan (1990–1995)	-61.00498	Yes	Yes
Libya (2006–2011)	-59.02927	Partial (fighting occured in 2011)	Yes
Iran, Islamic Rep. (1976–1981)	-57.46318	Partial (pockets of uprisings)	Yes
Saudi Arabia (1980–1985)	-56.91243	No	Yes
Venezuela, RB (2013–2018)	-52.36692	No	Yes
Ukraine (1991–1996)	-51.96059	No	No
Kiribati (1975–1980)	-51.54986	No	n.a.
Kyrgyz Republic (1990–1995)	-51.17912	No	Yes
Congo, Dem. Rep. (1989–1994)	-47.08452	No	Yes
Iraq (1986–1991)	-46.64312	No	Yes
Turkmenistan (1990–1995)	-44.67855	No	Yes
Rwanda (1989–1994)	-44.65985	Yes	Yes
United Arab Emirates (1981–1986)	-42.30883	No	Yes
Armenia (1990–1995)	-41.92654	No	No*
Angola (1988–1993)	-40.02107	Yes	Yes
Albania (1987–1992)	-39.24519	No	No*
Zimbabwe (2001–2006)	-38.90748	No	Yes
Russian Fed. (1990–1995)	-37.91658	Yes**	No*
Cuba (1988–1993)	-36.84444	No	Yes
San Marino (2008–2013)	-36.59921	No	No
Equatorial Guinea (2012–2017)	-36.56026	No	Yes

Notes: Data were obtained from personal communication with Miguel Ángel Santos and Santos (2021). Data is based on World Development Indicators (WDI), except for Venezuela, whose coverage is interrupted in the WDI. Instead, data for Venezuela were obtained from the Central Bank of Venezuela (Banco Central de Venezuela, BCV). Authoritarianism: Yes = Scoring an average below 3.0 in V-Dem's Liberal Democracy Index for the indicated period. Because official data from Venezuela is hard to get, economists differ sharply on the magnitude of the Venezuelan collapse.

n.a. = Not available.

*Values were slightly above 3.0.

**Georgian Civil War 1991–1993 and First Chechnian War 1994–1996.

Source: Santos, personal communication, and Santos (2021), based on World Development Indicators (for all countries) and Central Bank of Venezuela; V-Dem, Liberal Democracy Index, various years, www.v-dem.net/en/analysis/VariableGraph/.

that inflation is growing at a rate of between 30 and 50 percent each month (Hanke 2016), which are truly harrowing numbers. High inflation and, of course, hyperinflation are serious problems because, among other things, they lead to a rapid rise in poverty, speculation, and capital flight.

Venezuela's accumulated macroeconomic and microeconomic problems produced an accelerated transition to underdevelopment in a very short span. In just six years, poverty went from 29.0 percent in 2012 to 92.3 percent in 2017, becoming the essential condition of nine out of every ten Venezuelans (figure 3-1). This affected every indicator of development.

Education drops. Venezuela became one of the few countries in the world, at peace, in which education enrollment rates declined sharply. The number of school-age children missing school nearly doubled between 2013 and 2017 (figure 3-2). By 2018, it was estimated that only half of school-age children attended school regularly. The most important reasons cited for missing school involve crisis-related conditions such as lack of food, power, and water (table 3-3).

Hunger spreads. What started out as a mild food scarcity became by 2018 a quasi-famine situation. Because food production (and food imports) essentially ground to a halt, food availability shrank. By 2018, Venezuelans were consuming fewer meals, fewer calories, and fewer proteins than twenty

Figure 3-1. Poverty Data Venezuela, 2002–2019

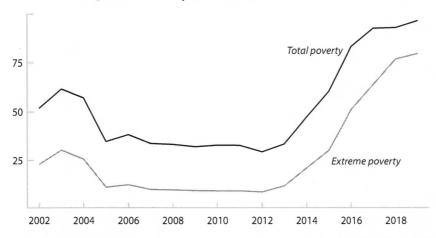

Notes: ENCOVI defines extreme poverty as the inability to afford a subsistence diet of 2,200 calories a day, while poverty is defined as the ability to afford a subsistence diet but not essential services, such as electricity or transportation.

Source: ENCOVI (2020).

Figure 3-2. Out-of-School Children by Age, Both Sexes, 2007–2017

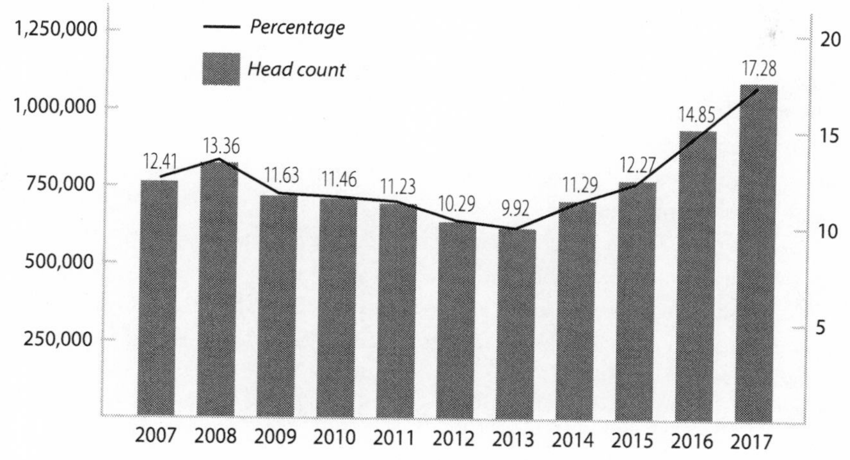

Source: UNESCO.

Table 3-3. Venezuela: Reasons for Missing School (Percentage of Respondents), 2018

	2018
Never misses school	52
Street protests	7
School staff absent	11
Lack of food at home	22
Lack of food at school	13
Lack of transport	17
Teachers' strike	8
Power outages	15
Water outages	28

Source: ENCOVI.

years before. Almost 90 percent of the population expressed not having enough income for food in 2019 (Abuelafia and Saboin 2020). Only one in four children under five was consuming dairy products. An estimated 64 percent of Venezuelans experienced involuntary weight loss averaging 11 kilograms (Castillo 2018, Connectas 2018). In many ways, the spread of quasi-famine conditions represents a modern-day example of Amartya Sen's (2000) argument that famines are more likely to occur in authoritarian contexts, especially when the government refuses to allow imports (Sen 1983). Famines, he argues, can result from a number of factors, but they all share a similar cause: distribution problems. Distribution problems are addressable problems. They require a maximization of information and a coordination of response. In authoritarian contexts, the rulers have no incentives to correct the problems, and the affected parties (e.g., food producers and consumers) lack mechanisms to punish the responsible parties, in this case the government, for their negligence.

Health declines. Venezuela also experienced a medical catastrophe. Hunger, rampant crime, and repression led to one of the world's largest mass exoduses, second only to the exodus from the Syrian civil war. This exodus included a large number of medical doctors. More than 22,000 doctors (approximately 56 percent of the total number) left Venezuela between 2012 and 2017. In addition, Venezuela also experienced medicine scarcity, itself a byproduct of import cutbacks. By 2016, deliveries of medicines grounded to a halt. By 2017, nearly 1,000 essential medicines were unavailable in Venezuela (Lamas 2017). Ninety percent of high-price medications (e.g., cancer treatment drugs) were unavailable (Globovisión 2018). As of 2018, nearly 60 percent of public health facilities had shut down. According to the Central University of Venezuela, of the remaining hospitals, 76 percent had medicine stock-outs and 81 percent lacked surgical materials (Smilde 2017). Even Chávez's famous social missions shut down: only 20 percent of services provided by Misión Adentro, the government's main medical assistance program, were operative (Fundación Váyalo 2018). With food scarce and health services collapsing, infectious diseases spread and the mortality rate increased. Among adults, it is difficult to find good data for health-related deaths. But infant mortality estimates are available, and the picture is brutal. After a steady decline from the 1950s onward, infant mortality rates started to increase again in 2009. By 2016, Venezuela was reporting 21 deaths per 1,000 live births of children before their first birthday, which was 1.4 times larger than the rate in 2008 and comparable to levels in the late 1990s (García et al. 2019). Almost two decades' worth of progress was completely canceled out by 2016.

Women and Queer Populations

Women and queer Venezuelans have taken a disproportionate beating from this crisis. A recent report (Martinez-Gugerli 2020) paints a bleak picture. Because malnutrition, health problems, and education irregularity target children in particular, they also target mothers indirectly since mothers are often the ones burdened with childcare. Because so many schools have stopped functioning, mothers have had to stay home to provide childcare, which reduces their labor participation and thus income. Venezuelan women's role as caretakers has been reinforced in this crisis, with Maduro himself using International Women's Day to recognize motherhood, and to instruct that "all women should have 6 children to grow the homeland" (BBC 2020b).

The same report expands on how the crisis also affected women's sexuality. Because contraceptives have disappeared, numbers of abortions (which are illegal and unsafe) soared; so have sterilization rates, especially among younger women, and sexually transmitted infection, especially HIV (Doocy et al. 2019). For those women who go through with their pregnancies, the maternal mortality rate skyrocketed (Martinez-Gugerli 2020), increasing at an average of 12 to 15 percent each year over the past decade (Smilde 2017). Whether mothers or not, life for women has gotten more dangerous. While Venezuela has reported a decrease in violent crime due to population decline from migration, the femicide rate has continued to rise, with a 10.89 percent increase in 2018 and an 18.89 percent increase in 2019 (Martinez-Gugerli 2020). Fleeing the country has not made things safer for women: 57.3 percent of Venezuelan women's deaths in Colombia are being ruled femicides, and many surviving women are being forced into exploitative sex trade (Martinez-Gugerli 2020).

The crisis also deeply affected gay men and trans women. By the mid-2010s, Venezuela had begun to experience a world-historic HIV crisis, which in Venezuela, as in the rest of Latin America, disproportionately impacts the population of men who have sex with men and trans women. Data are very scarce; even a government report on the HIV epidemic commissioned by the United Nations reveals this scarcity of information: of the thirty-seven indicators that the UN requested from the Venezuelan government, the government was able or willing to provide only eight (Ministerio para la Salud 2016). Nonetheless, enough evidence exists to paint a picture, and the picture is dismal. According to the report, the HIV epidemic in Venezuela in 2015 included 108,575 cases, of which 64.66 percent were men, mostly men who have sex with men. At a time when global survival rates among HIV patients are rising due to better medical treatments, Venezuelan survival rates dropped.

The state stopped importing condoms in 2015. They became available only on the black market, and at exorbitant prices. Public hospitals gave up testing for HIV (Faiola 2017, Faiola and Krygier 2017). There were no antiretroviral medicines or medicines to treat opportunistic infections between 2016 and 2020; some retrovirals did arrive in 2021 with help from the United Nations. Even going to the hospital was risky for HIV-positive patients. There were so many patients who were suffering from contagious diseases in hospitals—and who were not being treated due to lack of medicines—that HIV-positive people were being told to avoid hospitals or to leave as quickly as possible to avoid contagion. Consequently, HIV-related deaths have surged. Between 2011 and 2018, HIV-related deaths increased by 70 percent (Sinergia 2018).

Essentially, Venezuela's pre-pandemic economic crisis fed an HIV crisis not seen in the Americas since the 1980s. According to the United Nations, the number of AIDS-related deaths in the country surged by 25 percent to 2,500 between 2010 and 2016, even as they fell by 12 percent on average across Latin America (Faiola 2017). Approximately 80 percent of HIV patients were getting no treatment. "We've gone back to the 80s when it comes to HIV in Venezuela," said Jesús Aguais, president of Aid for AIDS (O'Boyle 2017). In Venezuela HIV is once again a death sentence. In 2021, the government arrested members of Azul Positivo, an NGO that provided food assistance cards to HIV patients in the state of Zulia. They were released a month later, but they still faced charges of fraudulent handling of cards, criminal association, and money laundering.

This death sentence has led to a disproportionate number of queer Venezuelans seeking an exit. The economic crisis makes LGBT individuals disproportionately vulnerable to sexual exploitation, human trafficking, and disappearance. Disappearances are often unreported (Sinergia 2018).

Explaining the Crash: First Approximations

What can explain the crisis? We can start with some of the most common hypotheses in the literature and political discourse, which focus on (1) external economic shocks, (2) economic warfare, and (3) U.S. sanctions. The first is insufficient. The second treats market actors as acting independently of state policy rather than in response to state policies. And the third was not very impactful until the end of 2019; it can at best explain why the crisis deteriorated in the late 2010s, but not its onset or severity.

External Price Shocks

All structural theories about the resource curse warn that oil-dependent countries have a greater susceptibility to external shocks (Luciani 1987, Auty 1993, Sachs and Warner 1995, Coronil 1997, Baptista 2003, Coronil 2005, Di John 2009). Economic activity other than growth is never optimal during boom times, in terms of efficiency, diversification, and distribution. And during a bust period, macroeconomic performance is especially dismal because of the procyclical nature of commodity-export dependence. Given that such economies depend enormously on oil, with very few other exports, and on imports to sustain both production and retail, a fall in the price of oil (bust period) has a doubly harmful effect: the state's income decreases (without any kind of buffer) and with collapsing imports, production and consumption decline.

Venezuela did experience this type of shock starting in 2014. Oil prices declined from US$100 per barrel to approximately US$40 per barrel in a couple of years. Nevertheless, this external shock is not the main cause of Venezuela's economic crisis. The same external shock was experienced equally in all oil states, but no other state collapsed at the same magnitude as Venezuela. Furthermore, signs of economic trouble began before oil prices fell. By 2012, for instance, almost all public companies were reporting underproduction, idle capacity, and growing debt. There were serious shortages in a number of private-dominated industries. Therefore, the fall of the oil price is more an exacerbation than a true cause.

Private Sector War

Another thesis, put forth by the Venezuelan government, is that the crisis was the product of an "economic war" unleashed by the domestic private sector. This theory posits that economic elites went on a type of strike (or boycott) orchestrated to undermine the government.

This assessment, however, mistakes cause and effect. Underinvestment was the result mostly of unfavorable state treatment rather than the other way around. For instance, capital flight amounted to a staggering $141 billion between 2003 and 2013. One-third of that capital flight was the result of the government borrowing heavily from the private sector by selling dollar-denominated bonds that buyers could acquire with bolívares, and almost half was the result of dollar purchases in parallel exchange rate markets funded by Petróleos de Venezuela, S.A (PDVSA); the rest was probably corruption in the form of overstating import bills and underreporting exports (Salmerón 2013).

Likewise, shortages were responses to government restrictions on the market. In any market economy, if consumer demand goes unsatisfied as in Venezuela (measured by the long lines that people must wait in to receive any kind of product or service), a strong incentive is created for private actors to step in and supply the demand. If the private sector does not step up, it is because of investment barriers. Most of the time, the most important barriers are created by the state. If informal markets exist, in which products are sold illegally, it is because there are no incentives or legal facilities to sell in formal markets, and that too is a product of state policies.

Finally, when the crisis hit, a large part of the Venezuelan economy was in the hands of the state. These state-run businesses were all undergoing a collapse in production that cannot be attributed to the private sector. In this state-dominant economy, the private sector was too minoritarian, too deprived of dollars, too weak, or simply too inconsequential to sink Venezuela's economy. For all these reasons, the thesis that Venezuela's economic recession is the result of an economic war fomented by the private sector is weak, and few Venezuelans actually believe it (Alfredo Keller y Asociados 2016).[1]

Economic Sanctions

Analysts have suggested the role of economic sanctions as a possible cause of Venezuela's economic decline. But this argument has a problem of timing. The severity of the crisis was already in place well before the sanctions became impactful.

Initially, U.S. and Western sanctions against Venezuela were mostly "smart sanctions," meaning that penalties targeted individuals and corporations rather than across broad economic sectors, the government as a whole, or the government's foreign relations. Smart sanctions had little impact on the economy. The Trump administration at first extended smart sanctions to cover more individuals (144 by 2020) and then added new general sanctions targeting the Venezuelan government itself as well as broader industries seen as supporting the state. The state, including PDVSA, was barred from accessing U.S. financial markets as of 2017, from marketing Venezuelan debt instruments in the United States as of 2018, and from selling oil to any U.S.-related individual or corporation as of 2019.

No one disputes that the tightening of sanctions in 2018–2019 caused enormous economic costs (see Bull and Rosales 2020). Sanctions are designed to do so. The debate is about the magnitude of the economic costs. Rodríguez (2019) provides a summary of different positions, with some scholars arguing that the sanctions produced most of the damage and even 40,000 deaths (based on an increase in infant mortality) (see Weisbrot and Sachs 2019), while other scholars argue that the damage was less severe. Rodríguez himself argues that the economic losses were substantial, amounting to $16.9 billion per year, but not as severe as argued by Weisbrot and Sachs (2019). However, Rodríguez (2021) also argues that the acceleration of the "rate of decline" of oil production starting in 2017 (from 1.0 percent per month to 3.1 percent) was strongly driven by sanctions.

There are, nevertheless, several problems with the causal claim. First, the most severe signs of trouble (high inflation, rising poverty, rising debt, declining production, scarcity) were already present by 2015, long before the sanctions started to take a toll. Second, even after the sanctions started to take their toll in 2019, to blame the sanctions for Venezuela's collapse would be predicated on a counterfactual premise that is far fetched—that without sanctions, Maduro would have chosen the right policy. The problem is that

Maduro never showed signs of rectification, even as most economic indicators in Venezuela were trending downward before U.S. sanctions and the threat of sanctions was increasing. There were no signs that the government was considering reversing course before (or even after) sanctions. Finally, the argument could be made that a more competent state would have been able to avoid some of the damage. In other words, other regime-specific figures intensified the impact of sanctions.

That said, the evidence is increasingly clear that the rate of collapse of oil production and revenues accelerated right after the August 2017 decision by the United States to impose broader financial sanctions. In other words, measured in terms of rate of decline, there is a clear before and after effect. But by that point, the revenues extracted from oil were already very low: little was being produced and most of what was produced was being used to repay debts to the Chinese rather than to bring in revenue.

After 2019, the sanctions did become particularly strong and seriously hurt Venezuela's ability to trade with other partners, including to import gasoline. The sanctions certainly exacerbated the economic crisis of 2020. But before that, their role was not that economically consequential.

Some Evidence on Behalf of Resource Curse Theories

Other economics-based arguments do a much better job of explaining the crisis, but only to a point. One example is "resource curse" theories. These arguments are not necessarily incorrect, but are insufficient to explain the full catastrophe in Venezuela.

There are several versions of resource curse arguments.[2] The two most important are the Dutch disease and fiscal disruption. Dutch disease occurs when a boom in the price of a commodity, in this case oil, causes a chain of events associated with the exchange rate that harm the diversification of the economy: price boom in an export commodity → overvaluation of currency → fall of other exports → increase in imports → deindustrialization.

This chain of events did take place in Venezuela under the Chávez government. Non-oil exports collapsed by the end of the 2000s. The problem is that this theory does not necessarily explain why the outcome has been so disastrous.

The Dutch disease theory predicts deindustrialization, but not all the other economic disasters present in Venezuela: collapse of the oil sector, consumer goods scarcity, economic recession during high oil prices, scarcity of imports, and decline in the production of state-owned enterprises. Furthermore, nowadays, the majority of oil states have learned to implement measures to counter the Dutch disease, such as, for example, saving, incentivizing private investment, and diversifying economic services. In Venezuela measures necessary to combat Dutch disease were not implemented.

The other theory associated with the resource curse is the tendency toward procyclical spending. Instead of saving, states undergoing a commodity boom respond by increasing spending, even above revenues. That is, the boom induces deficit spending, perhaps because it stimulates pressures to spend on the part of society, political parties, and even the government itself. This inarguably happened in Venezuela under Hugo Chávez. The problem is that, in Venezuela, deficit spending was taken to an extreme. The majority of oil states saved during the boom or spent with manageable debts. In Venezuela, by contrast, the deficits were enormous.

Nevertheless, the enormous deficit did play a causal role. Once Chávez embarked on deficit spending, inflation began to accelerate. That much was predictable. And it was at this moment that Chávez's economics began to malfunction, with the initial set of misguided policies to deal with inflation (e.g., price controls) leading to new problems, prompting still more misguided policies in response.

The final problem with traditional resource curse theories is that they cannot explain the dearth of reform under Maduro. Resource curse theories predict low incentives to reform during booms. But once the boom ends, there is no reason for the state to remain sanguine, as was the case in Venezuela.

One possible reason for the dearth of reform has to do with resource substitution. If the commodity-dependent state manages to find a resource substitute, reforms may not materialize. The Maduro regime found such a weak substitute: illicit gold mining starting in 2016. However, as future chapters will discuss, this activity generates too few resources to compensate the decline in oil revenues, and few resources from it are devoted to restarting the crashed economy, especially the oil sector (before and after the pandemic). We therefore need to supplement resource curse theories with other factors to understand Venezuela's economic collapse.

An Institutional Explanation: Overexpanded State and Suffocated Markets

The most important explanation for the collapse of Venezuela's economy is Chavismo's unbalanced formula toward states and markets. The state was allowed to grow indiscriminately and without accountability, and markets were excessively constrained by regulation.

At first, this formula was not much of a historical departure (Di John 2004, 2009, Corrales 2010). But near the end of the 2000s, the formula reached excessive proportions. Not since the Cold War, when command economies were common throughout the Soviet and communist world, did we see a country launch such an expansion of state, paired with so many restrictions on the private sector.

We know from the literature on the resource curse that commodity-dependent states, especially petro-states, tend to expand the size and powers of the state during price booms (Collier 2011, Hogenboom 2012, Monaldi 2015). But the literature does not suggest that this expansion will necessarily be as excessive as it became under Chávez and Maduro, or that it would encroach to this extent on private sector activity. No major oil state in the last twenty years curtailed economic freedoms to the same degree (figure 3-3). The control imbalance under Chavismo defied not just Venezuelan history but also theoretical expectations.

The economic outcome from this imbalance was predictable. In countries where regulation of the state is weak, both state leaders and market actors channel wealth into private pockets. In countries where regulations on markets are stifling, investment declines. For these reasons, an increasingly accepted mantra of development is the idea that states need to be endowed with accountability and transparency, and markets with investment facilities, competition, sufficient but not onerous taxation, and consumer protections. Chavista political economy dispensed with both recommendations. The destruction of the economy became inevitable. Below I describe the sequence of this destruction.

Hard Restrictions on the Private Sector

Perhaps the beginnings of the crisis were the price controls and currency restrictions that were put in place in 2003 under Hugo Chávez. Up until the 1980s, these measures were two of the left's favorite means of combating inflation (Edwards 2012, Kaplan 2013). They were common in Venezuela until the late 1980s. When a government refuses to diminish its debt or its spending, there is always the option of establishing price controls. This is what drove Chávez to reinstate price and currency controls in 2003.

Once these restrictions start, a number of subsequent economic ills follow, especially scarcity. Price control is perhaps the only economic measure capable of bringing about consumer goods scarcity. When the costs of production (supplies, labor, tax rates) begin to rise (given inflation), and business owners cannot raise the prices (because of price controls), the result is always the same: they cease to offer goods and services. This situation initiated the great scarcity in Venezuela of 2006–2008. Consumer goods in all categories—from toilet paper to basic foods—began to disappear from the shelves. Foreign exchange reserves also began to dwindle even before the price of oil

Figure 3-3. Evolution of Economic Freedoms,
Selected Oil-Dependent States, 1998–2020

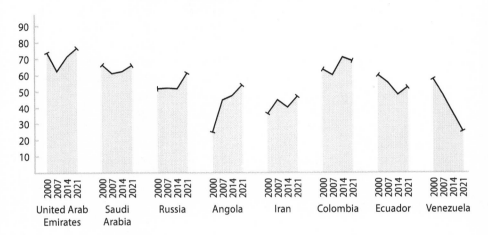

Notes: Index measures economic freedom based on twelve quantitative and qualitative factors, grouped into four broad categories: Rule of Law (property rights, government integrity, judicial effectiveness); Government Size (government spending, tax burden, fiscal health); Regulatory Efficiency (business freedom, labor freedom, monetary freedom); Open Markets (trade freedom, investment freedom, financial freedom). Each of the twelve economic freedoms within these categories is graded on a scale of 0 to 100, with 100 indicating the most economically free score. A country's overall score is derived by averaging these twelve economic freedoms, with equal weight being given to each.

Source: Heritage Foundation (2021).

crashed in the early 2010s. This prompted the government to make exchange rate controls stricter. This started hurting importers, which encompassed the vast majority of the non-oil economy. Many importing firms had to cease operations.

The government's response here was, for the most part, to increase rather than relax restrictions on private actors. The agriculture sector was a key victim. By 2010, national agricultural production began to decline year after year. Many farmers lost access to dollars so that it became difficult for them to acquire machinery, fertilizer, and pesticides. National consumption was on the rise, but agricultural production decreased. Nationalized land and businesses (3.6 million hectares and at least one hundred agricultural companies) produced less and less. By 2015, the amount produced covered between 23 and 45 percent of the demand for rice, beef, corn, coffee, and sugar.

And the worst part about Maduro's approach to unrestricted state and restricted markets is that inflation and capital flight never abated. Because inflation persisted, the state proceeded over time to implement other policies of state expansion: nationalizing more private businesses and punishing more firms for raising prices. Empresas Polar, one of Venezuela's most important food and beverage producing and distributing firms, reported in 2015 that it had been audited more than five hundred times in the past few years (Empresas Polar 2015).

Few Restrictions on the State-Owned Economy

The Chavista model of unrestricted states is best illustrated by looking at state-owned enterprises. In competitive markets, owners of firms look after their firms' assets and profits. This compels firm managers to pay attention to efficiency and cost savings. But when the state is running firms, and the state is not accountable to stockholders or to the rule of law, and the firm has no competition, incentives to operate profitably wane. State managers run businesses poorly, often using business transactions to engage in further corrupt activities, or treating the businesses as sources of jobs for supporters and favors to crony capitalists.

Between 2008 and 2010, at a time when few analysts and politicians still believed in expropriations for the sake of expropriations, Chávez went on a nationalization spree (Obuchi et al. 2011). No one knows for sure how many firms were nationalized. Almost every sector was affected. The state ended up controlling one-third of the banking industry and the majority of the agricultural production and distribution sectors; established a full monopoly over the entire cement, iron, steel, aluminum asphalt, and port industries; and became the most dominant actor in media and telecommunication services. The public sector became a massive employer. Between 2002 and 2012, public sector employment went from 1.9 million to 4.9 million, meaning that the state was hiring an average of 850 people a day (Salmerón 2013). By 2016, Transparencia Venezuela found that the state was running more than 511 firms; for comparison, Brazil had 130 state-owned enterprises, with six times the population of Venezuela (Wyss 2017).

Under Maduro, the lack of accountability in state-owned enterprises has been shocking. Most don't even have identifiable directors. By 2020, Transparencia Venezuela was able to identify the main director for only 53 percent of state-owned enterprises (Venezuela 2020).

Giugale (2017) has offered the following checklist to determine how well or poorly a government manages its (oil) riches: (1) contracts between the state and private firms need to be public; (2) prices used for budget projects must be verified by actors outside the executive branch; (3) savings need to increase during good times, even if modestly; (4) debt should decline; (5) investments by the public sector should be evaluated by independent actors; and (6) audits of fiscal accounts should be done annually by independent figures. The Chavista model violated each of these items.

It shouldn't be surprising that public firms, facing almost no controls, produced huge losses. In 2016, 70 percent of state-owned enterprises were losing billions of dollars, possibly far more than what the government had earmarked for education, health, housing, and social security for that year (Wyss 2017). In the fourth quarter of 2018, Transparencia Venezuela found that out of 576 state enterprises, only 467 were operational (Anzola 2018).

Declining Power

Ironically for a former petro-state, Venezuela experienced a chronic energy crisis of multiple dimensions under Maduro. A survey in late 2020 revealed that 76 percent and 77 percent of respondents faced chronic problems with electricity and running water, respectively (Consultores 21 2020). While the government blamed sabotage, drought conditions, and sanctions for the crisis, the real culprit was concentrated statism.

When Chávez arrived on the scene, the electricity sector comprised a variety of private and public firms regulated by independent commissions. By 2010, the regime had nationalized all the firms in the electricity sector and consolidated a monopoly under the state-owned power company, Corporación Eléctrica Nacional (CORPOELEC). That institutional change destroyed Venezuela's electricity sector. Not having any regulator, competition, or incentive to perform well, CORPOELEC neglected the very sector it was supposed to maintain.

A part of this chronic power crisis, especially in the late 2000s and early 2010s, was attributable to drought conditions. Sanctions played a role by blocking the import of diesel, which were needed for back-up plants (Rodríguez and Rodríguez 2019). But the real cause has been underinvestment, poor maintenance, and embezzlement. In 2019, Venezuela suffered extensive blackouts (figure 3-4). The government claimed sabotage. Engineers think the trigger was a vegetation fire. Power lines were covered in vegetation, which had not been pruned since 2018, an obvious safety hazard. This fire led to a series of subsequent malfunctions, all having to do with poor maintenance, unrepaired parts, lack of competent personnel, and insufficient fuel (Angulo and Batiz 2019).

This energy crisis in turn led to a dramatic water crisis. The three nationwide power outages in March and April 2019 brought on the collapse of the country's water distribution system, which was already compromised with low levels of water reserves, a number of pumps in disrepair, almost 80 percent of thermoelectric plants out of service, and lack of fuel. Most Venezuelans went without water for almost two weeks. People started to take water from contaminated rivers and sewage systems. It was difficult to cook. Medical staff in hospitals had no water to wash their hands (Portafolio 2019).

Figure 3-4. Venezuela's Blackout, 2019

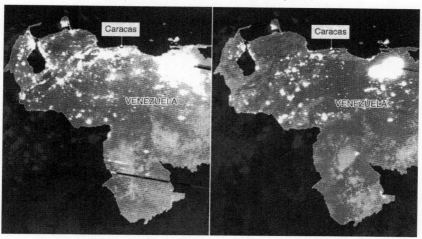

Source: NASA, Nighttime satellite image of Venezuela and Brazil (March 7–12, 2019).

Declining Purchasing Power

By the end of the 2010s, inflation turned into hyperinflation and gradually to partial dollarization. Countries that experience hyperinflation soon develop some form of partial dollarization: once the local currency loses all value, many retailers choose to set prices in dollars. Partial dollarization exacerbated inequalities.

In Venezuela, there was another cause of dollarization: collapse of state services. In March 2019, when the entire electric grid collapsed, electronic debit card payments were impossible. This forced people to start using dollars for daily transactions (Pozzebon 2020). Once enough of a critical mass switches to dollars, there is almost no going back. Dollarization spreads quickly. By early 2020, 64 percent of transactions were made in foreign currency (Abuelafia and Saboin 2020). Most debit card transactions started to use dollars even though the practice was technically illegal.

Dollarization produces economic relief by reactivating markets. However, gains from dollarization are obviously restricted to only a minority of economic actors—those with access to dollars. According to some estimates, that included only 15 percent of the population in 2020 (Rodríguez R. 2020). The rest of the population was left with limited consumption choices.

Declining Oil Power

The lack of control over state-owned enterprises explains Venezuela's transition from an energy giant to a bankrupt petro-state. No state-owned company reflects this catastrophic collapse of the public sector more than Venezuela's goose that laid the golden eggs: the state-owned oil company, PDVSA.[3] One would expect that a regime so dependent on the sale of oil to preserve its electoral coalition would do everything possible to look after PDVSA's operations. However, this firm earned the distinction, perhaps unique in the world, of registering profound declines in production during the oil price boom. This collapse defied trends elsewhere among petro states (figure 3-5).

There was no economic reason for the decline in production to occur. When prices are high, there are greater incentives to produce or at least to invest in exploration, production, and refining. None of that occurred in Venezuela. On the contrary, production had been trending downward since 2004. And, as production was falling, the government invested less, despite high oil prices. Venezuela, as Penfold (2016) put it, turned into the drought-ridden country always "waiting for rain."

In a study comparing the oil industries in Venezuela with those in Argentina, Brazil, Colombia, and Mexico, Corrales, Hernández, and Salgado

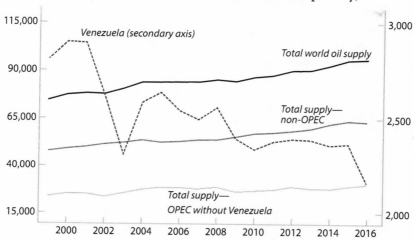

Figure 3-5. Venezuela: Oil Production Relative to OPEC and Non-OPEC Countries (Thousands of Barrels per Day)

Source: Corrales, Hernández, and Salgado (2020).

(2020) showed that the two variables that best explain the performance of these industries is (1) checks on the discretion of the executive branch in intervening in the affairs of the national oil company; and (2) facilities for the private sector to make investments and compete with the national oil company.

In Colombia, for instance, unlike in Venezuela, checks on the executive branch's ability to manipulate the oil sector were strengthened during this period. Granted, Ecopetrol is a smaller firm than PDVSA, but in the 2000s it became one of Colombia's most important exporters. Ecopetrol was governed by an independent board of directors and an audit committee. In addition, private sector actors, and even subnational political leaders (representatives from the governments of oil-producing states) held seats in Ecopetrol's board. This meant that the executive branch could not treat Ecopetrol as its own monopoly. As a result, Ecopetrol responded to price fluctuations very differently than PDVSA. During the oil boom, Ecopetrol expanded production. And when the price of oil declined, Ecopetrol (and thus Colombia) was in a stronger position to mitigate the negative effect of this external shock.

In summary, by 2014, when oil prices were still high, Venezuela was already registering serious problems, both macroeconomic and microeconomic. Venezuela found itself in serious trouble when the oil and sanctions shocks arrived. This explains why Venezuela was so severely impacted by the shocks.

The Political Gains from the Model

The question remains: Why didn't Maduro change course when the signs of economic collapse were obvious?

In 2013, the planning minister, Jorge Giordani, all but admitted that the model was flawed when he declared that more than $20 billion had been lost to fake corporations that obtained dollars through preferential exchange rates (De Freitas et al. 2019). Maduro fired Giordani in 2014. In 2017, Maduro arrested former president of PDVSA, Eulogio del Pino, and several other managers on charges of corruption, suggesting that Maduro had become fully aware of endemic corruption. Yet, no reform followed. At the end of 2018, the attorney general, Manuel Galindo, acknowledged the existence of *corrupción galopante* (rampant corruption) (Leon 2018). Days later Maduro replaced Galindo with a devout party member, Elvis Amoroso, sanctioned by the United States in 2017 for corruption. There is also evidence that Maduro deliberately turned down technical advice from both neoliberal and heterodox economists. One important proposal for economic adjustment came from the Union of South American Nations (Unión de Naciones Suramericanas, UNASUR), a group generally sympathetic to Chavismo. This proposal had a heterodox (and not neoliberal) inclination. Maduro ignored all recommendations (Galíndez 2016).

Maduro refused to change the model because: (1) it placed the ruling party in a position to gain from corruption, (2) it split the private sector, and (3) the government found alternative sources of revenue.

The Venezuelan model of unaccounted powers for state actors allowed the state to insulate the ruling party and reward important non-state actors. The most important avenue was through corruption. Although the private sector was largely strangled by Maduro's policies, the state never went so far as to extinguish the private sector entirely. As was the case under Chávez, private firms with strong connections to, and deals with, the state would thrive, and in the process, state officials could pocket economic kickbacks.

One market that gave rise to massive corruption was the foreign exchange market. For many years, the government offered dollars at different exchange rate prices—some very cheap, and others more expensive. The greatest business in Venezuela became acquiring money at the low dollar price. Only certain industries, or, primarily, certain people with good connections with the executive branch, were granted access to the cheapest dollars. With that, they were able to make a fortune—sometimes licitly, by bringing in needed imports, though more often illicitly, by participating in black markets.

Gallegos (2016) provides a good example of how corruption worked through exchange rate differentials. In 2015, the official exchange rate that offered the cheapest dollar was 1 bolívar = US$6.30. By buying dollars at that price and then offering them on the black market, where the dollar was quoted at US$1 = Bs 180, one would make a profit of 2,800 percent. No business (outside of crime) was more lucrative in Venezuela than speculation on this type of differential exchange (Gallegos 2016).

Corruption, of course, also happens through state-owned enterprises, because they negotiate many contracts with private vendors. An overexpanded state allows the state to place many allies in positions where they can broker contracts. Thus, both employees and managers of state-owned enterprises become dependent on and grateful to the ruling party, and the latter become especially complicit in corruption.

Corruption involving the state is seldom prosecuted under Chavismo. In the 2010s, most Latin American countries experienced serious scandals related to Odebrecht, a multinational Brazilian private firm that established contracts with a number of governments to carry out infrastructure projects leading to overbilling, underpayments, and government kickbacks. The scandal prompted investigations and convictions of high-profile government officials in Brazil, Chile, Colombia, Ecuador, Peru, and Panama. Odebrecht signed at least forty contracts in Venezuela. Only twenty have been disclosed. The disclosed contracts showed that most of the works contracted were never completed (De Freitas et al. 2019, Politika UCAB 2020). Few Odebrecht-related investigations followed. When corruption is investigated, it seldom leads to reforms. After the arrest of former PDVSA president Eulogio del Pino in 2017, the only oil reform that followed consisted of handing over the firm to the military by appointing general Manuel Quevedo as PDVSA's new president. Quevedo was sacked in 2020 based on underperformance, only to be replaced by Chávez's cousin, Asdrúbal Chávez, a symbol of continuism with Chavismo like few others.

The second reason the model persisted is that it split the private sector in a way that benefits the state. The state offers the private sector two options: if you are unwilling to support the state, the state will saddle you with restrictions, regulations, audits, and fines. If you become loyal to the state, you can gain market privileges. The former option, of course, hurts development. But at the same time, it reduces the ability of the nonloyal private sector to make huge profits, curtailing its ability to channel resources to political rivals. Private contributions to the domestic opposition decline. By strangling the nonloyal private sector, the government indirectly inflicts restrictions on would-be opponents in civil society.

The final reason the model never changed is that Maduro was able to find alternative sources of dollars. To compensate for the decline of the oil sector (and in fact, the decline of most of the productive private sector), Maduro turned Venezuela into a neoextractivist narco- and mining-state. Cocaine flows through Venezuela rose from 159 to 249 metric tons per year between 2012 and 2017 (Ramsey et al. 2020). The drug problem in Venezuela is not so much the volume (it is far higher in Colombia), but rather the extent of state involvement. Many sources suspect that the Venezuelan government, and especially the military, at the very least condone, if not actively maintain, ties with internationally connected drug lords for profit-sharing. Additionally, Venezuela also started to export gold and other metals. Turkey has emerged as one of Venezuela's most important buyers. Since October 2017, ten bilateral agreements have been signed between Venezuela and Turkey, most focusing on metals. In 2018, Turkey reported imports of approximately US$900 million in metals from Venezuela, up from nearly zero in 2017. The rise of illicit activities granted the state access to dollars, and equally important, it also allowed non-state actors to profit, thus ensuring their loyalty to the regime. This connection between illicit mining, illicit drugs, and private and public gains is discussed in greater length in chapters 5 and 7.

It is important to note that the connection between declining oil industry and rising illegal mining has produced environmental damage that is probably as serious as the Amazon fires. Rotting refineries led to accidents and then pollution (Urdaneta et al. 2020). The government is slow to respond, if at all. Several major oil spills were detected in 2020. One refinery in particular had three oil spills into the ocean between 2019 and 2021 (Klein 2021). These spills affect waterways and towns, coating beaches, marine life, mangroves, birds, and dwellings. The shrimp-fishing industry has been decimated. In its heyday, PDVSA was known for providing many gifts and free social programs to poor towns; now, all it leaves is pollution (Fermín Kancev 2020). Likewise, the expansion of illicit mining is also causing human and environmental damage (see chapter 7). Activists have begun to describe this environmental damage and its huge human toll as "ecocide" (Vollmer Burelli 2020).

In short, the state opted not to introduce major correctives to the economic model because it identified ways to insulate political allies from the cost of the crisis and at the same time offer some private actors opportunities to actually profit from it. The government also found a way to transfer the cost of the crisis to its potential enemies, thus weakening their capacity to challenge the regime.

Conclusion

In the 2010s, Venezuela came to experience one of the worst economic crises in the world, essentially erasing almost five decades of development. This chapter argued that Venezuela's economic collapse is in equal parts illogical and logical.

It is illogical because no one would have imagined that one of the richest nations in the world, an oil-producing country with the most extensive oil reserves, would end up sinking so low. Between 2003 and 2013, the country received the most extraordinary windfall in its history and one of the largest in the world (Adler and Magud 2013), close to US$1.36 trillion in oil dollars through PDVSA, an amount more than thirteen times the cost of the Marshall Plan, the program that the United States put into practice to promote economic recovery in Western Europe after World War II (Gallegos 2016). After 2013, the country became one of the fastest poverty-making machines in the world. No other economy in the world at peace—resource-based or otherwise—experienced a collapse of this magnitude.

The economic collapse was logical because the results could have been predicted, given the Chávez-Maduro model of development. The model had two prongs. First, Venezuela under Chávez intentionally intensified oil dependence. This made the country even more susceptible to two classic resource curses: Dutch disease and the tendency toward deficit spending. The second prong was the model's institutional response to these curses: an overexpanded state without controls and a cornered private sector with too many controls. It was this response that mostly led to a deep economic crisis, even while oil prices were still favorable.

This institutional framework had already failed before, including in Venezuela itself during the 1970s. As humorist José Rafael Briceño puts it, Chavismo was at the "vanguard of the past."[4]

What could not be predicted was that the model would be applied to such an extreme degree (under Chávez) and that, when the crisis worsened in 2014 (under Maduro), the government would refuse to make amends. In the exact words of Alfredo Serrano, a Spanish Marxist economist and an admirer and adviser of Chavismo: "President Maduro has followed the economic thought of Hugo Chávez to the letter" (García Marco 2016). In fact, Serrano is slightly mistaken. Maduro did not follow Chávez to the letter; he actually intensified Chavismo's excesses. The state became even less accountable and the independent private sector became even more cornered under Maduro.

By mid-2021, Maduro finally took small steps to relax some of the restrictions on the private sector. The government gave a tacit green light to partial dollarization. It began to transfer a few state properties to private actors and offer facilities for private actors to invest in oil. These are, however, baby steps. The Chavista model of an overexpanded and unaccountable state engaged in nontransparent deals with a select number of private actors remains in place.

The Maduro administration preserved this model of development because it allowed it to transfer the costs of the crisis to vast sectors of the population, while still channeling enough political and economic gains to the small group of actors who are vital to sustain Maduro in office: leaders of the ruling party and the military running state offices, many of whom do business with a select group of private actors.

That is not to say that the ruling party has been spared costs. The most obvious cost from not addressing the economic crisis was disaffection among traditional Chavista voters. By 2015, the ruling party had lost nearly a third if not more of its support across the electorate. Chavistas were experiencing "anti-government rage" and "demoralization" (Grandin 2016). The economic model led to a historic decline in the PSUV's electoral dominance, no doubt one of the regime's most spectacular mistakes. The next chapter discusses how the opposition strove to capitalize on this mistake.

4

Rising Opposition

PARTY-BUILDING IN TIMES OF AUTOCRATIZATION

The most significant political transformation during Venezuela's process of autocratization between 1999 and 2020 was a re-equilibration of the party system. Toward the end of the Chávez era and the beginning of the Maduro era, the opposition became electorally competitive. The previous chapter offered the first part of the explanation for the rise of the opposition: Venezuela's economic collapse and its toll on the ruling party's electoral competitiveness. This chapter focuses on the second part: the opposition's party-building strategies.

The evolution of opposition politics during the Maduro years until 2020 is a story of both success and failure. It is a story of success in that the opposition accomplished milestones unimaginable during most of the Chávez administration: becoming electorally dominant, taking control of the National Assembly in 2015, and putting together a remarkable antiregime international coalition that included some former allies of the government. It did this by following peaceful means. Never in the history of *Chavismo* was the opposition this close to unseating the Chavista coalition from power through institutional means.

Yet, it is also a story of failure in that the opposition ultimately failed to unseat the regime. As in some previous instances under Chavismo, the opposition managed to rise, and then stagnate. Some even argue that the opposition's tactics, after 2019, "seriously backfired" (Penfold 2021).

The Venezuela case thus offers an opportunity to reflect on the politics of opposition in the context of democratic backsliding and economic hardship. As chapters 1 and 2 explained, the key puzzle is as follows: If an important permissive condition of democratic backsliding is fragmentation or electoral weakening of the opposition, and an important purpose of autocratic legalism is to keep the opposition weak, what allows the opposition to emerge from this hole or return to it?

On the Theory and (Venezuelan) Practice of Opposition Politics in Autocratizing Contexts

In thinking about opposition revival, I follow Cyr's (2017) point that we should not limit ourselves to the regaining of power as a measure of party revival. The key issue is whether parties can regain electoral strength and, more broadly, national "influence" (Cyr 2017:54). By 2015, the Venezuelan opposition met this concept of revival.

Obviously, the opposition was able to profit from the inherent mistakes of the regime, and, especially, the economic catastrophe described in chapter 3. However, it is a mistake to assume that the fortunes of the opposition are proportional to the regime's mistakes or the economy's downturn. For one, the opposition's revival started in the late 2000s, before the economic downturn. In addition, once economic conditions become too severe, as they did in Venezuela by 2017, they can also hurt rather than help the opposition's prospects. In addition, not everything that Nicolás Maduro did was a mistake—in some respects, Maduro played his cards effectively to counter the opposition's moves, as the next chapter will show.

Furthermore, voter defection from the incumbent party, alone, does not make the opposition competitive (Wills-Otero 2020). Even when economic conditions were producing heavy losses for the PSUV in the mid-2010s, this bleeding would not automatically grant competitiveness to the opposition. Disaffected voters could remain detached, unsure they can beat the regime with the rules in place, or too distrusting of opposition candidates with different ideologies—all of which promotes abstentionism (see Magaloni 2006; Gandhi and Lust-Okar 2009). The opposition itself could remain fragmented, and so, even if it attracts disaffected voters, it may not form a cohesive force to assert itself electorally. And opposition parties could remain unstable, with voters switching parties from one election to the other, maybe even helping start new parties, contributing to fragmentation.

The key to understanding opposition politics—its triumphs and setbacks—has to do with party-building measures. These are steps taken by parties to transform themselves into electorally significant forces (Levitsky et al. 2016). These steps determine whether opposition parties can actually profit from incumbent party losses to flip the balance of power in the party system to their own advantage.

Party-building requires focusing on "goals and strategies" (Howard and Roessler 2006). The literature offers two important insights about which goals and strategies are likely to work. One is to uphold and privilege electoral strategies, which itself requires coalition-building (Bunce and Wolchik 2011). The other is to avoid "extra-institutional" and "radical" responses (Gamboa 2017, Cleary and Öztürk 2020, Mainwaring and Pérez-Liñán 2013). As this chapter will show, between 2006 and 2016, the opposition followed both recipes, to huge reward. Under the name Mesa de la Unidad Democrática (MUD), the leading political parties managed to work with existing rules, however disadvantageous, to form a coalition, stay united at election time, and mobilize voters for elections (Jiménez 2021). They did this at least until 2017. As a result, the fragmentation of the opposition declined. Starting in 2010, the effective number of parties hovered between 1.97 and 2.03, indicating a remarkable parity between government and opposition (Briceño 2021).

This chapter also offers some amendments to these theoretical arguments. First, it is important to do more than just focus on elections. Part of the MUD's revival also had to do with other strategies such as protecting its most important regained institution (the National Assembly), at least until 2020, and adopting a sophisticated foreign policy to enlist support for its cause. Second, flirting with some extra-institutional practices is no doubt risky, as Gamboa (2017) argues, but if done with moderation, it can offer some payoffs. Specifically, the strategic use of street protest (see Laebens and Lührmann 2021), without letting it get out of hand, can help expand the opposition's appeal beyond its traditional base.

Despite its rising electoral strength, the Venezuelan opposition failed to topple Maduro. This too deserves to be explained. However, it is important to acknowledge from the outset the methodological problem associated with invoking the Venezuelan case to draw causal inferences about the opposition's failure to topple Maduro: the case is overdetermined. Various competing causal explanations operated simultaneously in Venezuela between 2020 and 2021: the opposition leadership turned more radical and more prone to risk-taking, the United States hardened sanctions, the state heightened repression, and the pandemic spread sweepingly (in the context of a monumental economic crisis), which demobilized the public and gave the government new tools to repress. It is hard to tell which of these factors was the most decisive, or which factor might have actually succeeded had it not been for the influence of the other factors. That said, the chapter concludes with a review of these factors, even if it is hard to ascertain their decisiveness.

Change in Party System Balance, 2010–2015

Other than expanding the powers of the president, one could argue that the whole point of creating a semi-authoritarian government is to set barriers to stifle the growth of the opposition. It is not easy, therefore, for opposition parties in any process of democratic backsliding to experience a renaissance. And yet, the Venezuelan opposition experienced significant electoral and institutional growth between 2006, its lowest point perhaps, and 2015. Its biggest electoral and institutional expansion occurred in the first Maduro administration, successfully flipping electoral power asymmetry in its own favor. How did this happen?

No doubt, the opposition took advantage of the inherent weaknesses of the Maduro regime. The Maduro regime came to office with three important birth defects: the death of Hugo Chávez in 2013, which created a leadership vacuum; the nondemocratic way in which Nicolás Maduro was selected—by personal selection rather than a primary or even institutionalized party elite consensus as in China (Nathan 2003), which meant no testing of his popularity within the ruling party and beyond; and, of course, the economic crisis inherited from Chávez. These were conditions that, at least at first, helped the opposition gain some ground.

Signs of declining electoral competitiveness for the ruling party were clear from the start, when Maduro ran for president in 2013, weeks after Chávez died. Despite every effort by the party to capitalize politically from Chávez's death—by mounting one of the most public and extravagant funerals in Latin America since the death of Eva Perón in Argentina—Maduro barely won the 2013 presidential election. But the opposition's tactics also played a role in changing the party system to its advantage. Here's what the opposition did right.

Coalition, Unity, and Mobilization

In confronting elections, even if rigged, Howard and Roessler (2006) and Bunce and Wolchik (2010) argue that the opposition must unite, participate, and mobilize.[1] The Venezuelan opposition checked off these boxes after 2005. Even though it was divided into multiple parties and ideologies, the opposition still adopted a common strategy toward elections in general, starting in 2006 (Álvarez and Hidalgo 2020; Jiménez 2021): no more boycotts. Instead, it would continue to denounce the regime's increasing electoral irregularities and pressure the state to introduce reforms, but it would participate. Energies would be devoted to combatting abstentionism (Sucre and Briceño 2016; Álvarez and Hidalgo 2020), that is, to fight the tendency among voters and leaders to opt out of politics altogether, arguing that despite the electoral disadvantages, it was still important to demonstrate to the regime that the opposition enjoyed electoral strength. And, finally, the opposition would seek unity, not in terms of merging all parties into one, but by forming electoral coalitions that would choose only one candidate per contested seat (Cyr 2019; Álvarez and Hidalgo 2020). In 2008, this electoral coalition adopted the name of the Democratic Unity Roundtable (Mesa de la Unidad Democrática, MUD).

With a new logo, a unified list of candidates, and a commitment to run elections jointly, the opposition achieved a rare condition in electoral autocracies—joint campaigning. Opposition joint campaigning has been shown to increase opposition voter turnout in electoral autocracies, especially where opposition parties typically embrace "niche ideologies" (Ong 2021). In those contexts, opposition voters are likely to abstain. But joint campaigning changes the tendency to abstain. Ideologically divided opposition voters feel more comfortable voting for candidates they disagree with if there is joint campaigning. Opposition voters come to expect that other voters will vote too, and this induces voting rather than abstention (van de Walle 2006). Opposition voters finally see a chance of winning, and this too encourages voting (Gandhi and Lust-Okar 2009).

Seeking unity was perhaps the hardest challenge for the opposition, for several reasons (see Álvarez and Hidalgo 2020). First, the parties each came from very different backgrounds: ideological (ranging from the center-right to the extreme-left, including original members of the Chavista coalition);[2] origins (some parties dated from the 1940s, others emerged after the 1990s); presence across the country (some parties had nationwide presence, others were more urban, and still others were more region-specific). Second, the four leading parties in the coalition—Acción Democrática (AD), Primero Justicia (PJ), Un Nuevo Tiempo (UNT), and Comité de Organización Política Electoral Independiente (COPEI)—achieved comparable levels of vote share, which meant that it was difficult for one party to emerge as the leading coordinating agent (Álvarez and Hidalgo 2020). Third, deciding which party would present which candidate for which contested seat was difficult to settle, requiring parties to make difficult concessions.

But in the end, the MUD was able to settle these differences and present mostly unified candidacies in every election from 2006 until at least 2015 (Briceño 2021). The opposition essentially fielded elections as a united front. The MUD endorsed a single presidential candidate in the 2012 and 2013 elections. And the opposition for the most part did not offer competing candidacies for seats in Parliament for the 2015 legislative elections. Rules agreed upon by the opposition to foster electoral unity were both intentional and decisive. These included: (1) previous electoral performance would determine which parties would have greater weight in the selection of candidates, and (2) there was no requirement for coalition partners to agree on policy. The former rule reduced the number of actors negotiating to a manageable number of four main parties; the latter rule lowered the cost of joining the alliance (Bautista de Alemán 2021).

The opposition's post-2005 strategy of denounce, mobilize, and unite paid off electorally. The opposition's share of the votes increased after 2005 (figure 4-1). The opposition actually prevailed in the election for the constitutional referendum of 2007, although it lost a second (illegal) referendum in 2009, where the opposition was actually disunited. The share of the vote continued to increase thereafter. In the 2013 presidential elections, the opposition came very close to matching the ruling party, and, considering the electoral irregularities committed by the government, many analysts suspect the opposition may have actually surpassed the ruling party. The opposition won in eight states and increased its share of the votes in all states. In the 2015 parliamentary election, the opposition defeated the ruling party.

Think Institutions (Not Just Elections)

Gamboa (2017) argues that, for the opposition to succeed, its goals need to be moderate (electioneering, legislating, lobbying, and litigation) and institutional (focusing on using Constitution-sanctioned organizations, rather than coups, guerrilla warfare, and armed insurrection). Radical and extra-institutional goals and tactics can backfire: they can displease many sectors and invite harsh responses.

For the most part, the Venezuelan opposition during Maduro's rule adhered to moderation and institutionalism. For instance, the opposition started to think about the importance of not just challenging the presidency when it could, but also of retaking Congress, a perfect example of moderate and institutional strategies. In 2010, the opposition managed to reenter the National Assembly through legislative elections, and in 2015, the opposition took control of the Assembly, defeating the ruling party by taking 56.2 percent versus 40.9 of the vote. The opposition obtained 112 seats (an increase of 48 seats) and left the ruling party with only 55 seats (a drop of 41 seats). This was the opposition's most stunning victory since Chavismo came to power.

The 2015 legislative election results were a shock to everyone. The opposition's resounding victory was all the more impressive considering the

Figure 4-1. Venezuelan Electoral Results, 1999–2018

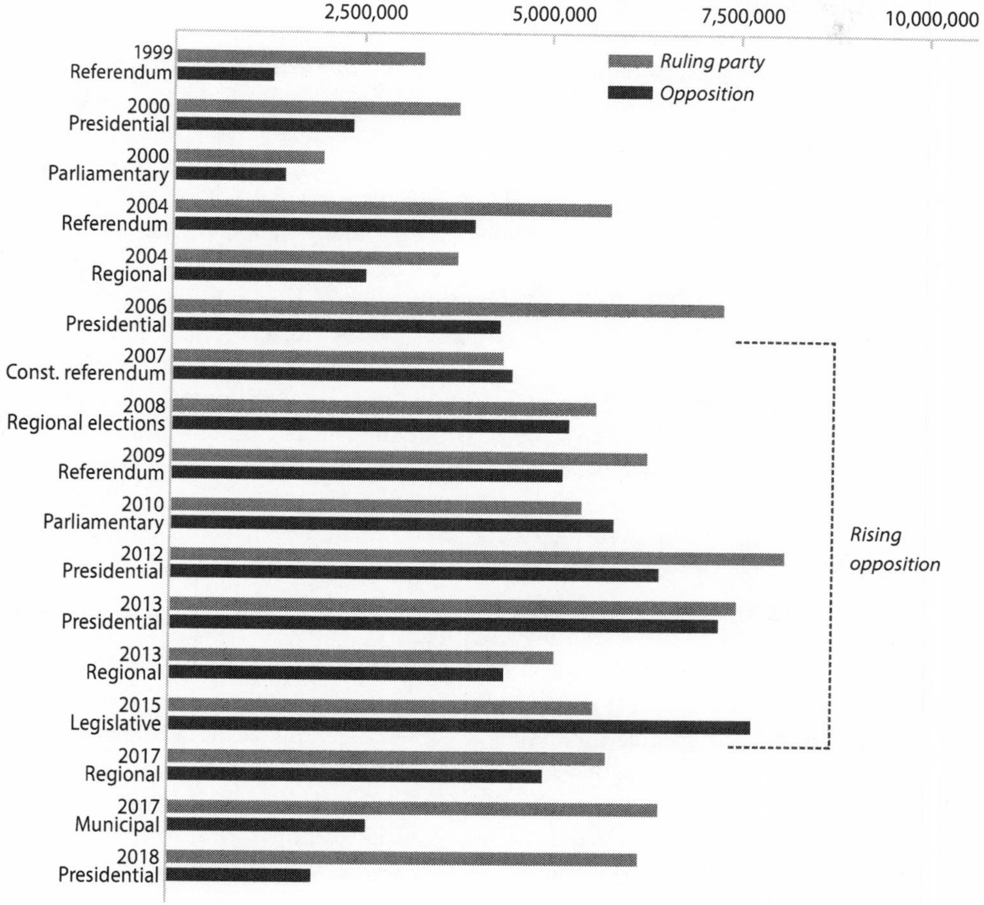

Source: CNE (various years).

unfavorable electoral terrain. The government went to the polls with twelve new electoral irregularities—the largest number on the books ever—hoping to avoid defeat. Everything had been designed to favor the government (Cyr 2019).

For instance, the National Electoral Council (Consejo Nacional Electoral, CNE) took long to announce the official date of the elections, giving little time for the opposition to get organized. One day after the opposition released its list of candidates, but before the government party released its own list, the CNE announced a new electoral regulation requiring 40 percent of each party's candidates to be female (Castillejo 2015). Only 11 of the 110 opposition candidates were women. Furthermore, multiple opposition candidates were arrested and/or barred from running (Agencia EFE 2015; Stolk 2015). The Supreme Court intervened in one of the major political party's internal affairs in an attempt to appoint more progovernment leaders (Transparencia Venezuela 2015). Former Chavista, now-opposition parties were banned from presenting candidates, also because of the gender-parity law (*El Estímulo* 2015). Some traditional parties among the opposition were also banned. In a clear display of nepotism, Cilia Flores, former member of Parliament and wife of Nicolás Maduro, was allowed to run for a state in which she did not hold a four-year residency, which violates Article 188 of the Constitution (Transparencia Venezuela 2015). Data showed that broadcast TV hardly covered the campaign activities of the opposition (Corrales and von Bergen 2015). At the same time, Maduro made twenty-five public appearances in campaign rallies for party candidates (von Bergen Granell 2015). Public rallies for the opposition, however, were banned in fifty-eight key districts, including twenty-six swing districts. Additionally, the government engaged in uneven gerrymandering.

With this election, the government went into panic mode. This was the first time since 2000 that the ruling party had lost control of the National Assembly, which until then was one of the regime's most reliable rubber stamps. Not only did Maduro lose control of a major institution, he also realized that even with the irregularities he could not win elections. Venezuela's party balance had flipped. The opposition now had the upper hand. And because preexisting electoral laws, created under Chávez, tended to give greater representation in Congress to majorities (which violated the constitutional principle of proportionality), the opposition's 56 percent victory translated into a supermajority of seats (Polga-Hecimovich 2015).

Outreach across Classes

The opposition during this time also flirted with some radical and extra-institutional tactics, such as street protests. Laebens and Lührman (2021) argue that it is difficult to contain backsliding without civic protests. The Venezuelan opposition parties encouraged massive protests in 2014 and 2017. It did so, in part, to exert pressure on the government, no doubt, but also to be able to mobilize cross-sectionally.

The opposition had always counted on the support of urban sectors, the middle classes, and the intelligentsia, including the student movement. Under Maduro, the MUD made greater efforts to reach out to lower-income groups, where the opposition always had some but not overwhelming support. With major street protests, the opposition managed to demonstrate that it was also able to achieve widespread appeal across low-income groups.

During Maduro's first term, the opposition managed to organize two massive protests, one in 2014 and the other in 2017. In 2014, a small protest initially started by student demonstrators against state security forces became a nationwide movement after it was embraced by opposition party leaders (Sequera 2014). Critics contended that this round of protests, though massive, still exhibited a class divide between the more middle-class/wealthier protestors and the poor who were less engaged in protests (Neuman 2014a). Perhaps. But the opposition continued its outreach by working with protesters throughout 2015 and 2016 (Martín 2016). In the 2015 legislative election, the opposition won in the 23 de Enero and Sucre parishes in Caracas—perhaps two of the most prominent bastions of Chavismo in the entire country (Briceno Perez 2015; Hellinger and Spanakos 2017). Protests erupted once more in 2017, culminating in the April 19 Mother of All Marches, in which over 6.0 million protestors participated, including 2.5 million in Caracas alone. The rallying cry was "Maduro, we don't want you" (*El Nacional* 2017). This was a massive protest, and for the first time, there was evidence that protest included low-income neighborhoods (Amaya 2017; Partlow and Krygier 2017).

The Government Counterattacks: Repression and Irregularities, 2015–2018

The ability of the opposition to reach out across sectors was never as strong as it had hoped. Alejandro Velasco, who studied support for Hugo Chávez in low-income neighborhoods of Caracas, argued that many people in these sectors still didn't identify with the opposition and still refused to participate in opposition-led protests (Stefanoni 2017).

Furthermore, the protests may have been a bit of a mixed bag. On the one hand, they showed strength. On the other hand, as Gamboa (2017) argues, more radical and extra-institutional tactics can and did elicit harsher repression from the government, and in the end, led to very little regime change. Jiménez (2021) has argued that the relationship between repression and opposition coordination is curvilinear (an inverted U). When repression is low, opposition coordination will be informal or unstable; when repression is at intermediate levels, opposition coordination will be strong; when repression is high, opposition coordination declines again. The effects of heightened repression after 2017 are discussed in the next chapter. Suffice it to say that the repression worked. It would become very difficult for the opposition to organize massive protests again or maintain unity. Citizens became too scared of the consequences.

The government not only increased repression but also curtailed the activities of Congress and revamped electoral irregularities. These measures are also discussed in the next chapter. The overall point is that this created important hurdles for the opposition (Jiménez 2021; Aveledo 2021; Bautista de Alemán 2021). The opposition organized a massive campaign to start a recall referendum, but the CNE tried every possible legal, technical, and fabricated argument to delay this process, ultimately prohibiting the recall election altogether (Pestano 2016). Electoral irregularities became even more pronounced in the regional elections for governors scheduled for 2017, ultimately leading to a resounding PSUV victory with seventeen of the twenty-three governorships (Reuters 2017b). These results were decried by many opposition and outside observers, some of whom chastised the opposition parties for believing they could win in elections directed by a fraudulent CNE, and calling for resignations of opposition leaders (Al Jazeera News 2017).

The government's cocktail of congressional skirting, repression, and electoral irregularities took a heavy toll. The MUD suddenly appeared ineffectual, cornered, unable to influence politics, irrelevant. The barriers posed by the government undid the electoral unity of the previous ten years, with leaders splitting on whether to participate in elections or not, whether to protest or not. More voices emerged in the opposition questioning the desirability of adhering to institutional means to challenge the government.

The boycott wing took the upper hand by 2018. Acción Democrática (AD) left the MUD over disagreements about what to do for the 2018 election. The wing in favor of participating in the elections ended up splitting into two candidates. One was Henri Falcón, a former Chavista governor who left the PSUV in 2010 and aligned with the MUD in 2012, becoming chief campaign strategist for Henrique Capriles Radonski, then leader of the MUD. The other was Javier Bertucci, an independent evangelical who had never been part of the MUD. With this three-way split: Falcón, Bertucci, and the abstentionists, all in the context of intense electoral irregularities, economic devastation, and massive migration, Maduro managed to win reelection (International Crisis Group 2018).

All of this was occurring in the context of Maduro's plummeting approval ratings. When asked to state the reason Maduro was still in power, Venezuelans blamed the MUD above any other factor. Just weeks before the presidential election, when asked to name a good leader, 47 percent of respondents would not name one. The two presidential candidates, Falcón and Bertucci, had approval ratings of 6 percent and 2 percent, respectively (figure 4-2).

The government placed the opposition in a no-win situation. By ramping

Figure 4-2. Support for Political Figures in Venezuela, 2018

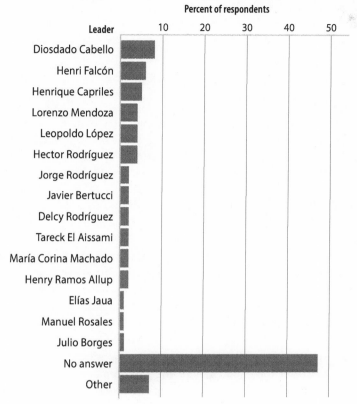

Notes: Percentage of respondents answering "Can you tell me the name of someone you think is a good leader in Venezuela or would be a good leader in the future?

Source: Consultores 21 (2018).

up electoral irregularities while also creating opportunities for the opposition to participate, it undid the opposition's decade-long effort to preserve electoral unity. Of eleven possible preelection irregularities, the Venezuelan government approached the 2018 elections committing at least ten, including banning candidates and parties, manipulating the electoral calendar to benefit the ruling party, allowing electoral authorities to be partisan, failing to properly update and audit voting registries, making welfare subsidies conditional on voting for the government, and threatening to keep tabs on people's voting preferences.

Everyone knew that the election was a sham. But the opposition forgot its main lesson from 2015: that boycotts end up giving their opponent the chance to win, that without campaigning the opposition loses touch with the electorate, and that disunity also favors the incumbent. Hence, Maduro, with an approval rating of only 30 percent, was able to win in 2018.

The Juan Guaidó Phenomenon: Accident, Pact-Making, and Intentionality

Despite the setbacks of 2017 and 2018, the opposition managed to regain momentum again in 2019. Under the leadership of a new face, Juan Guaidó, the MUD launched the most powerful institutional attack on the government outside of electoral and street-level challenges. Guaidó became president of the National Assembly (January 5, 2019). He quickly managed to reunite the opposition in the Assembly to declare Maduro's second term illegal. He argued famously that Maduro had carried out "an usurpation of power." This meant that, because Maduro did not win the presidency in an election that was free and fair, his presidency starting on January 10 was constitutionally illegal and the post was therefore vacant. Congress then proceeded to declare Guaidó as acting president of the country (January 23, 2019). This was followed by recognition from fifty-seven countries, some of which had previously been on Maduro's side. By February, Guaidó was the most popular leader in the country, with approval ratings hovering around 62 percent. This was a new peak of popularity and unity for the opposition.

The Guaidó phenomenon, like all the achievements of the opposition, turned out to be insufficient. On the one hand, no other politician, or movement, managed so much: creating splits in the government and receiving so much international support. On the other hand, as of this writing, Guaidó has yet to win the big prize: unseating Maduro. He also adopted more maximalist strategies, which some saw as mistakes (Penfold 2021). Below I discuss the achievements and then the setbacks.

The Guaidó Phenomenon as Party-Building

The Guaidó phenomenon can be construed as the result of two good decisions by the opposition, both involving institutional developments, and, especially, party-building strategies: the parties' decision to preserve unity across opposition parties in Congress and to privilege links with social movements. Between 2017 and 2018, party unity was disintegrating in the arena of electoral politics: boycotts and independent candidates were emerging. However, in the arena of Congress, unity remained a priority. One of the most important decisions by the MUD once it took control of Congress was to rotate the presidency yearly from party to party. This was done to preserve unity. The presidency went first to Acción Democrática (Henry Ramos Allup in 2016), then Primero Justicia (Julio Borges in 2017), followed by Un Nuevo Tiempo (Omar Barboza in 2018) and then Voluntad Popular (Juan Guaidó in 2019). Without this rotation agreement, it is unlikely that Guaidó would have been chosen because Voluntad Popular was too small a party in Congress, only the fourth-largest in size. Bigger parties would have tried to impede granting the presidency to such a small party, and, in fact, they did try. But in the end, the party-rotation pact was respected, and the presidency went to Voluntad Popular.

Juan Guaidó himself was not the obvious leader from Voluntad Popular to take over as National Assembly president. He was chosen for both accidental and intentional reasons. The accidental reason is that the main leader of the party, Leopoldo López, was still under house arrest, accused of inciting violence. The intentional reason was that, once it was obvious that López couldn't be appointed, party leaders opted for Guaidó because his profile met important party goals set by Voluntad Popular.

First, Guaidó was young and unknown, and this met Voluntad Popular's and the MUD's goal of adopting a new face to counter the government's argument that the opposition was led by the "same old people." Second, Guaidó came from the student movement that led the protests of 2007, and thus satisfied Voluntad Popular's desire to reaffirm its commitment to an alliance between parties and social movements. Third, Guaidó came from a humble background (one of seven children of a commercial pilot and a teacher), and this met Voluntad Popular and the MUD's goal to show that they were not led only by economic elites. Finally, Guaidó, unlike the other top leaders of the party, had good relations with the other parties and was seen by all parties as nonthreatening and nonpartisan (Krygier et al. 2019).

In short, the Guaidó phenomenon was somewhat accidental, but also the result of deliberate pact-making and renewal-seeking by party leaders. In many ways, it was an example of party-building in the face of rising adversity.

An Opposition with a Foreign Policy

Another success of the opposition in 2019 was to garner international support.[3] The literature of democratization argues strongly that opposition forces need strong international allies. When Latin America was governed by autocracies, it was not that difficult for opposition forces to find government allies abroad. As long as parties could convince the United States and its allies that they had no intention of siding with Cuba or the Soviet Union, opposition parties could find outside states as allies.

However, in the context of democratic backsliding, garnering international support is not as easy for the opposition. It is hard to convince foreign states that, in fact, the opposition is operating under a full-blown dictatorship. The international community is not equipped to easily handle, let alone punish, autocratic legalism when it originates from an elected government. In the case of Venezuela, the opposition also had to overcome its reputation of being a destabilizing force. This reputation dates back to 2002, when most of the opposition sided with that year's coup. The opposition needed to work hard to change both the government's image as well as its own.

Guaidó achieved this change of image, in part because the MUD had already laid the groundwork for this support. It did so by establishing one of the most comprehensive foreign policy initiatives of any opposition movement in the Americas since the end of the Cold War.

By early 2019, more than fifty-seven countries expressed support either for the National Assembly, for Guaidó himself, or for his central message calling for new elections, according to Prodavinci, a website for Venezuelan analysis (see also Martinez-Gugerli 2020b). Meanwhile, only fifteen nations—including Bolivia, China, Cuba, Iran, Russia, and Turkey—remained supportive of Maduro in 2019 (although most countries refused to officially break diplomatic relations with Maduro). Nearly the same number have said they will not take sides.

It is important not to undervalue this international turnaround. At the start of the Maduro administration, the situation was the exact opposite (table 4-1). Despite receiving moral support from key lawmakers and thought leaders in the United States and other nations, the Venezuelan opposition was largely isolated internationally. A look at the Organization of American States (OAS) voting shows this isolation. In 2014, Maduro had many international allies. His allies sided with him on a vote to disallow opposition leader María Corina Machado to speak at the OAS. By 2016, the tide had turned. The OAS voted against Maduro's attempt to block a meeting on violations of the Democratic Charter. Support flipped by almost equal margins. The number of Maduro-allied countries shrank to a mere three countries voting against a resolution declaring Venezuela's 2018 presidential election fraudulent and invalid and against another 2019 resolution calling for an independent investigation into human rights abuses by the Maduro regime. There was a brief spike in support for Maduro to a total of nine countries siding with him that same year on whether to allow the National Assembly to appoint Venezuela's representatives to the OAS, but since that high, pro-Maduro votes sank back to three to five countries, against a solid bloc of twenty countries.

Maduro inherited from Chávez one of the most interventionist and "hyperactive" foreign policies in Latin America's post–Cold War history

Table 4-1. Organization of American States Votes on Venezuela, 2014–2019

	Voted with Maduro	Voted against Maduro	Abstained	Total
2014	21	11	1	33
2016	11	20	2	33
2017	5	20	8	33
2018	3	19	11	33
2019a	6	19	8	33
2019b	9	20	6	35
2019c	3	21	7	31
2020	5	20	8	33

Notes: 2014: Venezuela requested the Organization of American States (OAS) to bar the press from attending opposition leader María Corina Machado's deposition. 2016: Venezuela requested canceling the meeting to discuss Venezuela's violations of the Democratic Charter. 2017: Resolution condemning Venezuela for repression of protests. 2018: Resolution declaring that the May 20 presidential elections were undemocratic and illegitimate. 2019a: Resolution to not recognize the legitimacy of Maduro's new term as president. 2019b: Vote on recognition of the Venezuelan OAS representatives from the National Assembly. 2019c: Resolution calling for an independent investigation into Venezuelan human rights situation. 2020: Resolution welcoming the reelection of Juan Guaidó as president of the National Assembly.

Source: OAS.

(Marthoz 2014; Corrales 2009; Corrales and Romero 2012; Mijares 2017; Serbin and Serbin Pont 2017). Much of the region's response to the Venezuelan crisis can be explained as resentment against this interventionism, which included supporting radical leftist groups, transferring nontransparent subsidies to friendly movements, openly insulting presidents who disagreed with Chávez, and even supporting terrorists in Colombia. Many of these Venezuelan-supported allies (e.g., Rafael Correa in Ecuador, Evo Morales in Bolivia, Daniel Ortega in Nicaragua, Cristina Fernández in Argentina, Mauricio Funes in El Salvador), if they won power, repeated offenses similar to Chávez's: concentration of power, high-level corruption, sectarianism, secret deals with the Chinese, or mistreatment of the media.

One of the consequences of Venezuela's interventionism has been Latin America's remarkable shift away from Chavista sympathizers since 2015. This shift has many explanations that cannot be reduced to a single story for all. But in almost every case, an important factor is a reaction to the missteps by the Venezuelan-supported left in each country.

Latin American governments are not opposing Maduro merely because they are on the right; instead, they moved to the right in part in response to what Venezuela did to their countries.

Venezuela's polarizing interventionism did not end when it started to run out of petrodollars in 2014. In fact, it acquired even more objectionable dimensions. As oil revenues declined, Venezuela began to engage in more illicit financial operations, prompting major rifts with Panama and several European countries concerned about money laundering. As dissent in the Venezuelan Armed Forces grew, Venezuela intensified its support for narco-terrorism, which in Venezuela operates from within the military. Venezuela's support for drug trafficking is directly affecting crime rates in Central America, the Dominican Republic, and Mexico. And as Colombia's government reached a peace deal with its largest rebel group, Venezuela began to support an alternative one, the National Liberation Army, which in mid-January of 2019 took responsibility for a suicide bomb attack at a police academy in Bogotá that killed at least twenty people.

As if regional interference were not enough, Venezuela also started exporting poverty. In 2017, Venezuelans started leaving in droves, inundating the strained institutions of many recipient countries in South America. As of February 2021, nearly 5.5 million people had left Venezuela, most of them since 2017. The most impacted countries have been Colombia, Peru, Ecuador, Chile, Brazil, and Bolivia. One consequence of this migration, in addition to straining resources, is to stimulate debate in recipient countries about Venezuela. Most of these debates are unfavorable to Venezuela's government (and since 2019, about the United States as well, for imposing sanctions). This exodus hurt Maduro's image with both governments and citizens abroad.

In sum, a consequence of Chavismo has been to export corruption and poverty across the Western Hemisphere. So today it is not surprising that in so many Latin American countries the electorates are vastly anti-Chavista. When they decided to support Guaidó in 2019, Latin American presidents were responding, therefore, not just to events in Venezuela but also to anti-Chavista sentiment in their own countries, itself the product of Venezuela's international behavior.

The United States also responded to Venezuela's foreign policies. It is not clear that the Trump administration, in tightening sanctions, cared much about human rights in Venezuela. But it did care deeply about Venezuela's non-oil exports, especially drugs. The United States also dislikes the way that Venezuela's actions impact Colombia, a key U.S. ally in the region. And of course, the Trump administration took into consideration the wishes of deeply anti-communist voters in Florida, comprising mostly Cuban Americans and newly arriving Venezuelans.

But it is not just the foreign policy of the Maduro administration that has mattered in determining the international response. The foreign policy of the opposition has also been crucial in changing international sentiment toward Maduro. In 2006, the opposition had a terrible reputation across the globe. It was seen as composed of recalcitrant, obstructionist, and elitist sore losers, unwilling to accept the reality that they could not win elections against Chavismo. The opposition's role in the 2002 crisis, which led to the military pushing Chávez to resign briefly, gave the opposition the reputation of recalcitrance and illiberalism.

The opposition then spent the next decade reconstructing its international image. That meant doing work at home and abroad. At home, the opposition became more rule-accepting, meaning more eager to participate in elections, even if these were increasingly biased. The opposition mobilized voters, growing electorally to the point of obtaining full control of the National Assembly in 2015, despite rigged electoral rules.

Abroad, the opposition engaged in a systematic campaign to denounce Chavismo for all its faults, including its human rights abuses. Members went to the right places—the Organization of American States in Washington, D.C., as well as to The Hague and European capitals.

For Venezuela's May 2018 presidential election, the opposition succeeded in getting forty-seven countries and important regional sources of legitimacy like the OAS to not recognize the vote. International activism continued thereafter. An Associated Press report provided nitty-gritty details of that activism (Goodman et al. 2019). It was one thing to have international leaders refuse to recognize the election; it was another to get them to support Guaidó's assumption of temporary powers. This was initially seen as too risky. So Guaidó and his party bolstered their international efforts. This meant secret trips by members of Guaidó's party and other lawmakers abroad, personal visits with foreign presidents, discussions with both moderate and hard-line factions abroad, and waiting until they garnered sufficient backing to initiate a transition (Lares Martiz 2019). Guaidó created the international response he wanted rather than responding to external cues.

None of this negates the importance of foreign influence in shaping developments inside Venezuela. Factors such as rising U.S. sanctions hurt the government and encouraged the opposition. But it was not internationally predetermined that Venezuela's opposition would gain the upper hand after the 2018 elections or that it would have this much international support. All this was a result of the Venezuelan government's own foreign policy blunders and the opposition's diplomatic achievements.

The Setbacks

Despite the opposition's achievements at home and abroad, the opposition still failed in its important goal to dislodge the regime. It attempted an unsuccessful insurrection, led by Guaidó himself on April 30, 2019, but this failed to garner significant military support and defections, while the streets too remained calm (Associated Press 2019). It participated in another paramilitaristic adventure, Operation Gedeón, a maritime invasion involving exiled former military members with private backing from a U.S.-based security firm, which was easily intercepted (and probably infiltrated) by government forces on May 3 and 4 of 2020 (Martinez-Gugerli and Ramsey 2020; Vyas and Forero 2020). The opposition entered into peace talks with the government on four occasions, sponsored by international actors such as Norway and the Vatican, but these led to no real concessions (Smilde and Ramsey 2020). It also tried to introduce a caravan with humanitarian aid from Colombia, only to be stopped short at the border by Maduro's military after a bloody clash with opposition supporters (Meredith 2019).

In the end, Maduro's governing coalition has stayed in place, with only a few economic (Seijas Rodríguez 2020) and political concessions (Marsteintredet 2020). Less than a year and a half after Guaidó's rise, his inability to unseat Maduro caused his popularity to plummet, with his approval rating down to 25 percent in May 2020 (Globovisión 2020). He was also unable to prevent the government from introducing a new set of electoral irregularities intended to rig the 2020 elections for a new National Assembly. The Guaidó phenomenon, like almost all previous moments of oppositions rising (the 2002–2003 protests, the 2007 protests, the 2015–2017 elections and protests), fizzled.

Many analysts blame Guaidó's mistakes. Critics have attacked him from every angle. Some say that he has not been radical enough, naively agreeing to empty negotiations with the government (Berwick and Guanipa 2019). Others say that he has been too radical, aligning too closely with the most hard-line sectors in Washington and Colombia (PBS 2020). In fact, it would not be incorrect to argue that Donald Trump's hardening of the embargo was made possible because of Guaidó's direct lobbying. Still others accuse Guaidó of being too naive, for example, thinking that he could organize a humanitarian mission without military cover (BBC News 2020a). Others blame him for being too prone to adventurism, supporting or not preventing ill-planned amateur pseudomilitary operations (the call for rebellion in 2019, Operation Gedeón) (Melimopoulos 2020). Still others blame him for being incoherent, supporting a variety of starkly different approaches and appearing to have no actual, coherent plan (Melimopoulos 2020.).

No doubt, part of Guaidó's approach involved turning more hard line and risk-taking. He refused to participate in the 2020 legislative elections without a plan for action after the election. He aligned the MUD too closely with the Trump administration's policy of maximum pressure, which involved not only imposing sanctions but demanding Maduro's removal rather than just new elections (see the next section). And he called for a military insurrection against the regime without spelling out clear terms for a future amnesty. These policies, inadvertently, scared Chavista voters, reunited the civilian and military Chavista leadership behind Maduro, and created tensions within the MUD, which always had a more moderate sector, calling for less maximamlist strategies (Penfold 2021).

But it could very well be that the reason for the opposition's failures since 2020 had less to do with its mistakes and more with structural and institutional barriers to opposition politics in autocratizing settings.

The Barriers

The first barrier was posed by the economy. Economic crises do not seem to have a linear effect on opposition politics in autocratizing cases. On the one hand, some economic deterioration helps the opposition: it creates incentives for the opposition to mobilize and garner support stemming from economic discontent. But after a certain point of deterioration, economic crises hurt the opposition: economic privation impedes electoral growth. The opposition becomes increasingly deprived of resources to run campaigns. Citizens need to devote more time and energy to survival, leaving less time and energy for protesting. Exiting (through migration or abstaining) become preferred options, especially if voice and mobilization are being heavily repressed.

The second barrier, and, in fact, the more serious of the two, was the regime's political response to the rise of opposition politics. Just as the opposition can rise in the context of autocratization, so can the regime. The rise of the opposition poses an existential threat to the government. Becoming electorally uncompetitive scares the ruling party, especially if the system is operating under a constitution and electoral system designed to empower majorities and penalize minority parties (Marsteintredet 2020). It is naive to assume that a regime in this context would remain unmoved. A counterresponse is almost unavoidable. One often hopes that a government could soften its autocratization in response to the rise of the opposition and offer some sort of concession or even a liberalizing pact (O'Donnell and Schmitter 1986). But in the case of Venezuela, tragically, the regime did the exact opposite. It became more autocratic and more entrenched. This chapter discussed two of those responses: increasing electoral irregularities and further repression. The next chapter will show that the response of the government was even more severe than this chapter conveys.

The third barrier was the mistakes made by the United States, especially the way it hardened sanctions in 2019. Chapter 3 discussed one debate about sanctions: their role in causing economic crashes. There is another debate: their role in generating regime change (for a summary of this debate, see Gratius and Ayuso Pozo 2020). The emerging consensus is that sanctions are unlikely to induce regime breakdown and democratization if the sanctioned government (1) has little political or economic interest in strong ties with the sanctioning party (Pape 1997); (2) has access to alternative economic outlets (e.g., trading partners, illicit economic activities); and (3) has the means to transfer costs to the population at large while insulating a small groups of actors from the costs of sanctions. If they are going to work for regime change, sanctions have a small window of opportunity. If they don't break the regime right away, extending sanctions over time is likely to entrench the regime.

The Venezuelan case between 2019 and 2021 may well go down in history as one more example where sanctions fail to produce regime change, and maybe even backfire. Although there are examples of cases in which Western sanctions do produce regime change, these are rare. This may not be accidental. Sanctions are often counterproductive: in the medium term and beyond, they weaken civil society more than the targeted state.

In the case of Venezuela, Smilde (2021) has argued that the problem with the Trump administration's sanctions was that the conditions for relaxing them were inflexible. The United States began to demand major concessions (e.g., immediate Maduro resignation) as a condition for any form of relaxation. This combination of sanctions and inflexibility had three counterproductive effects.

First, it unified government forces, thus reducing the probability of splits, or at least weakening moderates or pragmatists (see also Penfold 2021). Second, it undermined negotiations by making Maduro raise the price of compromise. Finally, this combination of harsh sanctions and diplomatic inflexibility also hurt the party that it was intended to help: the opposition, because it made the opposition feel cornered into (or overly optimistic about) adopting an equally hard-line position (see Lowenthal 2021). The best evidence supporting this argument occurred during the 2019 negotiations between Maduro and Guaidó, sponsored by the Norwegian government. Reports indicated that Maduro initially conceded to one of the opposition's key demands: schedule a new presidential election within nine to twelve months (Faiola and Krygier 2019). The United States, however, criticized the negotiations and ramped up sanctions right in the middle of them. It also argued that sanctions would stay in place as long as Maduro was in office. Maduro then argued that he could not organize elections in the context of sanctions. With the United States maintaining its inflexibility (Maduro must be gone before sanctions are lifted), Maduro halted the negotiations.

Of course, it is impossible to ascertain whether Maduro's concession offer was mere bluffing—perhaps he was never going to deliver on these negotiations—and he was, thus, glad to find an excuse to withdraw. After all, this was one of many times that Maduro unilaterally ended negotiations or failed to deliver on his promises. It is also true that the United States was not completely inflexible. The United States supported a very generous amnesty plan for Maduro. Finally, as Smilde recognizes in a separate piece, hard-line positions from Maduro's external allies (Cuba, Russia, China, and Iran) also contributed to the government's hard-line response (Smilde and Ramsey 2021). But Smilde's point about calibrating sanctions is worth remembering. International sanctions need some degree of flexibility. Maximum pressure should not come with maximum demands. Regime-toppling should not be the only option. Inflexibility is the equivalent of "pulling the rug" out from negotiations. International inflexibility makes both parties more hard-line than they may want to be.

Conclusion

Several lessons from the Venezuelan case can be drawn to understand the role of opposition politics in situations of advanced democratic backsliding. First, it is possible for the opposition to rise. While the early stages of democratic backsliding (1999–2006) are typically connected to asymmetrical party system fragmentation (APSF), this condition can be turned around. Backsliding and populist regimes make mistakes. These mistakes can be capitalized on by the opposition. In addition, rising autocratization creates incentives for the opposition to form coalitions. The regime makes all political parties in the opposition feel similarly threatened, and this reduces barriers for cooperation. Venezuela's opposition seized these opportunities to achieve remarkable electoral unity from 2006 until 2017.

Second, even if polarization and presidential threats incentivize opposition unity, the opposition still needs to take steps to cement that unity. Parties need to be able to sacrifice some candidates and to share power (*cuotas de poder*) with other parties. If accompanied by other electoral strategies, such as discouraging abstentionism, campaigning jointly, and creating united lists of candidates, electoral coalitions can allow the opposition to recover votes and bargaining strength.

Third, for the opposition to recover, strategies to safeguard institutions, not just elections, matter. One of the key decisions made by the opposition, after capturing the Congress in 2015 and realizing that other institutions would remain off-limits, was to maintain unity by agreeing to a rotation of leadership. This explains the spectacular Guaidó phenomenon—the surge of a new leader, with ample legitimacy: this only happened due to adherence to rules of rotation that were agreed upon to facilitate opposition unity.

No doubt, the rise of the Guaidó phenomenon—seen as the peak of opposition success—was the result of a combination of chance, pact-making, and party-building strategy. It was the result of chance because under normal circumstances, some other more prominent leader, a more familiar face, perhaps, would have taken the position. Had other leaders of Voluntad Popular not been under house arrest, Guaidó would not have emerged. Guaidó's rise was the result of pact-making because the decision to produce a new leader in 2019 was part of a pact among parties to rotate guardianship of the Congress. It was also the result of strategy because once it was decided that it could not be López who would take over, parties had to pick a leader who could meet some preestablished criteria: (1) offer a new face to the electorate, (2) have links to social movements, (3) not have strong links to economic elites, and (4) be amenable to all parties.

Fourth, the success of opposition parties under electoral backsliding depends not just on devising a strategy about elections and institutions, but also on foreign policy. Studies on democratization often discuss the role of international actors in shaping democratization, but mostly as outside pressures on authoritarian regimes, and in some cases, as offering inducements for opposition forces. But few studies look at the international politics of authoritarian resistance from the point of view of foreign actions by the opposition. One way to read opposition politics under Maduro is as a case study of an opposition that succeeded in changing the views of international actors.

Fifth, while moderation and the pursuit of institutional tactics are advisable for the opposition to gain ground, under conditions of increasing autocratization, there are limits to these approaches. Too much moderation leaves the opposition with insufficient bargaining power. It can also leave politics in the hands of established politicians, which could turn off low-income voters. At some point, the opposition needs to reach out to new sectors of society, and this may require flirting with more disruptive politics, such as street protests, which can galvanize other institutions to hold the regime accountable and also build ties across popular sectors. Furthermore, reliance exclusively on institutional approaches is problematic when institutions become increasingly off-limits to the opposition (most governorships, the National Constituent Assembly, the CNE) or summarily skirted by the government (the National Assembly). Consequently, it is unrealistic for the rising opposition in contexts of autocratization to adhere cleanly and exclusively to politics of moderation and institutionalization. The former is not powerful enough to pressure the regime and the latter is increasingly unavailable.

Sixth, despite the above, Gamboa's (2017) argument about the risks of deviating too much from moderation and institutionalization do hold. Once the opposition begins to consider more radical options, both the government and some sectors of public opinion can turn against it.

Seventh, economic crises have a nonlinear effect on the opposition. Some economic deterioration can help the opposition gain ground, since it produces discontent the opposition can capitalize on. But too much deterioration could create barriers for the opposition: lack of resources, exit options, generalized fatigue.

Eighth, Venezuela is one more case supporting the argument that sanctions do not produce regime change easily. If they do not topple the regime right away, sanctions over time may actually entrench the government and weaken the opposition's bargaining power. In the case of Venezuela, the U.S. policy of maximum pressure (tough sanctions plus inflexibility) triggered a policy of maximum pressure by Maduro on the opposition.

Finally, with or without the trigger of sanctions, it is naive to assume that a semi-authoritarian regime would remain static vis-à-vis a rising opposition. With every inroad by the opposition, Maduro introduced adjustments to the regime. Specifically, he responded by becoming more tyrannical even before sanctions were imposed. The regime adopted a wide array of authoritarian tactics, each tailor-made to counter the specific victories of the opposition. These tactics led to new challenges for the opposition. They allowed the government to survive. This is the topic of the next chapter.

5

Rising Autocracy

AUTOCRATIC TOOLS TO SURVIVE CRISES

This chapter explains Venezuela's transition from semi to full authoritarianism in the 2010s. This outcome was not preordained. As shown in chapter 1, many semi-authoritarian regimes stop short of eliminating minimal democracy and most aspects of liberal democracy. They find a comfort zone, so to speak, as hybrid regimes. So our first puzzle is: why did the Maduro regime turn fully autocratic?

The other puzzle is: how did Nicolás Maduro survive in office? Many semi-authoritarian regimes encounter resistance as they begin to harden political restrictions. This resistance often blocks would-be autocrats from backsliding further or even ejects them from office via electoral mobilization, social protests, military pressure or a combination of all. Maduro faced these pressures, and more. The resurgence of the opposition, together with the collapse of the economy, created threatening crises for the regime. How and why did Maduro manage to prevail?

The answers to these two questions are connected. Maduro survived rising opposition pressure by deepening autocratization. In response to every crisis that surfaced, Maduro deployed specific policies that are simply unavailable in democracies because they are inherently autocratic. The government's policies did not come out of nowhere. They stemmed from tools available within the government's arsenal, inherited from the Chávez era. The tools were redeployed and custom-tailored to meet each new crisis. With every response, with every tool redeployed, the regime inched closer to full autocracy.

The above argument verges a bit on functionalism: the outcome is explained as a response to exigencies of the system. But I try to be a bit more nuanced. Specifically, I ask: what were the political conditions that made possible resorting to autocratic tools? This chapter argues that the rise of autocracy was possible due to a combination of two factors: changes in the party system, as this book has argued thus far, and institutional reservoirs.

In making an argument about institutional reservoirs, this chapter contributes to theories on modern-day autocratization. A common argument to explain whether backsliders either stabilize or transition into full-fledged autocracy is based on "costs." As Robert Dahl (1971) stated, if the cost of suppression exceeds the costs of toleration, autocratization is more unlikely (see also Acemoglu and Robinson 2006, Levitsky and Way 2020). Another common argument focuses on hard-liners. If hard-liners prevail vis-à-vis soft-liners in both the government and the opposition, autocratization endures (Przeworski 1991).

No doubt, costs and hard-liners are a factor. But I argue here that the process is also dependent on state capacity. If the instruments to tighten the regime are readily available and deployable, then regime hard-liners will find it less costly to act. If they find it less costly to act, they will end up asserting themselves more vis-à-vis soft-liners. Both the Dahl condition (declining costs) and the Przeworski condition (hard-liners gaining the upper hand) are met and, consequently, autocracy rises. This chapter looks at how the Chavista regime bequeathed Maduro key state institutions and practices vital for a deepening of autocratic legalism, and how the regime redeployed them in response to every new crisis that emerged.

Institutional Reservoirs: Redeploying and Custom-Tailoring Autocratic Practices

The previous chapter argued that Maduro confronted a rise in the opposition's electoral competitiveness. A movement that never accepted the idea of rotation of power, *Chavismo* suddenly had reason to panic. Losing power by way of elections and civil protests became real possibilities.

To survive, Maduro faced three choices: remedy economic conditions, negotiate with the opposition, or turn more repressive. Maduro chose not to correct the economy because that would have meant abandoning the very essence of an economic model that granted enormous privileges for stateholders. He chose not to pact with the opposition because the opposition demanded free and fair elections as minimal conditions, and this would have entailed an assured loss of power for the ruling party. So the only option left was to turn more autocratic.

Geddes (1999) has argued that single-party authoritarian regimes tend to survive in office more than other types of authoritarian regimes, such as military juntas or personalist regimes. But they survive as long as they are free from exogenous shocks (massive crises and uprisings) and do so typically by legalizing some opposition parties and providing "increased space for political contestation," an argument that is similar to Linz's (1975) idea that authoritarianism survives when it offers "limited pluralism." When they face "unexpected problems," single-party regimes tend to "co-opt their critics" (Geddes 1999). But in Venezuela, Maduro's survival has occurred in the context of severe exogenous shocks and extraordinary closure of pluralism. Rather than co-opt critics, the dominant trend has been to repress. The factors that seem to provide survival—co-optation and societal quiescence—seemed missing or underutilized. It thus behooves us to identify which other factors explain Maduro's survival between 2015 and 2020.

The choice to turn more autocratic was possible and survivable because of the regime's institutional reservoir. Maduro inherited from Hugo Chávez a set of authoritarian practices and policies: a hyperpresidentialist constitution, electoral irregularities, legal restrictions targeting opponents, economic restrictions on the private sector, sectarian clientelism, a decline in media freedoms, strong control of the coercive apparatus, cooperation with authoritarian regimes, and ties with crony capitalists willing to engage in illicit businesses (Penfold 2005, Kornblith 2007b, Álvarez 2009, Brewer-Carías 2010, Committee to Protect Journalists 2012, Mainwaring 2012, Corrales and Hidalgo 2013, Albertus 2015, Corrales 2015). Maduro availed himself of these autocratic reservoirs. Specifically, he responded to each of the multiple crises he was facing with inherited autocratic tools and by adapting them for each crisis.

In Corrales and Penfold (2015), we warned about the possibility of Maduro becoming *"más duro,"* that is, more hard-line. We argued that as Chávez's competitive authoritarian regime was becoming less competitive, it could easily become more authoritarian. We did not know how exactly this process would unfold. Now we know. Here's how. The following section lists each crisis and the autocratic tool that was deployed in response.

Ruling Party Rebellion: Purge and Merge

To prevent the ruling party from abandoning the president, that is, to maintain party cohesiveness, Maduro refashioned the party with purges, espionage, and state-party merging. Haggard and Kaufman (1995) argued that when an autocratic ruling party maintains "cohesiveness," it is better equipped to resist pressures to liberalize. With such a dismal performance in the 2013 presidential elections, it was inevitable that Maduro's claim to be Chávez's true and best "heir" would be questioned within the party itself. Numerous studies have demonstrated that when presidents experience weak leverage within their own party, their formal powers decline (see Shugart and Carey 1992, Mainwaring and Shugart 1997, Pérez-Liñán et al. 2019). In response to internal party dissent, Nicolás Maduro, in conjunction with party power broker Diosdado Cabello, came up with autocratic policies toward the ruling party: purge the party of dissenting leaders and merge party leadership with state leadership.

The evidence for this comes from von Bergen Granell (2017), one of the best books on executive–ruling party relations under Chavismo. Purging began shortly after the 2013 elections, in preparation for the subsequent mayoral elections, when some former Chavistas began to hint that they would run as independent candidates. The party proceeded to expel these leaders and their voters. Maduro banned these leaders from using images of Chávez in their campaigns. Open primaries were eliminated. After the mayoral elections, several former mayors who were defeated were charged with corruption. Disciplinary tribunals were established within the PSUV, in typical Soviet style, to punish members for disobedience. By 2014, members of one of the largest factions within the party, Marea Socialista, were expelled.

In addition, Maduro deployed the classic autocratic tool of merging party and state. The party was reorganized according to different tiers (*anillos*) (von Bergen Granell 2017:215): the Socialist Congress at the top (1,113 members), the National Directorate (30 members), the Circles for Popular Struggles (3,988 members), the leaders for each Battle Unit (13,683 members), and the leaders of the ten sectoral patrols under each Battle Unit (136,820). Between 96 and 100 percent of party leaders were found to be state employees, often in high positions. This meant that approximately 155,000 party leaders were also public officials.

Purging and state-party merging are all autocratic approaches to party governance. While they did not prevent voter defection (by mid 2015, only one quarter of voters identified with the ruling party), these approaches helped ensure that the PSUV leadership stayed invested in the system, was incentivized to mobilize the vote, and was monitored. They kept the party aligned with the state, thus preventing Maduro from becoming a "president without a party" (see Corrales 2002) and thus susceptible to presidential downfall.

Consequently, defections from members of the ruling party have been less pronounced. Very few leaders who supported Maduro at the start of his government have left his side, although many have changed roles and titles. The most notable defection was that of Attorney General Luisa Ortega, who had been a vocal supporter and member of the regime since the Chávez years (Marczak 2019). In August of 2017, she was forced to flee the country after becoming one of Maduro's most vocal critics. For her, the last straw was the Supreme Court's decision to strip all power from the National Assembly. Despite her very public defiance, Ortega was unable to destabilize Maduro's government, or prompt high-profile defections.

Constitutional Crisis: Judicial Shield

To avoid a constitutional crisis, the regime created a judicial shield by (re)packing the courts. Constitutional crises occur when the top court declares that the president is acting unconstitutionally and the president refuses to desist. A typical autocratic practice to avoid these crises is to advance autocratic legalism, which in turn requires ending the independence of the judicial branch (Gibler and Randazzo 2011:5). This is often done through court packing: expanding the number of justices and judges, and filling the new seats with individuals openly aligned with the president.

Chávez did this in 2004, when he passed a new Organic Law of the Supreme Court. This law expanded the Court from twenty to thirty-two members (Human Rights Watch 2004). He allowed the National Assembly, under his control, to choose new justices and to nullify existing justices with a simple majority, if the Congress failed after two attempts to make nominations with two-thirds of the vote. This was a way to grant his party full control of the nomination process, since his party had a simple majority. In addition, he often refused to grant tenure to judges so that they could be fired easily: the number of "provisional judges" in Venezuela during most of the Chávez era ranged from 66 to 80 percent of the judiciary, depending on the year (International Commission for Jurists 2017; Office of the United Nations High Commisioner for Human Rights 2020).

Maduro wasted no time in fortifying this Chávez-era tactic of dominating the courts. Immediately after his party's defeat in the December 6, 2015, parliamentary elections, Maduro realized his first potential crisis was going to be a constitutional crisis. With a new Congress about to start in January 2016, there was the potential for the Assembly to name new, more independent judges. Maduro responded by safeguarding his judicial yield.

On December 23, 2015, days before the new National Assembly was to be inaugurated, the government forced the retirement of thirteen court members. The government proceeded to nominate their replacements together with twenty-one alternate members. This move kept the court fully loyal to Maduro.

Both the Constitution and the law were violated by this move. The

National Assembly should have created a Nomination Committee comprising National Assembly members and members of civil society. Their nominees would then need to be vetted by the Ministry of Public Affairs, the Ombudsman (Poder Público), and the Attorney General, which would produce a new short list. The National Assembly would then deliberate for three more sessions and make the final selection based on a two-thirds majority. If a decision was not made, the National Assembly was supposed to conduct one more session and vote based on a simple majority. This process was designed to take a long time (more than a month) and to involve a plurality of actors and vetting procedures. Instead, the ruling party used what was described as an "express procedure." The Congress, still in the hands of the ruling party, came up with the list of nominees on December 8. No real vetting process took place. Although the official expiration date of the National Assembly was December 15, the Assembly met on December 22 and 23 to approve the nominees. Four extraordinary sessions were conducted in two days total, which also violated the norm banning more than one session per day. It was later discovered that only five of the thirteen new members had actually met the legal and professional requirements for the position. Prior to their designation, the Poder Público had stated that the rest of the list did not meet the minimal eligibility requirements (Alonso 2017). By ramming through this process, skipping important steps, and violating the laws, the government managed to ensure a judicial shield, and thus minimize the probability of a future constitutional crisis (Hernández 2015).

With these steps, the court became intensely *Madurista*. The tool used was intensely Chavista; meaning, it was the redeployment of a key tactic of autocratic legalism inherited from Chávez. Maduro then updated this tactic to increase its reach: autocratic legalism was used not just to defend the executive branch, as was done under Chávez, but to actually disarm an institution of liberal democracy, the Congress. In addition, as the state increased repression (see below), the courts became direct instruments of violence, not just legal obstacles, for the opposition. A shocking report by the United Nations on Venezuela's judicial system, which included reviews of court cases and interviews with judges and people detained, revealed "reasonable grounds to believe" that the Venezuelan justice system played a significant role in "providing legal cover for illegal arrests" and in justifying state repression (United Nations Human Rights Council 2021). Maduro, therefore, not only further undermined judicial independence, but updated autocratic legalism to target institutions and enemies more frontally.

Executive-Legislative Clash: Legislative Dodging

To avert an impending clash with the legislature, Maduro engaged in legislative dodging. Presidents with ambitious agendas and minority control of Congress must either give up their ambition or face the risk of losing power (Pérez-Liñán et al. 2019). In the case of Venezuela, the 2015 parliamentary election gave the opposition not only control of the new Congress but also a supermajority. As per the Constitution, supermajority status in Venezuela came with great powers, including:

* Approve enabling laws

* Remove the vice president with a censure vote

* Remove cabinet members with a censure vote

* Appoint members to the National Electoral Council

* Remove members of the Supreme Court

* Call for a National Constituent Assembly to rewrite the Constitution

To prevent this new Congress from exercising those powers, Maduro reinforced Chávez's autocratic legalism. When dealing with political enemies, autocratic legalism typically translates into using minor or unproven infractions as a pretext to punish alleged wrongdoers with severe penalties. This was the tactic that Maduro deployed toward the National Assembly.

He recruited the new Madurista court to legally strangle the legislature. Shortly after the election, the court conveniently ruled that the election in the state of Amazonas was legally null. This deprived the opposition of three deputies, and thus their supermajority. The legislature ignored this ruling (International Commission for Jurists 2017:6) and proceeded to swear in these legislators, providing the pretext for the court to declare the Congress to be in contempt of court.

From that moment, with full support from Maduro, the courts started to invalidate laws and initiatives coming from the legislature: 127 rulings invalidating decisions by the National Assembly between December 2015 and May 2020 (Office of the United Nations High Commisioner for Human Rights 2020). The court also removed parliamentary immunity for twenty-nine legislators of the opposition without due process (Office of the United Nations High Commisioner for Human Rights 2020) and at one point tried to take over some of the powers of the National Assembly (International Commission for Jurists 2017:5). This latter initiative failed due to international pressure, but the courts were successful in blocking almost every other form of congressional action. The courts also ordered the arrest of deputies (e.g., Julio Borges) or their family members on charges of corruption that were made without evidence. The courts delayed trials, thus leading to indefinite detentions (U.S. Department of State 2020). Juan Requesens, for instance, was arrested in August 2018 and remained in prison until August 2020, when he was released to house arrest due to the COVID-19 pandemic; he has still not received a trial.[1] This type of legal persecution has forced three dozen deputies into self-exile or asylum abroad or in local embassies (El Estímulo 2020).

While the National Assembly was allowed to stay in operation, the government paid no attention to any of its measures and persecuted many of its members. In addition, the government issued a number of economic emergency decrees, which allowed Maduro to implement, without National Assembly approval, the country's budget, adjust tax rates, and issue contracts with private firms (Transparencia Venezuela 2019). In a nutshell, the government neutralized the second most important branch of government, which is one of the most severe violations of liberal democratic principles.

Potential Electoral Defeats: Increase Electoral Irregularities

To avoid future electoral defeats, Maduro exacerbated the regime's electoral irregularities. This too was inherited from the Chávez era (see chapter 2). Maduro's problem since the start of his administration was declining electoral competitiveness. Clean and fair elections, therefore, were out of the question because Maduro, like his predecessor, was unwilling to be voted out of office. Under Chávez, with his electoral hegemony (Hetland 2017), the risk of losing elections was low. Under Maduro, with his declining competitiveness, the risk was too high. In response, Maduro took electoral irregularities from the Chávez era and escalated them to new levels and scope.

Electoral irregularities are different from electoral fraud.[2] Electoral fraud consists of deliberate attempts to miscount or suppress the vote on voting day, typically through illegal acts (Alvarez et al. 2008). Electoral irregularities is a broader concept, which may include electoral fraud, for sure, but also the manipulation of the entire set of rules and norms governing the elections even in the absence of fraud (Hall and Wang 2008). It includes problems on the day of voting (e.g., fraud, infrastructure disruptions, coercion of voters) and, just as important, practices, norms, and rules affecting the precampaign, the campaign, and the postelection periods. Overall, irregularities violate the principles of stable, free, and fair rules of competition. Some irregularities affect only a particular election. Other irregularities (such as changing electoral laws or the composition of electoral authorities) impact both current and future elections.

Chapter 2 (table 2-1) shows the evolution of electoral irregularities in Venezuela.[3] Under Maduro, irregularities expanded significantly, especially after 2015, in terms of both average number of irregularities per year and average irregularities per electoral event (see table 5-1).

Electoral irregularities emerging in the context of noncompetitiveness, that is, when the ruling party is not popular and thus faces the risk of losing elections, are a familiar occurrence. Suffice it to say that under conditions of noncompetitiveness, the president panics. Helmke (2017) has demonstrated that when presidents feel politically threatened or insecure, they tend to deploy institutional assaults: they lash out at Congress or manipulate courts. The Maduro case suggests that presidents are also tempted to manipulate electoral systems. Irregularities that emerge in this context of presidential insecurity tend to occur at a greater speed and go deeper than in any other context. Irregularities become widespread, bold, and even overtly extralegal.

For instance, the government blocked a well-organized recall referendum initiative in 2016. This was probably one of the most important turning points for the regime: it was the first time electoral irregularities culminated in canceling (not just rigging or postponing) an election.

After imposing a number of technical obstacles to the organizers, the National Electoral Council (Consejo Nacional Electoral, CNE) suspended the second attempt to collect signatures after PSUV-controlled courts in five states ruled, almost simultaneously, that there was fraud in the first signature-collection round in June (LatinNews, October 21, 2016).

The government then called for a quick election to a Constituent Assembly, designed to replace the National Assembly. For these elections, the government violated the principle of one-person one-vote (Pardo 2017): the

Table 5-1. Summary of Electoral Irregularities 1999–2018, Chávez vs. Maduro

	Chávez	Maduro
Period	1999–2013	2013–2018
Years in office	14	5
Total electoral irregularities	56	61
Comprising		
Legacy irregularities	33	34
Election-specific irregularities	24	27
Average no. of irregularities per year	4	12.2
Average no. of irregularities per electoral event	3.29	7.63

Source: Corrales (2020b).

government created new types of voters who were unbound to territory. Eight sectors were created and given the right to elect their own representatives: Indigenous, students, peasants, fishermen, businesspeople, people with disabilities, communal councils, and communes and workers. Only voters deemed by the government to belong to those sectors could vote for those representatives. This allowed the government a buffer of seats that would secure its victory even if the opposition decided to participate in the election. After the election, there was evidence of fraud: an official from Smartmatic, the IT company that provides the platform used by Venezuela's electronic machines, claimed there was manipulation of data. Moreover, the election gave the government an excuse to replace elected officials who refused to recognize the new Constituent Assembly, such as the elected governor of the state of Zulia, Juan Pablo Guanipa, who was stripped of his post.

The process of rapid electoral irregularities continued in the 2018 presidential election. This election was conducted with the largest number of legacy irregularities in the history of Chavismo (see table 2-1). In addition to banning candidates and parties (Martínez 2018) and manipulating information, the government created polling centers where people could receive free packages of food and household items—this encouraged many people to vote for the ruling party in fear of not receiving humanitarian assistance (Rodríguez 2018). There was also evidence of outright cheating: inconsistencies in the records (actas) from the state of Bolívar showed a narrow victory for the MUD candidate, Andrés Velázquez, and not the PSUV candidate ultimately proclaimed by the CNE. The results of this election were rejected by all members of the opposition.

In December 2020, the government again violated some of the most important norms for the parliamentary elections. The violations began when the Supreme Court (Tribunal Supremo de Justicia), declaring that Congress was taking a long time to appoint new members to the CNE, decided to appoint the new members, their alternates, and each member's new roles. In addition, autocratic legalism against opposition parties became deeper and more widespread (Aveledo 2021). Table 5-2 shows whether the government used the courts to block parties (or their leaders) from competing in the 2015 and 2020 elections for the National Assembly. The table shows that the government increased the use of autocratic legalism against opposition parties. Consequently, the majority of opposition parties boycotted the election or ran with a leadership imposed by the government. Under these irregular conditions, it was not surprising for the ruling party to obtain 79 percent of seats in the new assembly.

Overall, Maduro inherited all of Chávez's legacy irregularities and made

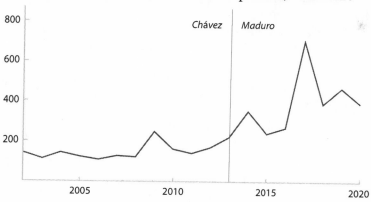

Figure 5-1. Violations of Freedom of Expression, 2002–2020

Notes: Table provides number of documented violations on freedom of expression per year. Violations include: impeding journalists or researchers from accessing information centers; direct censorship of media content; confiscation of material and equipment; police intimidation of reporters after publishing stories; arrests and detention of journalists; attempts to block online content.

Source: Espacio Público (2021).

them worse. He added more irregularities, reinforced existing ones, and went as far as canceling elections and political parties.

Spread of Information: Censorship

To contain the spread of information made possible by the expansion of social media, Maduro also increased restrictions on freedom of the press, both of the local press and increasingly the international press. Figure 5-1 shows press restrictions between Chávez and Maduro. Documented cases of violations of freedom of expression were frequent under Chávez; Maduro elevated these cases considerably.

Harassment of journalists intensified after the 2016 protests. The National Telecommunications Commission (Comisión Nacional de Telecomunicaciones, CONATEL) played an active role in stripping media outlets of their broadcast frequencies. Journalists were frequently subjected to acts of aggression by uniformed and ununiformed agents (Escalona 2019). The government has also gone after the international press (Cañizález 2021). In 2014, the government banned the Colombian news channel NTN24 from covering news in Venezuela and broadcasting locally and also expelled CNN journalists

Table 5-2. Hardening of Autocratic Legalism, Political Parties, and Elections, 2015–2020

Party (share of seats in 2015 National Assembly Elections)	Repressed in 2015	Repressed in 2020	Boycotted 2020 National Assembly Election
Pro Government			
PSUV (31.14)			
Partido Comunista (1.2)			
Vanguardia BR (0.6)			
Somos Venezuela			
PODEMOS			
MEP			
Alianza para el Cambio			
ORA			
UPV			
Patria Para Todos		Yes	
Tupamaro		Yes	
Opposition			
Primero Justicia (19.76)		Yes	Yes
Acción Democrática (14.97)		Yes	Yes
Un Nuevo Tiempo (10.78)	Yes	Yes	Yes
Voluntad Popular (8.38)	Yes	Yes	Yes
La Causa Radical (2.4)			Yes
Mov Progresista de V (2.4)			
Avanzada Progresista (1.2)			
Proyecto Venezuela (1.2)			Yes
Cuentas Claras (1.2)	Yes	Yes	Yes
Gente Emergente (0.6)			
Alianza Bravo Pueblo (0.6)	Yes		
Vente Venezuela (0.6)	Yes		
Esperanza por el Cambio			
Primero Venezuela			
Copei		Yes	Yes
Bandera Roja		Yes	
Movimiento Republicano		Yes	Yes

Notes:

Parties are considered repressed if their top leadership was: (1) exiled (usually due to false charges), (2) barred from participating in an election, (3) arrested leading up to, and during, the election, (4) replaced by the government-controlled Supreme Court of Justice, or (5) banned from forming an electoral alliance.

Prior to the 2015 elections, Un Nuevo Tiempo leader Manuel Rosales was arrested on corruption charges and sentenced to more than 13 years in prison, Voluntad Popular leader Leopoldo López was found guilty of incitement to violence for his role in protests the year prior and sentenced to more than 13 years in prison, Cuentas Claras leader Enzo Scarano was sentenced to 10 months in prison for charges related to the protests, Alianza Bravo Pueblo leader Antonio Ledezma was arrested by state intelligence forces without charges made immediately available and held until his escape in 2017, and Vente Venezuela leader María Corina Machado was barred from holding public office without charges.

Prior to the 2020 elections, the Supreme Court of Justice suspended the national boards of directors of Acción Democrática, Bandera Roja, Copei, Movimiento Republicano, Patria Para Todos, Primero Justicia, Tupamaro, and Voluntad Popular.

Source: Based on Aveledo Coll (2021).

(Muñoz 2014). In 2016, the government increased the number of denied visas and "revoked credentials" for more international journalists: ten international journalists were barred from entering the country to cover news, and various others were detained, harassed, expelled, or had their equipment confiscated, affecting Al Jazeera, NPR, Radio Caracol, Le Monde, and the Miami Herald. In 2017, similar sanctions were applied to CNN en Español after it reported that Vice President Tareck El Aissami and other government officials were connected to a Venezuelan passport and identification papers scandal in the Middle East (Casey 2017).

The government has also begun to use Chinese technology to engage in censorship. In 2017, the government hired a Chinese telecom company (ZTE) to develop a national identity card, Carnet de la Patria, to track citizens' social and political behavior. Everyone was required to have one of these cards to qualify for food assistance as well as access to pension benefits and subsidized oil. The government also offered cash prizes to encourage citizens to apply for the card. As many as eighteen million Venezuelans became cardholders (Berwick 2018). It also appears that since the onset of COVID-19, media censorship has intensified, especially in the digital realm (Espacio Público 2021). Internet content and access blockage now extends not only to media and private actors who are seen as hostile by the regime, but also to portals covering the spread of the pandemic, including websites maintained by the World Health Organization (El Nacional 2020).

Street Protests: Two-Pronged Coercive Apparatus

To contain street protests, the government deployed two available forms of coercion: traditional military pressure and paramilitarism.[4]

In every process of autocratization, the presidency will commit illegal and unconstitutional acts, and the opposition will protest, often disruptively. The coercive apparatus will face a predicament: whether to side with the executive and repress, or side with the protesters, and perhaps force the executive branch to back down. A key question is what side the coercive apparatus will take in this showdown (Barany 2011). If it takes the side of the government, autocratization follows and the democratic movement is defeated.

Scholarship answers the question of which side the military takes by focusing on degrees of institutional professionalism and autonomy (see Huntington 1957). If the military is too unprofessional and beholden to the whimsical wishes of the executive branch, it may not necessarily defend the people and the public interest when the time comes to defend democracy.

This thinking led Bellin (2012) to argue that the key challenge is for regimes to avoid what she calls the rise of a "patrimonial" military, meaning a military institution where "career advancement" is governed by "cronyism" and "political loyalty" rather than merit. In a patrimonial military, the officers obey every order of the executive branch, even if illegal or unconstitutional, because they were recruited and trained with the sole aim of defending the personal and political fortunes of the president. Their loyalty is not to the Constitution, the rule of law, or the public, but to the president's wishes. Patrimonialism of the armed forces means no autonomy from politicization by the executive branch (Pion-Berlin 1992). Bellin posits that patrimonialism is the most important predictor that the military will side with the executive rather than protesters.

However, autonomy in the military cannot go too far either (Cruz and Diamint 1998, Arcenaux 1999). Too much autonomy can also help autocratization. In particular, the coercive apparatus of the state cannot be allowed to have too much autonomy from the rule of law and civilian command in general (Schmitter and Karl 1991). This form of autonomy produces a coercive apparatus that comes to feel that it has the discretion to act with impunity. This is what occurs when the military is seldom held accountable, not even by the president. It is also the main feature of many paramilitary and armed non-state groups (Carey and Mitchell 2016). Paramilitary groups can also be used to defend illegal decisions by the president, escape accountability, and provide the executive with plausible deniability. In sum, the coercive apparatus that is more likely to lead to autocracy during a showdown between government and protesters is a military corps that is first and foremost patrimonial (fully unprofessional and exclusively beholden to the president) or too autonomous from the rule of law.

Maduro inherited both types of coercive instruments: an official military that was fully patrimonial, and a set of non-state armed actors that were substantially autonomous, the so-called *colectivos*. When the need to repress arose, he deployed both instruments. This allowed him to escalate brute force to levels not seen in Latin America since the 1980s (with the sole exception of Nicaragua in 2018; see chapter 6, this volume).

This escalation had a clear starting point in 2014. Data on state-level repression show an important upswell that year. In 2014, Maduro encountered several months of sustained protests across many cities. The government's response had no match. During the Chávez era, government forces would violently repress approximately 3 to 5 percent of protests, with the highest number, 7 percent, registered in 2009. Maduro in the first half of 2014 violently repressed 34 percent of protests, even though 93 percent of all protests were peaceful (Foro Penal Venezolano 2014). In the states of Mérida and Lara, 50 percent of protests were violently repressed (Foro Penal Venezolano 2014). The repression of 2014 resulted in forty-three deaths.

Additionally, the government has relied on non-state coercive elements to handle protesters. The most important of such groups in Venezuela are called colectivos: civilians paid or encouraged by the government to harass political dissidents (Wallis 2014, Torres and Casey 2017). Colectivos first appeared under Chávez and have become a hallmark of Maduro's rule (Venezuela Investigative Unit 2018b). Under Maduro, colectivos have been used to attack both politicians and civilians. On July 5, 2017, an attack by colectivos on the National Assembly resulted in twelve injured persons, including five opposition deputies (Office of the United Nations High Commisioner for Human Rights 2017). Colectivos were responsible for at least twenty-seven deaths in the 2017 protests. They also attacked the media and carried out violent house raids.

The government has also relied on military courts to try civilians. Judges in these courts are active-duty military members, subject to military discipline and required to be loyal to the regime. The regime also established "anti-terrorism" courts in 2014. Their hearings are often not public. The state underfunds public defenders, and since 2015, the Supreme Court has suspended elections of the Venezuelan Bar Association, undermining the independence of private lawyers (Office of the United Nations High Commisioner for Human Rights 2020).

This heightened level of repression would continue unabated. For the 2017 protests, repression became even more severe. The Venezuelan human rights group Foro Penal reports that between April 4 and August 13, 2017, there were 163 protester deaths (the government acknowledged 129 of them). Of these, 101 had been "directly assassinated" during demonstrations. The regime had also made 5,400 arbitrary arrests and held 620 political prisoners as of July 31, 2017. Many of these detainees were taken from their homes in the night. Most crimes committed by colectivos remain unaccounted for.

To understand the severity of these numbers, it helps to compare Venezuela with Brazil and Chile. In Brazil, the death toll from four years of protest against the Dilma Rousseff administration, in which millions participated, was zero. Most sources report the use of tear gas, rubber bullets, arbitrary detentions, and human rights violations, but no deaths and possibly no more than 50 arrests (Amnesty International 2016). This occurred in one of the most polarized contexts in one of the most violent countries, where the police have a reputation for brutality and indiscriminate killing.

Venezuela's repression was even more shocking than the widely condemned Chilean repression of protesters in 2019 and early 2020. In terms of injuries, the Chilean protests were more savage than those in Venezuela that year. In terms of deaths, however, Venezuela's record was higher. Most newspapers or nongovernmental organizations count at least twenty-seven deaths in Chile from police violence, possibly more.[5] Amnesty International (2019) reports forty-seven protest-related deaths just during the mass protests that occurred between January 21 and 25 of 2019, at least thirty-nine of which were carried out by state forces or government-affiliated paramilitaries. In Chile, the protesters obtained much of what they wanted: a promise to carry out a constitutional reform to renew democracy. In Venezuela, the result was continuity of autocracy.

Military Defections: Purge and Splurge

To avoid potential defections of the top leadership of the military (a strategy otherwise known as coup-proofing), Maduro deployed a strategy of purge and splurge. Intelligence services were strengthened to catch and sanction potential defectors within the military, while economic incentives were simultaneously offered for those who remained loyal (see Norden 2021).

As chapter 1 argued, a common trigger of interrupted presidencies is defections or pressure from the military. In fact, the executive's ability to keep the military on its side is often seen as the most important determinant of whether regimes of any stripes can survive massive street protests (Way 2011, Frantz 2018, Geddes et al. 2018). Chávez himself was briefly unseated by an April 2002 putsch, when the military refused to go along with his plan to repress massive protests. While autocracies face a higher risk of coups, perhaps more so than democracies, especially if economic conditions are dire (Thyne and Powell 2016), they enjoy tools for coup-proofing that are simply not available for democracies (Bell 2016). These tools include both repression and rewards within the military, and Maduro used both.

Under Maduro, economic troubles increased the incentives for members of the Armed Forces to defect. Maduro himself claims frequently that he is under threat from a "continuous coup." In August 2017, he discovered "Operation David": a group of about twelve dissidents from the Venezuelan National Guard (Guardia Nacional Bolivariana, GNB) and some civilians who attacked a military base near Valencia (Gupta and Ulmer 2017). In January 2019, he discovered the Cotiza Rebellion: a small group (four) of dissidents from the GNB led by Wandres Figueroa, who stole weapons and started an insurrection. They called for people to take to the streets. Although demonstrators did start a protest, they were dispersed with tear gas by the police force. The dissidents from the GNB were met with resistance by loyalist GNB. They were captured and their weapons were seized (Pozzebon and Alam 2019, Sanchez 2019). In 2020, Maduro intercepted "Operation Gideon," an amateurish effort by approximately sixty exiled military officials to invade Venezuela by sea, funded by civilians in the United States.

That said, Maduro has successfully foiled coups, public disobedience, or episodes in which the bulk of the military's higher-rank officers turn against him. There have been desertions, but no clear insurrections. During "Operation Freedom," an uprising led by Juan Guaidó in late April 2019, few members of the military joined the ranks of the opposition (Marczak 2019). Despite creating a strong momentum against the regime, both locally and internationally, the movement ultimately did not achieve its original promise of ousting Maduro.

The first tactic that Maduro used to contain military defections has been to increase crackdowns on internal dissent, by borrowing another of Chávez's autocratic practices: the use of Cuban intelligence. Reports suggest that in 2008 Cuban security forces were specifically directed to train a government unit, known as the Directorate General of Military Counterintelligence, devoted to spying on the Armed Forces (Berwick 2019). There are reports of approximately 2,500 Cuban officers currently providing intelligence and espionage on Madurista forces and the military. Any officer "in touch with the opposition" can be arrested, and family members are threatened, in turn (María Delgado 2019). By mid-2019, the regime held 217 active and retired officers (including twelve generals) in prison, many of them without trial. Since 2017, there have been 250 cases of torture committed against military officers, their relatives, and opposition activists (Kurmanaev and Herrera 2019).

Operation Gideon illustrates the extent of both military disaffection and state-sponsored surveillance. This plan by about 300 exiled Venezuelan military officers based in Colombia was to invade Venezuela by sea and topple Maduro. The plan was aided by a U.S. security firm and had some support from civilians. The landing attempt, which in the end consisted of around sixty people, would not have been possible without military defections. Among the reasons it failed was the degree to which Maduro had managed to infiltrate the operation. His forces were ready and intercepted the two invasion boats.

The other strategy employed by Maduro, also inherited from Chavismo, has been to allow members of the military and the ruling party to enjoy the benefits of state office, privileged access to the budget, and state contracts (see Norden 2021; Tian and Lopes da Silva 2019). Table 5-3 provides a basic indicator: military presence in the cabinet increased under Maduro. But the influence was much larger than cabinet presence would suggest. If one were to create an index of military privileges, it would probably cover the items in table 5-4. Maduro checked off most of the items in this table.

Shortly before the 2015 National Assembly elections, when Maduro could sense his party was about to lose, he declared that if the opposition won the midterms, he would refuse to "hand over" ("entregar") the revolution, and

Table 5-3. Venezuela: Military Presence in the Cabinet (percent of total)

	2011–2012	2013–2015	2015–2016
Ministers with military background[a]	16.7	25.0	26.5

Source: von Bergen (2017).

a. Percent of total cabinet.

would govern instead with "the people" in a "civic-military union." Maduro followed through on that pledge. His government became more militaristic, but this required administering many punishments in the military for defecting and many rewards for staying on his side. In that sense, the Maduro regime fits the conventional model of authoritarian politics and, especially, the model where the military not only is the locus of power (Geddes 1999, Frantz 2018), but also acquires a strong presence across every level of the state—in the cabinet, across the bureaucracy, and in subnational governance (see Falleti 2011).

Economic Crisis: Reduce Civil Society

Perhaps the biggest puzzle of all is understanding the regime's ability to survive in office despite the country's decade-long economic crisis. Maduro survived by turning hunger and scarcity into a tool for expanding state control and reducing the reach of civil society.[6]

By 2016, Maduro realized that rather than trying to solve the economic crisis, he could turn it to his own advantage. This was risky, but under extreme crisis conditions, not impossible either.

First, in a very deep economic crisis, the state can easily insulate a select number of actors from the crisis, and thus earn their gratitude and loyalty. Additionally, in a profound economic crisis, less is needed to create a grateful set of allies. Second, bringing profound immiseration and hardship to the rest of society can disarm society's ability to mobilize resources against the regime. The crisis drains civil society, and even the private sector, of resources and energy to fight back. And if the crisis produces a mass exodus, the result is a convenient escape valve for discontent, and, thus, relief for the state.

In other words, when a regime manages to bring the middle classes to destitution, the better choice for a citizen is to fend for yourself or to leave the country. Add repression to the mix and the result is an exodus of almost 7 percent of the population, the largest in the Americas since the civil wars in Central America in the 1980s.

Economic deprivation along with repression changes incentives away from

Table 5-4. Venezuela: Indicators of Military Influence, circa 2019

Indicator	Featured under Maduro?	Description
Increase in military size, per capita	Yes	Military size per capita has grown 150% since Maduro took office, from 425 enrolled for every 100,000 citizens, to 1,065 for every 100,000; military size 115,000 for population of 29.78 million in 2013, to military size 343,000 for population of 32.22 million in 2019.
Increase in military budget as a percentage of GDP		Decline from just under 1.0% in 2015 to 0.5% in 2017, no data available since.
Weak civilian oversight of military institutions	Yes	The 1999 Constitution takes power away from the legislature (the Senate) to approve military promotions and retirements.
Presence in Politburo/Cabinet	Yes	See table 5-3.
Governors with military background	Yes	7 out of the 20 governors loyal to the regime have a military background.
President with military background		Nicolás Maduro has never served in the military.
Control of state-owned enterprises	Yes	See chapter 7.
Control of dollar-generating firms	Yes	See chapter 7.
Control of firms in joint ventures with foreign corporations	Yes	See chapter 7.
Independent sources of financing	Yes	Since 2005, the military has unregulated access to the National Development Fund.
Compulsory draft		Constitution forbids "forcible recruitment."
Involvement in social programs	Yes	The military has been heavily involved in the CLAP food distribution program since 2016.
Enforce price controls	Yes	Armed Forces were deployed to over 100 markets in 2018 to enforce price controls.

Notes: CLAP = Comités Locales de Abastecimiento y Producción (Local Committees for Supply and Production).

Source: Brennan (2018), Desilver (2019), International Crisis Group (2019), Observatorio Venezolano de Conflictividad Social (various years), Tian and Lopes de Silva (2019), von Bergen Granell (2017), World Bank (2021, Armed Forces Personnel).

political engagement toward escape. This is exactly what Maduro gained from the economic crisis—to gut the resistance—and one reason he has allowed the crisis to continue for this long.

Maduro discovered that the crisis could produce a sort of Bolshevik effect—that is, rid the country of the independent private sector, and, thus, potential sources of funding for the opposition. Maduro could very well have borrowed the idea from another Bolshevik-inspired revolution: Cuba's famous 1968 revolutionary offensive. This was a campaign led by Fidel Castro, then nine years in power, to nationalize the little that was left of the private sector. Castro confiscated 55,636 small businesses, including most food outlets and semiprivate farms. He wanted zero private profits and total state monopoly over food distribution. The goal was to turn citizens completely dependent on the state.

Likewise, Maduro has used economic misery to extinguish the little that is left of Venezuela's private sector and to extend state control. He has taken over food distribution by issuing entitlement cards, handed out mostly to loyalists (Miller 2018). At one point, during the crisis, he decreed a 3,000 percent increase in minimum wages—insufficient to allow workers to keep up with hyperinflation, but high enough to be unaffordable for small retailers, already strapped by recession, price controls, lack of dollars, and frequent power outages.

By 2018, authorities had arrested 131 people on charges of sabotage, mostly managers of retail chains (Lavallee 2018). Venezuela's private industry was operating at 10 percent of its capacity of twenty years ago, when the Bolivarian Revolution started (Varela 2018). Even McDonald's restaurants were closing.

The little welfare that is offered is an opportunity for Maduro to expand state control over society. Maduro's "Carnet de la Patria" acts with the Local Committees for Supply and Production (Comités Locales de Abastecimiento y Producción, CLAP), as a modernized version of "ration books," a system put in place in Cuba for food rationing (Ragas 2017). The Carnet has become a clientelistic method for withholding goods like food or subsidized gasoline (Smith 2019, Soto 2020).

And yet, Maduro's actions are not an exact replica of Cuba's Revolutionary Offensive. His model, inherited from his predecessor, Hugo Chávez, allows some private actors—those willing to cooperate with the state—to amass wealth, even if through illicit activities or access to the government's multiple exchange rates (McDermott 2018).

Chávez was known for dividing the private sector into friendly ones and unfriendly ones. The unfriendly private sector was constricted through controls, tough audits, high taxes, and even harassment. The friendly private sector, in contrast, was rewarded with access to preferential dollars, state contracts, and low enforcement of regulations. Maduro has extended this model.

Maduro has turned a blind eye to the corruption of loyalists, another form of state reward. Press reports and indictments coming from the United States offer a picture of enormous cronyism under Maduro. For instance, between 2014 and 2015, multiple businessmen led a money-laundering operation using the currency-exchange scheme resulting in $1.2 billion being plundered (Weaver and Delgado 2018). Maduro has also extended the powers of the state to benefit his cronies. Two sectors stand out: food through CLAP, and personal data through the Carnet de la Patria. The CLAP program became a hotbed of corruption and collusion among the military, the government, and private actors (Spetalnick 2019). Perhaps nobody embodies this complex network of cronyism and corruption better than Alex Saab, a Colombian businessman who was detained in Cape Verde on charges of money laundering (Redondo 2020). "Saab has personally profited from overvalued contracts, including the government's food subsidy program . . . Through a sophisticated network of shell companies, business partners, and family members, Saab laundered hundreds of millions of dollars in corruption proceeds around the world" (U.S. Department of the Treasury 2019).

Maduro's nepotism is also noteworthy, and it involves allowing close family members access to both licit and illicit business activities. The international scandal of his "narcosobrinos," or "narco-nephews," where Maduro's wife's nephews were captured for trafficking over $20 million worth of cocaine into the United States, is perhaps the most famous example (Pierson 2017). Maduro's own son, Nicolasito, who has held many high-level positions in the government, now runs a gold-mining scheme that has been deemed illegitimate by numerous countries, including the United States (Vincent 2019).

Analysts are debating whether the country's economic debacle is the result of design (Hausmann 2018) or incompetence (Ulmer 2017). It is both. Extremism produces and requires decimation, and decimation increases the chances of governance errors.

Maduro embraced decimation—despite its risks—over recovery because when decimation reaches overwhelming proportions, as it has in Venezuela since 2015, it disarms the opposition more than the government. Chaos stifles the private sector while leaving the state still standing. And if the government applies repression surgically, especially within its ranks, it has a chance of surviving as enemies inside and outside the revolution capitulate out of misery or fire.

Conclusion

To explain Maduro's autocratic turn, this chapter focused on need and reservoir. Maduro faced the urgent need to take desperate survival measures. His regime was born with critical birth defects: an unpopular leader nominated without democratic consent and elected under a dubious election, a ruling party with declining electoral competitiveness, and a crashing economy. With time, these vulnerabilities aggravated, prompting new crises. In addition, the opposition made inroads by becoming electorally more competitive, creating even more crises for the regime.

Many of these vulnerabilities and crises have proven lethal for many other administrations in Latin America (see chapter 1). To survive, the Venezuelan regime did not opt to change the leadership (i.e., retire, renounce, give up power) or the economic model. It did not choose to negotiate with the opposition. The regime chose instead to suppress political competition.

Maduro was able to restrict rules of competition through autocratic tools because of what I have labeled "institutional reservoirs." Maduro redeployed policies and tools that had been used before under Chávez's semi-authoritarian regime. The difference under Maduro was that these policies and tools came out with greater intensity (e.g., repression, economic neglect), clever targeting (e.g., legislature, the private sector, parties), and a few updates (e.g., Chinese technology for media censorship, welfare weaponization).

Thus, the previous regime's penchant for centralization was redirected toward the ruling party, which was transformed into a disciplined, espionage-oriented machine at the service of the state. The custom of governing with a nonindependent judiciary was reaffirmed, only this time by violating the law in the famous "express court packing" of December 2015. The doctrine of autocratic legalism was used not only to target political dissidents, but now an entire institution, the National Assembly, and to justify higher levels of violence and repression against dissidents. The notion of co-governance with the military was intensified, but now supplemented with greater punishment targeting dissidence in the military itself. And the familiar Chavista formula of manipulating economic distribution with partisan and sectarian objectives was used, now in times of hunger, to create an even more powerful capacity to select a few winners, and thus consolidate a governing coalition willing to defend the regime and expand the state's capacity to inflict losses among nonloyal actors.

There is a risk in this analysis of suggesting that the use of institutional reservoirs was an exercise in efficiency and rationality. Far from it. Yes, the regime was responding to crises, suggesting some rationality. The regime used available tools, which also implies judgment in decisionmaking. But the material in this chapter is not meant to suggest that tools were used fittingly, without errors or excesses, or that other tools could have yielded better results. Some of Maduro's tools created new problems.

One such error is what Martínez (2020), a famous Venezuelan playwright, has called "the military plague": impregnating so much of Venezuelan society with too many different forms of military coercion. This military plague has been enormously risky. It has made the opposition turn more hard-line and tempted them to also make overtures to the military (Trinkunas 2019, Martínez 2020). It has helped propagate violence in low-income neighborhoods as dwellers seek to defend themselves against police brutality (Bracho and Zubillaga 2021). And it has created rifts and tensions within the military that might jeopardize the regime's longevity (Jácome 2018).

The key point of this chapter was not to suggest rationality and competence, but to highlight that the Madurista response to the easing of asymmetrical party system fragmentation (APSF) violated basic principles of democracy, and thus, by definition, would have been unavailable to democratic presidents. Democratic presidents facing the kinds of crises that Maduro faced would not have easily survived. They would have needed to change leadership, change economic models, or negotiate with opponents. None of this happened in Venezuela because the regime had autocratic tools in its arsenal to address the crises. And by deploying these tools, autocracy arose from semi-authoritarianism.

6

Comparisons

NICARAGUA, COLOMBIA, AND ECUADOR

This chapter looks at regime dynamics comparatively.[1] It applies this book's theoretical framework—variations in asymmetrical party system fragmentation (APSF) and institutional reservoirs—to explain three possible outcomes following the rise of semi-authoritarianism. These outcomes are (1) transition to full authoritarianism, (2) liberalization, and (3) coasting. In the latter cases, the semi-authoritarian regime does not move much in any direction.

This chapter compares three cases that share some similarities with Venezuela's regime in their initial stages (see table 6-1): Nicaragua under Daniel Ortega, 2006–2021, which like Venezuela, transitioned to authoritarianism; Colombia under Álvaro Uribe and his designated successor Juan Manuel Santos, 2002–2018, which experienced semi-authoritarian coasting followed by slight liberalization; and Ecuador under Rafael Correa and his designated successor Lenín Moreno, 2007–2021, which experienced, like Venezuela, backsliding to semi-authoritarianism, but not to the same degree, followed by a bumpy form of liberalization.

In terms of research design, this chapter relies on two methods of comparison. The first consists of a similar outcome (autocratization) in two different modes of transition: one led by a successor (Venezuela), or what in Latin America are called *delfines* (Corrales 2021), and the other led by a nonsuccessor (Nicaragua). The second consists of two different outcomes (liberalization versus autocratization) in three similar modes of transition, namely, successor-led (Venezuela, Colombia, and Ecuador).

Table 6-1. Cases and Regime Outcomes

Administration	Regime Outcome	Successor	Regime Outcome
Hugo Chávez, 1999–2013	Backsliding (transition to semi-authoritarianism)	Nicolás Maduro, 2013–present	Autocratization
Daniel Ortega, 2006–2011	Backsliding (transition to semi-authoritarianism)	N/A (Ortega re-elected, 2011–present)	Autocratization
Álvaro Uribe, 2002–2010	Coasting (stable semi-authoritarianism)	Juan Manuel Santos, 2010–2018	Slight liberalization
Rafael Correa, 2007–2017	Backsliding (transition to semi-authoritarianism)	Lenín Moreno, 2017–2021	Liberalization

Source: Author.

I will show that in all cases the politics of semi-authorianism was associated with the rise of APSF. Whether they autocratized or liberalized thereafter was instead predicated on rising competitiveness or strength of the opposition, cohesiveness of the ruling party, and institutional reservoir, namely, the ruling party control of the judiciary, the electoral authorities, and the military and paramilitary apparatus at the time of the opposition's rise (see table 6-2).

Control of the judiciary is necessary for autocratic legalism, an essential ingredient in the transition from liberal democracy to autocracy. Control of electoral authorities is necessary to commit self-serving electoral irregularities, an essential ingredient to block the opposition's electoral growth when the ruling party is threatened. And control of the coercive apparatus is necessary to repress dissent and protests, an essential ingredient to handle the inevitable unrest that emerges when the regime turns autocratic.

Before starting, it is important to mention that there is yet another outcome that can follow from semi-authoritarian settings: military coups. Several of the interrupted presidencies listed in chapter 1, for instance, constitute cases of rising authoritarianism ending in coups or some form of intervention by armed actors. This chapter does not go into the political details of coups, even though one could argue that, in discussing the role of societal resistance to autocratization and features of the regime's coercive apparatus, this chapter offers some implicit reflections on the conditions under which these coups may occur or not.

Table 6-2. Institutional Inheritance and the Politics of Post-Semi-Authoritarianism

| | Party Variables | | State Capture Variables** | | | Non-state Variables |
| | Asymmetrical Party System Fragmentation | Ruling Party Cohesiveness | The Judiciary | Electoral Authorities | Coercive Apparatus: the Military | Coercive Apparatus: Paramilitarism |
Cases*						
Venezuela	Declining	High	High	High	High	High
Nicaragua	Declining	High	High	High	High	High
Colombia	Declining	High	Partial	Partial	Low	Medium
Ecuador	Declining	Medium	High	High	Medium	Low

Notes:

*Case refers to conditions in the country at the time Maduro in Venezuela (2013), Santos in Colombia (2010), and Moreno in Ecuador (2017) take office, and Ortega in Nicaragua wins his third consecutive term (2016).

**Capture refers to degree of ruling party control.

Cells in grey indicate factors that contributed to liberalization.

Source: Author.

After Backsliding

The different regime dynamics experienced by several of Latin America's most noteworthy semi-authoritarian regimes since the 2000s are depicted in figure 6-1: Venezuela, Nicaragua, Colombia, and Ecuador. Using V-Dem's Liberal Democracy Index, the figure shows regime trajectory in the first five years (*t* + 5) of each regime; at the end of the founder's regime (*t* final); and in 2019 or at the end of the subsequent administration, whichever came first. The figure shows some common patterns and some important differences.

Regarding the first stage (from start to *t* + 5), all four cases exhibit new administrations that either entered or stayed in the semi-authoritarian category, defined here as having a score of 0.5 to 0.2 (see upper and lower bounds). Venezuela under Hugo Chávez starts out as the most democratic case of all four, with a score of 0.61 in 1998. In five years, Venezuela experienced the largest and fastest drop of all cases. Ecuador under Correa and Nicaragua under Ortega exhibit nearly identical rates of decline by *t* + 5, with Nicaragua reaching

Figure 6-1. Transitions from Semi-Authoritarianism

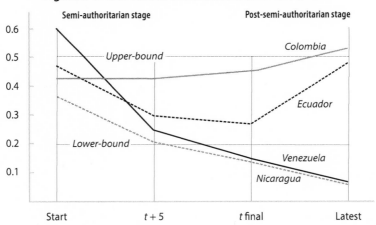

Notes:
    Start: Country score six months prior to backsliding president getting elected (1998 for Chávez in Venezuela, 2001 for Uribe in Colombia, 2006 for Ortega in Nicaragua, and 2006 for Correa in Ecuador)
    t + 5 = five years after start
    t final = last year in office for Chávez, Correa, and Uribe; end of Ortega's second term
    Latest: 2019, except for Colombia, which shows year Santos stepped down (2017)

Source: V-Dem Liberal Democracy Index.

the lowest point of all cases. Colombia under Uribe shows stability. It is the one case of coasting, more so than deep backsliding.

In terms of outcomes, Nicaragua and Venezuela resemble each other the most. Like Venezuela, Nicaragua experienced a rapid transition from semi-authoritarianism to autocracy. It took less than six years for the regime inaugurated by Ortega in 2006 to drop below 0.20 in V-Dem's Liberal Democracy Index.

To be fair, the use of this index to measure democracy might be penalizing Venezuela, Ecuador, and Nicaragua and rewarding Colombia. This index does not look at issues of participation and social inclusion, which arguably remained strong in Venezuela, Ecuador, and Nicaragua, at least initially. These were regimes that were engaged in left-wing populism, in which distribution and social spending played a major role. The Liberal Democracy Index does not take social spending much into consideration. Likewise, the Liberal Democracy Index might be underestimating atrocities associated with the war on drugs and against guerrillas under Uribe (e.g., false positives, ties between paramilitaries and state officials). If the index were more sensitive to these issues, Uribe's overall democratic scores would probably be lower.

Despite these caveats and the differences among these four cases, it is clear that they all entered or maintained semi-authoritarian conditions in their first five years. The big difference in regime dynamics among them occurs later in their administrations (Ortega) or after the founding leaders step down (Uribe and Correa) or die (Chávez).

Ecuador experienced a clear U-turn under Correa's successor, Lenín Moreno. Colombia experienced not so much a U-turn but a gradual and slow improvement in democracy under Uribe's successor, Juan Manuel Santos, albeit at a slower rate than Ecuador. And Nicaragua and Venezuela became deeper autocracies. I will show how changes in APSF and variations in institutional control over the bureaucracy, electoral authorities, and the coercive apparatus help explain these outcomes.

Justifying the Cases and Rival Explanations

The case studies of transitions from semi-authoritarianism in this chapter—Nicaragua under Ortega, Colombia under Uribe and Santos, and Ecuador under Correa and Moreno—share similarities among each other and with Venezuela. These similarities justify comparisons.

Each regime's founding leader enjoyed strong support among his respective constituents from the start. This support expanded initially. By these leaders' second terms, their parties became dominant. They each engaged in forms of populism: left-wing populism for Correa and Ortega, and right-wing for Uribe. Economic growth accelerated under their tenure, in part because of rising commodity export prices (Colombia and Ecuador), strong economic ties with a booming commodity-dependent economy (Nicaragua), and openness to foreign direct investment (Colombia). In addition, the state engaged in policies of social inclusion, expansion of welfare, or overall consumption stimulus, though less so in Colombia than in the other cases. These favorable conditions—popularity and economic growth—allowed incumbents great latitude in office. Incumbents used this latitude to either move toward semi-authoritarian conditions or stay comfortably in such a position during their tenure in office.

But with time, these regimes took different paths. In Venezuela, Colombia, and Ecuador, successors took over, yet it was only in the latter two cases that the successors engaged in liberalization. In Nicaragua, in contrast, the founding president managed to stay in office, and the regime became more repressive and entrenched.

It is tempting to think that an important part of the explanation for these differences in post-semi-authoritarian regime dynamics stems from differences in levels of external dependence. No doubt, Nicaragua depended heavily on ideas and advice from Venezuela, and so it is tempting to think that this regime was bound to follow the same path as Venezuela. However, similar ties existed between Ecuador and Venezuela, and yet the Ecuadorian regime took a different path. Ecuador also had similar levels of dependence on international oil markets as Venezuela, and it responded to the collapse of this market in 2015–2021 with liberalization.

Another case-specific difference is that Colombia depended heavily on the United States, which may have had more influence restraining the worst excesses of the semi-authoritarian experiment and blocking autocratization (or as the left would say, blocking liberalization). But Ecuador after Correa also turned toward the United States, and it actually moved toward liberalization, suggesting that the role of the United States is not enough to explain differences in regime characteristics (stable semi-authoritarianism under Uribe versus liberalization under Moreno).

It is also tempting to think that regime direction is based on leadership proclivity, the hypothesis being that Santos and Moreno were closet democrats all along. Possibly. But this claim is impossible to falsify. What I can show is that if they had wanted to become more authoritarian, these leaders would have been less able to prevail because they were less institutionally equipped to succeed. In Colombia, the party system, the state institutions, and, to a lesser extent, the inherited coercive apparatus made it difficult for Santos to replicate the Venezuelan and Nicaraguan models. In Ecuador, the party system and the coercive apparatus, more so than state institutions, were the real obstacles to autocratization. In short, the inherited institutional setting encouraged liberalization over autocratization, but it also made liberalization somewhat bumpy and inconsistent.

Nicaragua: Ruling Party Noncompetitiveness, Full State-Capturing

In terms of regime dynamics, Nicaragua resembles the Venezuelan experience the most. The transition from flawed democracy to semi-authoritarianism followed the typical process of (biased) inclusiveness cum executive aggrandizement and rights degradation (see Martí i Puig and Jarquín 2021). For instance, at the start, tuition fees were abolished, a literacy program was launched with Cuban assistance, and an innovative Zero Hunger program was established, financed from the public budget and Venezuelan aid, which distributed one cow, one pig, ten hens, and a rooster, along with seeds, to 15,000 families during the first year (Burbach 2009). In 2007, Ortega established the Citizens' Power Councils (CPCs) as neighborhood committees charged with managing social spending, all under the control of the ruling party. Because Ortega established secretive slush funds with foreign aid from Venezuela, the opposition worried about its inability to track the use of these funds. The Sandinista National Liberation Front (Frente Sandinista Liberación Nacional, FSLN) portrayed the opposition parties' criticism as elitist and antidemocratic (McKinley 2008, Martí i Puig 2009). Through the CPCs—sidestepping the legislature—Ortega boosted social spending so much that Nicaragua became one of the fastest-growing economies in Central America (McKinley 2008). In addition, CPCs became active in elections, using resources to compel beneficiaries to vote for the ruling party or to discriminate against supporters of the opposition (OEA 2006, Martí i Puig 2009). Overall, Ortega, like Chávez, created models of participatory democracy that were actually "partisan and state-linked" (Chaguaceda 2012, 2020).

Biased inclusion emerged in conjunction with aggressive forms of executive aggrandizement. By 2009, national and international electoral observers were banned. Both opposition demonstrations and Sandinista dissenters were increasingly repressed. Reporters covering corruption and illegal government contracts were charged with slander. NGOs operating in the country were heavily investigated and often accused of corruption (Freedom House 2020). The Constitution was changed to allow the president to seek reelection in 2011. In short, between 2006 and 2011, the regime completed its journey from democracy to semi-authoritarianism, bordering on full-fledged autocracy.

The first key variable to explain the turn to authoritarianism is APSF. This process was as salient in Nicaragua as in Venezuela. In the 1990s, Nicaragua developed a bipartisan system. When Ortega returned to power in 2006, this system fragmented (see table 6-3). The second-largest party, the Constitutionalist Liberal Party (Partido Liberal Constitucionalista, PLC) collapsed. New parties emerged in the run-up to each presidential election (Nicaraguan Liberal Alliance [La Alianza Liberal Nicaragüense, ALN] and the Sandinista Renovation Movement [Movimiento Renovador Sandinista, MRS] for 2006; the Independent Liberal Party [Partido Liberal Independiente, PLI] for 2011) to challenge the incumbent party or to block a polemical ex-president (José Arnoldo Alemán) from returning to power. But none of these new parties became strong enough to challenge Ortega's party (FSLN), which still had a strong core of support among low-income and low-education voters (Anderson et al. 2021), and after one electoral cycle, all new parties collapsed as well. At no point did opposition parties form broad electoral coalitions like those of the 1990s.

Under these conditions, as in Venezuela in the mid-2000s, it was nearly impossible for the opposition to mount an effective resistance to Ortega's power. Ortega also took measures to ensure that the party-based opposition stayed fragmented and weak between 2008 and 2018. For the 2008 municipal election, he stripped parties of their legal standing (e.g., MRS) or imposed

Table 6-3. Nicaragua: Vote Share, Presidential Elections

Year	PLC	FSLN	ALN-PC	MRS	PLI
1996	50.99 (New)	37.83 (−7.32)			
2001	**56.28** (**+10.37**)	42.34 (+11.92)			
2006	26.21 (−53.44)	**38.07** (**−10.09**)	29.0 (New)	6.44 (New-S)	
2011	5.91 (−77.45)	**62.46** (**+64.07**)	0.4 (−98.62)		31.0 (New)
2016	15.03 (+154.3)	**72.44** (**+15.98**)	4.31 (+977.5)		4.5 (−85.0)

Notes:
Includes only parties obtaining more than 5 percent of the vote.
New-S stands for a new, splinter party.

Sources: For 1996, IPADE (2007); for 2001, IRI (2002); for 2006, CSE (2006); for 2011, World Heritage Encyclopedia (2011); for 2016, CSE (2016).

on them an Ortega-controlled leadership (e.g., ALN) and also committed blatant fraud (McConnell 1997, Booth et al. 2015, Thaler 2017). These violations were far graver than any of Chávez's initial electoral irregularities. And the following year, in 2009, Ortega obtained indefinite reelection through dubious constitutional means, another frontal attack on liberal democracy. Again, in Venezuela, this took a bit longer to materialize. Chávez obtained indefinite reelection in 2009, after a decade in office. The main point is that the transition to semi-authoritarianism advanced at a much faster pace in Nicaragua.

This faster rate had to do with the ruling party's low electoral competitiveness. I argued that the propensity to turn more autocratic increases when an (illiberal) ruling party is noncompetitive. This played a factor in Nicaragua, but curiously, in the early stages of the regime. Ortega started his presidency with a weak 38.1 percent of the vote and always with the threat of a potential split in the party (Kaufman 2008). This created incentives at the beginning to turn autocratic quickly with bold power grabs. By 2008, for instance, his loyalists in the Supreme Electoral Council (Consejo Supremo Electoral, CSE) were already disqualifying opposition candidates (MRS and the Conservative Party) from participation in municipal elections, leading to significant protests (Burbach 2009). For comparison, Chávez did not engage in that type of attack on democratic parties until his second administration.

Also aiding the process of quick transition to semi-authoritarianism was the fact that the ruling party managed to contain the bleeding. Although Ortega's efforts to remain Nicaragua's "perennial candidate" led to a party defection (the MRS), this new splinter party never managed to take off. Two defecting Sandinista groups joined forces into a single anti-Ortega party (Kaufman 2008). But the MRS, which was lagging in the polls to begin with, lost appeal following the sudden death in July 2006 of its leader, Herty Lewites, who was replaced by a less appealing candidate, Edmundo Jarquín (Anderson et al. 2021).[2] To contain the growth of the MRS, Ortega campaigned on a more moderate, conciliatory platform that appealed to many dissident Sandinistas. Thus, the ruling party that went to the polls in 2006 was able to survive that year's schism.

An important difference between the Nicaragua and Venezuela cases is that Ortega's lack of competitiveness predates his return to power, which in turn explains why his turn to autocratic practices also predates his return to power.[3] The key evidence is the famous 1999 "El Pacto" between then president Alemán and Ortega, then president of the National Assembly.

The basic principle behind El Pacto was to restrict spaces for other parties and distribute government posts to each other. Alemán was facing legal troubles stemming from corruption scandals and wanted Ortega to look the other way.[4] Ortega himself was facing electoral difficulties and needed a lower threshold to access power. Alemán and Ortega pacted to help each other. A series of self-serving reforms, laws, and constitutional amendments followed:[5]

- Article 130 of the Constitution was amended to grant the president immunity from arrest or prosecution.

- Article 133 was amended to grant not only former presidents and vice presidents immediate terms in the National Assembly but also candidates for president and vice president obtaining second place. National Assembly members also enjoy immunity from prosecution, meaning presidents could not be prosecuted in office or in the five years after their presidential terms—long enough for the statute of limitations to pass on any crimes committed while in office.

- Act 330 reduced the percentage required to win the presidency, that is, avoiding a second round if one of the candidates achieved 40 percent of the vote, or 35 percent of the vote with a five percentage point lead over the second runner-up. This gave Ortega, who was always polling in the low 40s, an easy entry into the presidency.

- El Pacto also called for collaboration to impeach President Enrique Bolaños in 2004. While the impeachment effort failed, Alemán and Ortega succeeded in weakening and dividing the ruling party (Council on Hemispheric Affairs 2004).

- Finally, and more important, El Pacto entailed granting the Sandinistas greater control of the judiciary and the Supreme Electoral Council (CSE). Article 163 added four new seats to the Supreme Court (Corte Suprema de Justicia, CSJ), making it sixteen total. Article 138 gave the National Assembly the power to appoint associate magistrates to substitute justices during times of absences. Article 162 shortened CSJ magistrate terms from seven to five years, essentially allowing the National Assembly or the president to rush out the judges who were not aligned with the PLC or FSLN.

Ortega's strategy was to start "governing from below" (Feinberg and Kurtz-Phelan 2006). Because he was not growing electorally, he pacted with Alemán to grant himself easier access to state institutions. The result was that, unlike Chávez, when Ortega arrived in office, he had already colonized important parts of the state (Marti i Puig 2016).

The process of expanding Sandinista control of state institutions continued once Ortega returned to power. To secure control of the courts and the Supreme Electoral Council, Ortega reaffirmed his pact with Alemán (Booth et al. 2015). Emboldened by a fragmented opposition and strong allies in the Church and business community, the path was clear for Ortega to engage in further state-capturing. A key target was full capture of both the Supreme Court and electoral authorities (tables 6-4 and 6-5).

In terms of the Supreme Court, Ortega started with half control in 2006, but over the years, he appointed or reappointed only FSLN judges (Martínez-Barahona 2010), leading to near full control. By 2008, Ortega was able to obtain a resolution from the Supreme Court granting the executive branch the power to issue decrees to regulate any arena of citizen participation (Chaguaceda 2020). In 2010 Ortega faced the risk of losing control of the courts and the CSE. The term was ending for many loyalists. Ortega issued a decree extending their terms until successors were found and blocked opposition

Table 6-4. Nicaragua: Ortega's Capturing of the Supreme Court of Justice

	Total Seats	Controlled by Ortega (FSLN)
Late 1990s	12	4
After El Pacto (2000)	16	8
Late 2010	16	9
2020	16	10*
		(plus 4 vacant)

Sources: Expediente Público (2021), Martínez-Barahona (2010), LatinNews, August 2010, October 2010, Confidencial 2020.

Table 6-5. Nicaragua: Ortega's Capturing of Consejo Supremo Electoral

Year	Total Seats	Controlled by Ortega
1999	5	n.a.
2000	7	3
2008	7	4
2020	7	5.5
2021	7	7

Notes: For 2020, one of the members, Luis Benavides Romero, is seen as sympathetic to both Ortega's party and the PLC; represented here as .5 seats controlled; n.a. = not applicable.

Sources: LatinNews, June 2008, Confidencial 2020, CNN 2021.

legislators from entering Congress to vote against the decree (Booth et al. 2015). Loyalists stayed in office.

An important FSLN figure in the Supreme Court was Rafael Solís. Until his resignation in January 2019, Solís acted as the official boss of the judicial branch. In 2021, he gave an interview in which he explained his job: "Politically it was my job, as political chief of the judicial branch, to act according to the directives [of the executive branch], because in effect I reported to Daniel Ortega and Rosario Murillo. . . . They would tell me to look at cases and make sure they were condemned . . . I would summon judges to tell them to rule according to [Ortega and Murillo's] wishes" (Confidencial 2021). This interview is one of the most chilling accounts of the erosion of judicial independence in Nicaragua.

Rising Opposition (with Weak Parties)

As argued in the previous chapters, at some point, the transition from semi-authoritarianism to tighter autocracy will produce a societal backlash. Heightened authoritarianism can lead, at first, to societal resistance. Even if (or precisely because) opposition parties are becoming weaker,[6] civil groups may become more active and disruptive. This civic upswell forces the regime to make a choice: to repress or to negotiate.

In Nicaragua, the surge of civil society against rising authoritarianism began in 2016. The trigger was economic contraction, and Ortega's announcement that his wife, Rosario Murillo, would run as his vice presidential running mate. Murillo was increasingly seen as a sinister power operative. By 2016 she seemed more like a copresident running not just the government but her family's expanding businesses in energy, television stations, and public works. A reporter for the *New York Times* described the Ortega-Murillo ticket as a "real-life 'House of Cards'" (Robles 2016).

Discontent escalated into massive protests in 2018, prompted by announcements about social security cuts and some acts of repression (Weegels 2018). The massive protest included university students, pensioners, environmentalists, feminists, religious leaders, Black and Indigenous activists, and journalists as well as left-wing and right-wing opposition groups (Morris 2018). For a while, the protesters gained the support of the Catholic Church and business groups, until then close allies of the government. This was the first time that "so many different sectors of Nicaraguan civil society united" against Ortega (Morris 2018). The government was on the verge of falling. Now united, the opposition was rising.

The state responded with brutal repression rather than negotiation. More than 300 people were killed, at least 2,000 were injured, and more than 500 political prisoners were still incarcerated at the end of 2018 (Freedom House 2019).[7] More than 50,000 Nicaraguans were forced to flee the country (Waddell 2019). The government harassed independent TV stations and arrested many journalists, carrying out raids and seizing computers and legal documents (Human Rights Watch 2019). This is what prompted Ortega's most steadfast allies in the Supreme Court, Rafael Solís, to resign from his post, calling Ortega's response to the protests "an irrational use of force" and regretting having approved in 2009 the end of term limits (Robles 2019).

In Nicaragua, as in Venezuela, the choice was made therefore to turn more autocratic. And the reason was the same as in Venezuela. In addition to a "cohesive," if streamlined, ruling party (Martí i Puig and Jarquín 2021), the executive branch had control of the state variables needed to turn autocratic legalism into a tool of repression. The courts and electoral authorities began to justify the acts of repression, label protesters as enemies of the state or ordinary criminals, and introduce further irregularities into the electoral system to make it harder for the opposition to turn protest into an electoral challenge.

In short, the Nicaraguan case confirms the variables that lead to autocratization. The initial quick transition to semi-authoritarianism was the result of APSF. The hardening was the result of a rising opposition and captured state institutions. The two differences between Nicaragua and Venezuela are that the process of state-capturing in Nicaragua was aided by a pact with another party, and it started before Ortega returned to the presidency, all because Ortega's party never achieved electoral competitiveness during the democratic period.

Colombia and Ecuador: Rising Opposition, Insufficient Reservoirs

The transitions from semi-authoritarianism in both Colombia and Ecuador were shaped by an easing of APSF. Figure 6-2 provides a quantitative measure of APSF among the three cases of post-authoritarianism led by *delfines*. This is a modified version of Altman and Pérez-Liñán's (2002) metric of the government and opposition's relative strength based on respective fragmentation. In its original use, the metric tends toward 1 when opposition and government are equal, and toward 0 when one or the other is more unified. In this modified version, numbers tend toward 1 for equally fragmented camps, but tend toward 0 only in the cases where the ruling party has the advantage and the opposition is smaller and more fragmented. Thus, lower scores mean more unevenly fragmented parties in the opposition relative to the ruling party. The figure shows how all three cases exhibit an easing of APSF at the moment

Figure 6-2. Venezuela, Colombia, and Ecuador: Easing of APSF

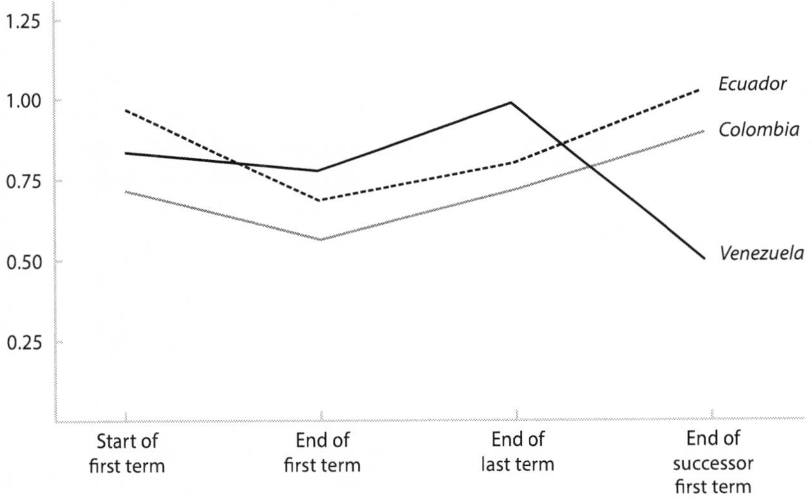

Notes:

Indicator formula:

$$(1)\ O = \frac{\Sigma o_i^2}{\Sigma o_i}, \quad (2)\ G = \frac{\Sigma g_i^2}{\Sigma g_i}, \quad (3)\ C = 1 - \left| \frac{G-O}{100} \right|$$

where O indicates the leverage of the "typical opposition party" and oi represents the strength of the i-th opposition party; G indicates the leverage of the "typical government party" and gi represents the strength of the i-th government party; and C indicates the balance of competitiveness between the two "typical parties."

Sources: Altman and Pérez-Liñán (2002), using data from this chapter.

of succession (end of last term), when *delfines* were chosen. The data are taken from results of presidential elections.

This decline in the ruling party's competitiveness after years of dominance produced a breaking point. On the one hand, the ruling party's declining competitiveness created incentives for the regimes to become more authoritarian. But the recovery of the opposition created more obstacles to choose that route.

Successor presidents in Colombia and Ecuador, unlike Maduro in Venezuela, opted to liberalize the regime. This choice had much to do with state-capture variables. But before discussing this capture, it is important to review qualitatively the evolution of party variables in these cases and their impact on regime dynamics.

Rising APSF and Semi-Authoritarianism

Both Correa and Uribe owed much of their ability to govern in a semi-authoritarian fashion to APSF. In Ecuador, the party system was traditionally one of the most fragmented in Latin America (Sanchez-Sibony 2017, Polga-Hecimovich 2020). Correa broke this system in 2006 by amassing a large electoral following to win the presidency. This was the first time a ruling party had won that big in decades. Correa achieved this large majority by adopting the anti-party discourse typical of Chávez in the late 1990s and the anti-capitalist discourse typical of Chávez in the mid-2000s (Freedom House 2010, Hawkins 2011, Smith 2017). With this new party system advantage, Correa achieved a sweeping constitutional rewrite shortly after taking office, which expanded the president's formal powers (Corrales 2018a, Polga-Hecimovich 2020).

In Colombia, the rise of APSF entailed first the breakup of the country's historical two-party system, one of the oldest in the Americas, dating back to the nineteenth century. As in Venezuela, the erosion of the country's traditional two-party system began with the 1991 Constitution, which granted new powers to subnational actors and weakened the national parties (Corrales 2018a). However, nothing broke the party system more than the rise of Uribe in 2002 (Liendo and Losada 2015). Uribe decided to run for president by breaking away from his party, the Liberal Party, and forming an alliance with a new social movement, Primero Colombia. He campaigned on a hard-line approach to the guerrillas, traditional parties, and the courts. The Conservative Party was in office, but its popularity had declined by election time, possibly in response to escalating violence, crime, and kidnappings. Uribe's campaign drew support from both disaffected Conservative Party voters, as well as from the Liberal Party, leaving each party weaker (Posada-Carbó 2011, Fierro 2014, Flores-Macías 2014).

Over time, the party system became even more asymmetrically fragmented in each country. In Ecuador, Correa maintained approval ratings averaging around 60 percent, with several peaks (Becker 2013, Secretaría de Comunicación de la Presidencia 2014, Larrea and Montalvo 2017, Wolff 2018). Uribe enjoyed average approval ratings around 70 percent with peaks of up to 92 percent (Arnson 2007, Henderson 2011, Fierro 2014). Uribe reformed (rather than rewrote) the Constitution (which is an important distinction that we will discuss later) to allow reelection, breaking with the country's long-standing practice of one-term presidents. For the 2006 and 2009 re-elections, respectively, both Uribe's and Correa's ruling party expanded their share of the vote. In Colombia, the Liberal Party continued to decline, and the left, Alternative Democratic Pole, already internally divided, only managed to get 22 percent.

As is typical of many processes of semi-authoritarianism, the opposition parties stayed weak in both cases (see Gamboa 2017; Polga-Hecimovich 2020). The countries became polarized between Correístas/Uribistas and anti-Correístas/anti-Uribistas, but the latter were fragmented and electorally uncompetitive. The party-based opposition thus lacked the bargaining leverage to pressure either president to steer away from semi-authoritarianism.

With inflated informal powers such as high approval ratings and a fragmented opposition, Correa and Uribe were able to implement much of their policy agenda (Polga-Hecimovich 2020, Gamboa 2017). On the positive side, Correa stabilized the economy, restored growth, alleviated inequality, diminished poverty, and made dollarization work (GlobalSecurity.org n.d., Dosh and Kligerman 2009, Hawkins 2011, de la Torre 2013, 2014, Bowen 2015, Ordóñez et al. 2015, TeleSUR-ACH 2016, Smith 2017). This was a remarkable achievement, given that five previous presidents between 1996 and 2007 had failed to stabilize the economy, let alone reduce poverty. Uribe produced a substantial decline in urban insecurity, especially abating the incidence of kidnappings and the activity of guerrillas (DeShazo et al. 2007, Pachón 2009). This "Democratic Security," as Uribe's security policy came to be known, and the spurring of economic growth were both remarkable achievements after decades of escalating insecurity and underinvestment. Both presidents also boosted the oil-exporting sector, with Correa taking a more heavy-handed statist approach to the oil sector, and Uribe a more public-private partnership approach (Mejía Acosta and Albornoz 2020; Caballero Argáez and Bitar 2016; Hawkins 2011).

On the negative, both Correa and Uribe undermined local governance by micromanaging municipal affairs; pressured the courts constantly; lashed out frequently against critics, even within their cabinet; and tolerated too much corruption among supporters. There were some differences in emphasis. Correa, for instance, targeted and severely weakened the press. Correa also adopted antagonistic approaches toward three major social movements in particular—Indigenous groups, environmentalists, and feminists—all of which had been initial supporters (Dosh and Kligerman 2009). Uribe, for his part, paid little attention to violations of human rights (e.g., the "false positives" scandal involving the government and guerrilla forces), and may have made illicit deals with politicians and paramilitaries (Rettberg 2010). In addition, he engaged in a process of state-capture (more on this later).

One important difference between Correa's and Uribe's antagonism toward these social movements is that in the case of Uribe, the antagonism strengthened and unified his right-wing coalition, whereas with Correa, the antagonism created friction within his left-wing coalition. This is important because in many ways the ruling parties that their successors inherited were not equally cohesive: in Colombia, the ruling party was fairly united at the end of Uribe's term; in Ecuador the ruling party experienced internal tensions (Burbano de Lara 2017, Pachano 2018). These tensions became clear when Correa launched his bid for another reelection, with some members of his party showing displeasure to a far greater degree than Uribe experienced when he tried to seek reelection.

Weakening Ruling Party

As in Venezuela after Chávez, APSF eased after Correa and Uribe. Ruling parties weakened considerably, and the opposition regained electoral strength. Overall, the party system morphed from pro-incumbent party asymmetry (Wills-Otero and Benito 2012, Pachano 2018) to more symmetry between the government and the opposition (Reuters 2017a).

In the case of Ecuador, the easing of APSF actually began even before Moreno became president. Correa's own personal approval ratings had fallen to just 35 percent by mid-2016 (Beittel 2018). Even with party backing and state support (Alpert 2015, Conaghan 2016, Maag 2017, Sanchez-Sibony 2018, de la Torre 2020), Moreno was only able to win the 2017 election by a meager margin.

In both Colombia and Ecuador, the post-semi-authoritarian government started out with a party system that was more symmetrical and, thus, more restrictive of the presidents. Autocratization was difficult (because the ruling party was weaker) and pressure for liberalization expanded (because the opposition was stronger). In Ecuador, an important pressure point from the opposition was to act more strongly against corruption; in Colombia, it was to bring the war against the guerrillas, the Revolutionary Armed Forces of Colombia (Fuerzas Armadas Revolucionarios de Colombia, FARC) and the National Liberation Army (Ejército de Liberación Nacional, ELN) to an end.

It is in this context that Moreno and Santos made a major policy decision, which in retrospect, represented the beginning of regime liberalization: prosecute previous Correa officials implicated in corruption (Ecuador) and pursue peace talks with guerrillas (Colombia). These decisions triggered further easing of APSF by producing a huge rupture in the ruling party.

Correa and Uribe were incensed. They felt politically betrayed because during the campaign, their *delfines* had promised continuity. Consequently, Correa and Uribe turned into lead opponents, Correa from the left and Uribe from the right (Nasi and Hurtado 2018), both with substantial voter support.

Even within the administration, there were divisions. In Ecuador,

Moreno's own vice president Jorge Glas (who had previously served under Correa), published a written critique of Moreno's friendlier policies toward the media and right-leaning opposition groups, accusing him of "betraying" Correa's Citizen Revolution (Deutsche Welle 2017). In Colombia, Inspector General Alejandro Ordóñez publicly sided with Uribe and decried Santos's peace deal, calling it a "barbarity" (Colombia Reports 2018). In 2012, he filed a legal challenge to Santos's deal, asking the Constitutional Court to find it illegitimate (Murphy and Garcia 2013).

Correa and Uribe both created a new party to challenge their *delfines* (Union for Hope [Unión por la Esperanza, UNES] and the Democratic Center [Centro Democrático], respectively). The formation of a new opposition pole—led by still popular ex-presidents—constituted the most decisive change in opposition party politics in Ecuador and in Colombia in decades (Botero 2017, Burbano de Lara 2017, Rice 2021). In Colombia, this was the first time that a new party was born "already big." In the first round of the 2014 presidential elections, Uribe's candidate actually managed to defeat Santos 29.25 to 25.69 percent, though Santos later won the runoff 50.95 to 45.00 percent. In Ecuador, Correístas took advantage of the economic crisis to participate in widespread protests against Moreno in 2019, which came close to unseating the government.

Rising Opposition

In addition to opposition from ex-presidents, Moreno and Santos faced opposition from the opposite side of the spectrum. In Ecuador, opposition leader Guillermo Lasso more than doubled his vote share to 48.84 percent between 2013 and 2017. Though a bit more divided than the opposition led by Uribe, the left in Colombia (comprising the Partido Liberal Colombiano [PLC]; Alianza Verde; and the Polo Democrático Alternativo [PDA]) had become electorally competitive, and thus capable of imposing conditions on the ruling party.

The one important difference between Moreno and Santos was the role of the new left in Ecuador—a group that broke off from Correa early on and never sided with Moreno. This new left had challenged Correa's semi-authoritarian rule, neo-extractivism, and disavowal of environmentalists, Indigenous, and feminist allies. Whereas Santos in Colombia was able to forge an alliance with the moderate left and the moderate right, Moreno remained unable to create a coalition with the new left. He established a truce based on policy reversals, but could not win their support to run for reelection (CBS News 2019). Perhaps the only reason Moreno was able to survive in office was his decision not to seek reelection. This diffused government-opposition tensions.

Bimodal Opposition

Although the opposition did not unite in both Colombia and Ecuador (i.e., fragmentation did not become zero), it achieved the second-best condition in terms of capacity to contain the president, what Milanes and Gamboa (2015) described as "bimodal," meaning, an opposition comprising two concentrated and cohesive nodes on both sides of the spectrum, left and right. Prior to Santos, Colombia still maintained a certain liberal versus conservative ideological cleavage that aligned with government-opposition dynamics: one side occupied one post, and the other side, the other post. Under Santos, for the first time, the ruling party had both liberals and conservatives in the opposition (Botero 2017).

This party system—a ruling party losing competitiveness and cohesiveness and an opposition organized bimodally—created obstacles for autocratization. With a ruling party that was weak and facing strong opposition from each pole of the ideological spectrum, one of which was led by a popular ex-president, it was challenging for presidents to move the regime significantly in the direction of more authoritarianism. They might have faced incentives to turn more autocratic, to crush the rising challenge from ex-presidents, but they lacked the party capacity to assert themselves, and as we will see in the next section, they lacked state capacity as well.

The presidents, however, faced greater incentives to turn democratic. To survive politically, Moreno made the decision to reach a truce with the new left (e.g., withdraw the austerity package signed with the International Monetary Fund [IMF], work with Indigenous groups to rethink fiscal reforms; refrain from seeking reelection). These decisions not only appeased his opponents, but more important, reaffirmed the country's democratization.

Santos decided to run for reelection. But to win the second round in the context of declining competitiveness, he was forced to forge an alliance with the opposition, and especially the democratic left. He did so by turning the election into a referendum on peace talks (O'Hagan 2014). Clara López, who campaigned against Santos in 2014 with the Alternative Democratic Pole, publicly endorsed him in the runoff (Neuman 2014b). He also won the endorsement of former president César Gaviria, who played a major role in building Santos's second-round coalition (*Semana* 2018). This need to build an alliance with the democratic left meant that autocratic policies toward either Uribe or the guerrillas were off the table. By the same token, the resistance from the Uribe-led right also created huge obstacles for major overtures toward liberalization. While the center-left pressed the regime to liberalize, Santos still could not move fast enough due to roadblocks set by the opposition to his right.

It is important to notice some similarities and differences in the role of ex-presidents and transitions from semi-authoritarianism across our cases (table 6-6). In all three cases, ex-presidents turned from former allies to enemies of the incumbents, producing splits and defections in the ruling parties and creating obstacles for incumbents. In Nicaragua, the challenge posed by the ex-president-turned-opponent fizzled away quickly: Alemán's electoral performance in 2011 was disastrous and brought an end to his career. This cleared the path for Ortega to pursue full autocratization. In Ecuador, Moreno's falling out with Correa produced splits in the ruling party that made pursuing reelection impossible without courting the right-wing opposition, something Moreno had trouble doing while maintaining his base of center-left support. In Colombia, the incumbent was able to enlist the support of another ex-president (Gaviria in 2014) to counteract the attacks coming from an ex-president, and this bolstered Santos's chance of implementing his agenda and surviving in office.

Colombia: Less State-Capturing

The second reason the semi-authoritarian regime in Colombia and to some extent Ecuador did not autocratize further was lack of full control over the institutions needed for autocratic legalism and repression. A review of appointments in the bureaucracy reveals this difference with the Venezuelan and Nicaraguan cases.

The ruling party under Uribe never achieved full control of institutions required for full autocratic legalism. No doubt, Uribe tried to undermine

Table 6-6. Ex-presidents as Allies or Opponents

Cases	Incumbent	Ex-president as Ally		Ex-president as Opponent
Ecuador, 2017–2021	Moreno	Correa (2017)	⟶	Correa (2017)
Colombia, 2010–2014	Santos	Uribe (2010)	⟶	Uribe (2012)
Colombia, 2014–2018	Santos	Gaviria		Uribe (2014)
Nicaragua, 2006–2011	Ortega	Alemán (2006)	⟶	Alemán (2011)
Nicaragua, 2011–2016	Ortega	None		None

Source: Author.

the separation of powers and the independence of federal agencies, that is, erode horizontal accountability (Botero 2010), in order to achieve autocratic legalism. His approach focused on badmouthing agencies that challenged him, nominating partisan loyalists to open vacancies, and, a bit like Ortega in Nicaragua, forming behind closed-door agreements with other politicians in other parties (namely, the Conservatives) for support in Congress. By the time he left office, Uribe had loyalists in the Office of the Attorney General, the Comptroller, and the Ombudsman. He also controlled one of the two branches of the Supreme Council of Judicature (Consejo Superior de la Judicatura, SCJ), the body in charge of ensuring the independence of the judicial branch. He achieved full control of the Bank of the Republic, though authors have noted that most codirectors were experts promoted from within the institution rather than nonexperts promoted from within Uribista loyalist ranks. Additionally, he took full control of the National Television Commission and achieved a sizable majority over the National Electoral Council.

Despite these appointments, the executive branch never achieved full control of the judicial branch and the electoral authorities (see table 6-7). Regarding the judicial branch, one of the chambers of the SCJ remained entirely independent, and only three of the six members of the other chamber were party loyalists by the end of Uribe's second term. Additionally, only four of the nine members of the Constitutional Court were loyalists, giving Uribe control over just seven of the twenty-two members of the Supreme Court.

Regarding the electoral branch, four of nine members of the National Electoral Council (CNE) were loyalists by the end of Uribe's first term. By the end of the second, the number of loyalists had risen to five—a slight majority of the nine-member council. This insufficiency of institutional reservoirs is one reason Uribe couldn't obtain reelection. The courts blocked him and he knew he did not have control of the electoral system.

One of the reasons some horizontal accountability survived the Uribe years is that Uribe never opted (or managed) to rewrite the Constitution. Colombia's 1991 Constitution was designed to limit the powers of the president and the independence of government agencies (Corrales 2018a). The Constitution did grant the president powers of appointment, but always with limits: protecting the job security of appointees, setting clear term limits that did not coincide with presidential terms in office, and often involving other actors in the nomination and approval process. Because Uribe never changed the Constitution to overhaul the rule-bound process of nominating people to state office, he was never able to conduct a sweeping seizure of government agencies (Mance 2009). That said, had Uribe stayed in office for one more term, the process of state-capturing would have continued and perhaps reached a point similar to that achieved by Chávez. In short, the constitution together with

Table 6-7. Colombia: Uribe's Control of State Institutions

	End of first term (2006)		End of second term (2010)	
	Seats Controlled by Uribe over Total Seats	Decision-Making Record	Seats Controlled by Uribe	Decision-Making Record
Justice Institutions:				
Constitutional Court	0/9	I	4/9	C
SCJ*: Disciplinary Chamber	0/7	I	3/6	I
SCJ*: Administrative Chamber	0/6	I	0/6	I
Electoral Institutions:				
National Electoral Council	4/9	C	5/9	C
National Registry	NA	I	NA	I
Comptroller General	1/1**	A	1/1***	A
Inspector General	1/1	C	1/1	C
Attorney General	1/1	C	1/1***	C
Ombudsman	1/1	A	1/1	A
Key Economic Institutions				
Bank of the Republic	2/7	I	5/7****	C
Ecopetrol (National Oil Company)	N/A	I	3/9	I

Notes:

Grey: Under Uribe's control: majority of appointees comprised of clear loyalists or decision-making record was mostly aligned with Uribe's preference.

Decision-Making record: I = Mostly independent; C = Coopted; sided with Uribe often but not always; A = Aligned; sided with Uribe most of the time.

*Supreme Council of the Judicature (SCJ). It is comprised of two chambers: disciplinary and administrative.

**Under Uribe's control starting in 2006

***Under Uribe's control until 2009

****Although Uribe made appointments, many were promoted from within the institution or were financial experts rather than politicians.

Source: García Villegas and Revelo Rebolledo (2009), and Corrales et al. (2020).

term limits prevented the president from acquiring full control of the state institutions that would have led to more repressive forms of autocratic legalism.

The overall point is that Santos inherited neither a hyperpresidentialist constitution nor sufficient institutional reservoirs to turn autocratic. He also witnessed how persistently, and in the end, successfully the court system stood up against the former president. The court under Uribe asserted its independence and defended human rights, despite every effort by Uribe to undermine each of these missions. Santos thus concluded that it was better to "make peace" with the courts: to work with them, rather than against them (Kutner 2011). The state apparatus thus placed dual restrictions on the extent to which Santos could use the state to take an authoritarian turn. Santos could only rely on the powers to make new nominations to rid the bureaucracy of Uribistas, but not to turn those institutions into tools for repressive autocratic legalism.

Ecuador: The Challenge of Purging the State

State-capturing in Ecuador at the start of the Moreno administration was not as profound as in Nicaragua and Venezuela, but it was far greater than in Colombia. The ruling party under Moreno had therefore greater capacity to engage in autocratic legalism. The problem was that those state institutions were in the hands of Correístas. Once Moreno realized he needed to fight the Correístas to survive in office, he essentially gave up his chances of using many of those institutions to his advantage—they were out of his control. Instead, his best hope was to try to purge state institutions from Correístas. This purging created its own set of challenges for Moreno and complicated Ecuador's process of liberalization.

When Moreno took office, Correístas controlled all of the ministries of the executive, each major institution of the judiciary (the Council of the Judicature, National Court of Justice, and the Constitutional Court) (Basabe-Serrano and Llanos Escobar 2014, Vera Rojas and Llanos Escobar 2016), the National Electoral Council (CNE) (Alpert 2015, Noboa 2015), the dollar-generating oil-export energy sector, and the powerful Consejo de Participación Ciudadana y Control Social (CPCCS) (Polga-Hecimovich 2020), an oversight and anti-corruption body founded by Correa and responsible for both appointments and dismissals of members of the other branches.

Moreno's decision to liberalize produced an obvious clash with *Correísmo*: not just with Correa himself and his constituency, but also Correa's loyalists in office. To deal with Correísta capture of state offices, and proceed with democratization, Moreno used all the strategies available in hybrid, semi-authoritarian regimes: a bit of liberal democracy; a bit of plebiscitarian populism; and, paradoxically, a bit of autocratic legalism.

Moreno deployed many liberal democratic approaches. He met with civil society groups and journalist organizations that Correa had repressed or publicly incited anger toward and encouraged them to do their work without fear of more state repression (Southwick and Otis 2018, Stuenkel 2019). In 2018, the National Assembly reformed Correa's notorious 2013 communications law and disbanded Supercom, the agency that had been responsible for monitoring private media companies (Freedom House 2021). And in 2019, several executive agencies worked together to form a Committee for the Protection of Journalists, which has been successful in reducing attacks on journalists in the country according to the U.S. State Department's human rights report (Beittel 2021).

Moreno also deployed Correísta-style plebiscitarian-populist tactics (Burbano de Lara and de la Torre 2020). He called for a plebiscite in 2018 to set a limit of two presidential terms and to bar officials convicted of corruption from running for office again (BBC News 2018), effectively blocking both Correa and his clearest successor, Jorge Glas, from future elections, as well as removing the Correístas from the CPCCS, the state's most powerful oversight institution, and replacing them with his own appointees (Human Rights Watch 2020). The referendum also included questions about restricting mining, which was Moreno's attempt to court the anti-Correísta, anti-extractivist, pro-Indigenous left. The referendum questions were all approved, with margins ranging from 63 to 73 percent.

And finally, and more polemically, Moreno also relied on tools of autocratic legalism that had been handed down by Correa. After successfully replacing CPCCS members via plebiscite and appointing his own transitional CPCCS (pending an election the following year), Moreno quickly used the oversight body to clear all of the nation's top courts of Correístas, either replacing them with his own appointees or leaving the positions vacant (Human Rights Watch 2020). He also used the CPCCS to seize control of the CNE, replacing all of Correa's appointees with his own, and of the independent oversight ministries, led by the Comptroller General, Attorney General, and Ombudsman, which had been controlled by Correístas (de la Torre 2020). The new authorities have been accused of irregularities in their treatment of Correa and Correísta political groups within the country, but have otherwise markedly lessened the level of irregularities and malpractice prevalent under the Correa regime (Freedom House 2021).

In sum, one of the key challenges that Moreno faced when he decided to break with Correísmo was state-capture by defenders of the semi-authoritarian regime. To purge them from office, he used democratic, populist, as well as semi-authoritarian methods. This mixture of approaches is one reason Ecuador's democratic reopening was bumpy: it was less far-reaching and internally consistent than one would have hoped.

The Coercive Apparatus: The Military and Paramilitaries

The final factor to consider in the process of transition from semi-authoritarianism is the coercive apparatus. Table 6-8 shows how our cases fared according to the two dimensions of civil-military relations proposed in the previous chapter: nonautonomy of the official armed forces (patrimonial armed forces) and excessive autonomy of armed, pro-government non-state actors (paramilitaries and gangsterism). In Venezuela and Nicaragua, the regimes exhibited both dimensions. In Colombia, in contrast, Uribe tried but failed to achieve the first dimension, and the incidence of the second type declined under Santos. In Ecuador, Moreno inherited some elements of the first dimension, but not much of the second.

Nicaragua: The Showdown

As argued, the Nicaragua regime used the upswell in the opposition in 2016–2018 to turn more autocratic. One more reason the state took this response is that its institutional reservoir included, as in Venezuela, the two key elements in the coercive apparatus needed to repress. The first was a military that was completely beholden to the executive branch (patrimonial armed forces). The second consisted of ties with non-state actors that employ coercion with full autonomy from civilian authority (paramilitarism) (Weegels 2018).

The patrimonialization of the military was one of Ortega's "achievements" in office. During Nicaragua's brief democratic period in the 1990s, some progress had been achieved to make the military a "nonpartisan" and "nonrevolutionary" force, increasingly under civilian control (Chaguaceda 2020). But following reforms in 2014, granting Ortega increased oversight and decisionmaking authority, the military and police became pawns to be used at Ortega's discretion. There was a sizable increase in the defense budget from US$42 million to US$85 million in 2013. While the military remained an extremely trusted institution (with 67 percent of Nicaraguans saying they trust it), mostly because of its involvement in domestic disaster relief and border security, Ortega gradually managed to turn the military into a patrimonial force. He appointed FSLN allies to key roles in the organization, such as Julio César Avilés as army general.

Table 6-8. The Coercive Apparatus and Autonomy

President	Patrimonial armed forces (exclusive subservience to the president)	Paramilitarism, gangsterism (full autonomy from the rule of law)
Maduro and Ortega	Yes	Yes
Santos	No	Declining
Moreno	Partial	Minimal

Source: Author.

In addition, Ortega, like Maduro, had paramilitary forces available to suppress the revolt. FSLN-supporting paramilitary groups were established prior to the protests. This included actors such as organized civilians, hired paramilitaries, retired soldiers or police forces, former civil servants, and even gang members, and they are infiltrated in groups such as the "Voluntary Police," "Power Councils and Cabinets," "Family, Community, and Life Cabinets," "Sandinista Youth," "Sandinista Leadership Committees," and "Blue Shirts" (FIDH and CENIDH 2021). During the protests, many of these groups, looking for protestors, entered (and often destroyed) homes, businesses, and churches. They kidnapped protestors and carried out torture and sexual violence. Ortega has attempted to distance himself from these groups while not necessarily condemning their actions, claiming that "they are citizens defending themselves" (Pestana and Latell 2017). An Organization of American States (OAS) report documented that detentions were carried out by the National Police as well as by the state-backed "parapolice" (Inter-American Commission on Human Rights 2020). The report noted that the Nicaraguan justice system ignored these crimes and made no attempt to hold perpetrators accountable. In June 2021, acting on this information and heightened repression by the Ortega regime, the OAS condemned the actions of the Nicaraguan government with a vote of twenty-six in favor, five abstaining, and three against (Freden 2021).

Colombia: Declining Military Options

In Colombia, in contrast, the semi-authoritarian regime never counted on high levels of control over the tools of repression. During the Uribe years, the Colombian military remained fairly professional and autonomous. This was due to two primary factors: The United States' heavy-handed role in Plan Colombia and attentive press and opposition scrutiny of military operations.

In its effort to get Plan Colombia approved by the U.S. government (including Congress), Uribe's predecessor, President Andrés Pastrana, had to commit to engaging in a series of military reforms (Long 2017). The military was weak, corrupt, and in retreat. It was also underfunded and too autonomous—attempting to compensate for its underfunding by engaging in both licit and illicit economic activities (Marcella 2003). Civilians would refuse to fund the military to prevent it from becoming a big actor and to avoid it being perceived as too militaristic (Mejía 2008). The military responded by eschewing civilian authority. Pastrana needed to make the Colombian military more appealing to Democrats and Republicans in the United States. Democrats wanted better attention to human rights. Republicans wanted better attention to capability (Long 2017). So Pastrana modernized the military. His plan was to increase funding and make the military more professional, while at the same time making the military more subordinate to civilian authority. Although Uribe gets most credit for putting security first, it was perhaps Pastrana, with his Plan Colombia, who first recognized that investments in security were not in competition with investments in human development (Mejía 2008).

Pastrana's new approach to security moved fast under his second defense minister, Luis Fernando Ramírez. First, personnel and equipment were improved. In 1998, one report mentioned that about 20,000 to 30,000 personnel were professional and ready for battle; 135,000 or so were ill-trained (DeShazo et al. 2007). The ministry added "more and better men" and better training (Long 2017). Second, Pastrana turned the military into a joint custodianship institution. Both Colombian and U.S. officials would together push for military reforms and conduct oversight of performance. At Ramírez's request, for instance, U.S. officers sat with Colombian generals to convince them of the need to fire corrupt personnel (Long 2017). Overall, the U.S. government authorized the deployment of some 400 military advisers and another 400 to 800 civilian contractors to administer the assistance (Angelo and Ilera Correal 2020).

Uribe's approach was to take Pastrana's doctrine of professionalizing security and add an additional component; that is, security needs to be extended across the entire territory to address pockets of statelessness (Marks 2005). Uribe had no option but to reinforce this commitment to domestic civilian oversight and international joint oversight. In 2002, Uribe promoted a notoriously strong defender of civil-military relations to commander in chief (DeShazo et al. 2007). He had to preserve various checks and balances by the judicial branch (Angelo and Ilera Correal 2020). The government respected the ban on voting by the military (Angelo and Ilera Correal 2020). The first aid packages approved by the U.S. Congress were earmarked exclusively for counternarcotics measures, preventing immediate co-optation by the political branches (Spencer 2012). Even when aid was given for more general military improvements, it was used for professional purposes (DeShazo et al. 2007). All these measures made it difficult for the Colombian president to convert the military into a patrimonial institution. Co-opting the military for personal use would have eroded its legitimacy domestically (while under Uribe it achieved 80 percent approval ratings, the highest of any institution in Colombia) (Angelo and Ilera Correal 2020), and likely would have resulted in the United States cutting its aid packages (Spencer 2012).

Precisely because Uribe's hands were tied with the military, he began to rely on closer ties to paramilitary groups. By the time Uribe ended his term, almost half of his legislators were indicted for ties with paramilitaries (López

Hernández 2010). The press and the political system developed strong over-sight of paramilitarism. Most politicians with ties to the paramilitaries were in the Uribista coalition. Most came from electoral districts with high para-military activity.

So when Santos became president, unlike Chávez and Ortega, he did not have a patrimonial military institution to use for repression, and there was significant oversight, both domestically and internationally, of paramilita-rism. For Santos to continue with a policy of turning a blind eye toward paramilitarism would have been too risky in terms of cultivating the political support he needed with non-Uribistas. And besides, these groups were prob-ably more loyal to Uribe, if anyone, than to Santos.

Ecuador: Unavailable Options

In Ecuador under Correa, the official military apparatus had become more captured by the executive branch than perhaps in Colombia under Uribe, though hardly to the same degree as in Venezuela and Nicaragua during their respective semi-authoritarian stages. In fact, Correa can be credited as having increased the professionalization of the military, at least at first (Shifter 2016).

Correa inherited a military that was fairly autonomous and involved in politics. The military played a key role in unseating three presidents prior to Correa: Abdalá Bucaram in 1997, Jamil Mahuad in 2000, and Lucio Guti-érrez in 2005. So Correa's first set of military policies entailed increasing the professionalism of the military and its subordination to civilian authority. He started the tradition of appointing civilians as ministers of defense, dis-banded the Council of National Defense (Junta de Defensa Nacional), which often made arms deals without congressional oversight, banned the military from participating in business enterprises that were not directly tied to secu-rity, tried to get the military to focus more on border control than domestic politics, increased fiscal audits on the military, and purged corrupt military leaders (Jaskoski 2020).

In time, Correa's initial push in favor of professionalism and subordina-tion to civilian authority morphed into an effort to turn the military into a patrimonial force. However, the military actually remained "largely able to resist politicization" during this period (Polga-Hecimovich 2019). The best evidence of autonomy from the executive branch under Correa occurred during the September 2010 crisis in which the police kidnapped Correa: the military's high command did not take sides for or against the president until called upon to rescue him. Furthermore, there is no major evidence of ram-pant use of paramilitary forces in Ecuador.

Moreno, therefore, did not inherit a coercive apparatus that was transformed into an instrument to enforce the wishes of the executive branch, let alone a coercive apparatus with a tradition of unchecked repression. When Moreno started to experience clashes with the opposition, including the massive protests of 2019, he simply did not have the type of autocratic coercive apparatus that both Maduro and Ortega used to their advantage. This too blocked a possible return to semi-authoritarianism.

Conclusion

This chapter explains regime dynamics after semi-authoritarianism. Why did semi-authoritarianism morph into full-fledged autocracy in Nicaragua (and Venezuela) but not in Colombia and Ecuador?

My explanation has to do with variations in party system fragmentation and state capacity, in line with this book's argument. I also considered another variable: the role of the ex-presidents as allies or rivals. In all three cases (as in Venezuela), the ruling party of the semi-authoritarian regime eventually lost competitiveness, which increased the incentives to turn authoritarian.

In Nicaragua the regime was able to turn fully authoritarian because, first, the opposition fragmented and stayed electorally weak; and, second, as in Venezuela, the executive branch managed to capture the key institutions needed to tighten autocratic legalism and eventually repression: the judiciary, the electoral authorities, the official military, and paramilitaries. Both regimes lost economic resources (the collapse of oil prices and foreign aid), but these were compensated for by gains in institutional resources essential for a hardening of autocratic legalism and repression.

In Colombia and Ecuador, the ruling party split under successors (in Ecuador, it was showing strains before succession). In addition, the opposition acquired strength. First, the opposition became bimodal, with each node sufficiently competitive to exert pressure on the executive branch. Second, in each case, one of the nodes was led by a widely supported, albeit polarizing, ex-president. The other nodes were more democratic-minded and would not have supported the regime turning more autocratic, even to weaken the ex-president-led rival node.

Furthermore, in Colombia, the fact that Santos did not inherit total control of institutions necessary for autocratic legalism precluded a highly repressive approach toward the ex-president-led opposition. Because the authoritarian tools were not available, the only alternative was to turn more electorally competitive, and this led Santos to side with the democratic left (including another ex-president) to prevail electorally in the second round of his reelection drive. These groups demanded democratic reforms in return for their support.

In Ecuador, Moreno inherited a few more tools for autocratic legalism than did Santos, but he did not enjoy sufficient electoral strength to make full use of them and still remain popular. Besides, many of those inherited tools were controlled by his sponsor-turned-adversary, ex-president Correa, and thus were not at all truly available for Moreno to use. Moreno's response was to empower the opposition to Correa, which itself was ideologically split. This too required accepting many of their democratizing demands. Moreno also responded by trying to purge state institutions of Correístas. Moreno had to do all of this while managing a severe economic crisis and social protests, first triggered by the 2015 oil crisis and exacerbated by the 2020 pandemic. In short, the regime never enjoyed the institutional capacity nor the party system conditions necessary to stay semi-authoritarian or even to autocratize. So it chose to liberalize politically. The transition to liberalization was bumpy and inconsistent, but the net result was greater political rights to parties and civil society than were available at the start of the transition.

Finally, this chapter highlighted an important paradox in the politics of democratizing semi-authoritarian regimes. While our two cases of liberalization reveal that the goal of dismantling semi-authoritarianism can be accomplished through the use of democratic tools (e.g., free and fair elections, negotiations with opponents, adherence to the rule of law), they also reveal that some semi-authoritarian practices either survive or need to be placed at the service of democratizing the state. In the case of Colombia, Santos was forced to preserve some aspects of Uribismo, such as relying on a strong military and keeping some Uribistas in his cabinet, in order not to produce too lethal a backlash from Uribistas or to contain the defection of conservative voters. In the case of Ecuador, Moreno relied on populist and semi-authoritarian tactics to purge state institutions of Correístas. This paradox is not surprising. It resonates perfectly with the scholarship of the 1980s on the transition to democracy: often those transitions come with the survival of "authoritarian enclaves" (Haggard and Kaufman 1997). As Loxton (2021:145) has argued, democratization almost never means a "clean slate."

That said, in Colombia and Ecuador, there were significant episodes of clever and daring uses of democratic strategies to deal with authoritarian enclaves. Furthermore, most of the nondemocratic tactics deployed were not targeted at democratic adversaries. The net effect was that the regimes became more democratic than how they first started, even if liberalization was less consistently uphill than many would have wanted.

7

Function Fusion

A SURVIVAL TOOL FOR EMBATTLED STATES

This book has argued that to survive, autocratizing regimes need to have an inventory of conventional autocratic tools ready to be deployed and repurposed. But sometimes these regimes need to do more than that. They may need to invent new forms of autocratic governance. Venezuela did that. Maduro not only redeployed existing institutional reservoirs, but he also generated new modes of governance. In other words, the regime's crisis response reflects some path dependence, but in other respects path innovation. The most important form of innovation by Maduro is what I call "function fusion."[1]

Function fusion consists of granting existing institutions the ability to perform a variety of functions traditionally reserved for other institutions. Function fusion provides added capacity for autocratizing presidents to survive resistance. It supplements traditional autocratic tools by allowing states to economize on some traditional tools of autocratization, especially outright violent repression. Autocrats worldwide have discovered that relying too much on violent repression generates excessive international condemnation and can be counterproductive domestically (Guriev and Treisman 2020). They need alternative or supplementary tools of governance.

Function fusion is one such tool. Because it allows autocratic states to be more sparing in the use of traditional autocratic tools, function fusion has rising appeal among modern-day autocrats.

In addition, function fusion allows the state to expand the rewards it can offer to its winning coalition (see Bueno de Mesquita and Smith 2011). It is a form of private good provision to the coalition's members. However, function fusion expands rewards not by offering more volume in private goods (see de Waal 2015), but by diversifying the portfolio of rewards. It gives allies added *roles*, not just more profits. This allows allies to expand the reach of their power.

Function fusion is thus another form of currency used by the regime to compensate members of the governing coalition for their loyalty. It is a way for the state to minimize defections among its allies, especially when economic conditions would otherwise compel groups to shift their loyalty away from the state. Ultimately, function fusion allowed the Venezuelan regime to survive the pressures stemming from rising domestic opposition, economic contraction, and, most importantly, external economic sanctions.

Fusing Functions

Function fusion is not exactly a new concept in the social sciences. Scholars who study democracy recognize that regimes typically imbue institutions with multiple functions. Democracies, for example, often manipulate and distort institutions so they can serve goals other than the one they were intended to serve. For instance, democratic governments often use social spending to buy votes, macroeconomic fine-tuning to affect electoral outcomes, and information manipulation to deflect criticisms. Likewise, authoritarian regimes often incorporate or "mimic" democratic practices: for example, they allow elections for state office and permit some aspects of the press to survive.

Function fusion is related but also different from this type of institutional blending. It is related in that the state deliberately blends institutional functions that legally or formally should not go together. It is different in that the fusion takes place not by importing institutions from other regime types, but by blending the functions of institutions within the same regime type.

Function fusion is also different from duplication. Duplication occurs when presidents, instead of dismantling an institution they dislike, create their own parallel organization to sidestep the disfavored institution (Freeman 2018). There is no question that a lot of function fusion produces duplication. But function fusion is different in that the president grants multiple functions to the same institution, so that there could be multiple duplications as well as new functions operating simultaneously.

Function fusion is a form of pretense. Recent scholarship on the new forms of authoritarianism often makes the point that new authoritarians like to disguise their true nature by adopting presentable façades. A common idea is that new authoritarians like to pretend to be democrats, adopting the trappings of democracy (e.g., running elections, allowing some press to exist, reducing overt violence) to disguise their true desire to concentrate power (Schedler 2006, Frantz 2018, Guriev and Treisman 2020). Function fusion is also a way for the state to adopt multiple facades, but not with the intention of camouflaging its unsavory aspects (penchant for violence against rivals and impunity for loyalists), but actually to amplify these practices and make them, if anything, more visible to the population. To borrow the language of the political marketplace developed by de Waal (2015), function fusion is a diversification of the currency a ruler (the chief political entrepreneur) uses to buy political loyalties and services. In de Waal's model, the ruler pays for loyalty and services with money (or money-based rewards such as business contracts). In a function fusion system, the ruler pays by granting extra state functions.

The Functions of Function Fusion

Function fusion emerges as a form of authoritarian survival in the context of rising challenges. This book has discussed the three main threats the Venezuelan regime faced: (1) rising opposition starting in 2007; (2) economic collapse starting in the 2010s; and (3) increasing foreign sanctions led by the United States, Canada, and the European Union starting in 2017. The other cases of regime transition from semi-authoritarianism discussed in the previous chapter faced comparable challenges stemming from rising opposition, while two cases, Nicaragua and Ecuador, also faced economic collapse. Yet none faced economic sanctions like Venezuela. Nicaragua experienced sanctions, but not as severely.[2] These sanctions created a special threat to the Venezuelan regime. In many ways, function fusion, as I will argue, was one way for the regime to survive sanctions.

The literature on external economic sanctions has been able to identify why sanctions tend to fail in generating regime change. Sanctions fail when the targeted regime has economic alternatives (foreign partners) and when the elites are able to pass on the cost of adjustment to other groups, especially opponents and disenfranchised groups (Pape 1997, Hovi et al. 2005). But this argument cannot explain why allies of the government reaffirm their loyalty to the government even when economic goods decline. This chapter shows exactly how function fusion allows the government to reward allies in the context of severe resource shortage. Economic rewards, no doubt, still play a role in function fusion, as we will see. But function fusion does more by granting additional informal powers to government allies. When autocrats can turn to both illicit economic transactions and informal powers, they can neutralize the effects of external sanctions (Norwich University Online 2020).

Function fusion became common in Fidel Castro's Cuba early on. Castro's Cuba was the main authoritarian model that served as political inspiration for the Venezuelan regime since the early 2000s. It is not surprising that Cuba, also subject to severe external sanctions, early on made use of function fusion. The most important example of function fusion in Cuba are the Committees for the Defense of the Revolution, established in 1960, and the Brigades for Rapid Action, established in 1991.

The Committees for the Defense of the Revolution are neighborhood committees existing on almost every residential street. Committees are tasked with a number of civic functions (e.g., vaccine campaigns, hurricane preparations, street cleaning, building maintenance, garbage collection), party functions (mobilize participation for rallies, transmit the party line), headhunting functions (determine who is eligible for good jobs with the state), court functions (determine who is guilty of counterrevolutionary activities), and security functions (citizens' watch, snitching, reporting to authorities) (Fagen 1969, Montaner 1999). The brigades are groups of civilians (sometimes, security agents dressed as civilians), hired by the state and given paramilitary functions to harass and infiltrate protesters (Rodiles 2014). They show up at protests with sticks and baseball bats, always dressed as civilians. They are sometimes helped by so called *contramanifestantes,* civilians who harass crowds and even arrest people. Many members of these groups do not consider themselves repressors or part of the security forces, and yet that is one of their functions (Castañeda 2021).

As this chapter shows, Venezuela borrowed many of these uses of function fusion, and more. That said, it is important to note that function fusion began in a bold way in Venezuela before harsh sanctions arrived. More precisely, function fusion began under Hugo Chávez in relation to the oil industry. Chávez converted the oil sector into more than just another appendage of the executive branch; he made it an organization for conducting foreign policy (offering oil discounts and investment facilities to external allies), providing contracts for friendly domestic businesses to garner the support of business elites, funding social welfare for low-income groups, providing employment of last resort, and providing campaign financing for the ruling party (Monaldi 2013, Gallegos 2016, Corrales et al. 2020). Function fusion did not necessarily cause the oil sector to thrive economically, but it helped Chávez achieve a remarkable electoral coalition at home and a reliable set of allies abroad. Under Maduro, we have seen Venezuelan executives embezzling funds from PDVSA (Petróleos de Venezuela, S.A.) contracts and laundering them abroad. That Tareck El Aissami, wanted by the U.S. Department of

State for drug trafficking and narco-terrorism, was put in charge of PDVSA is a sign of entanglement between the country's oil sector and the illicit drug trafficking by related officials.

Nicolás Maduro would not only continue to practice function fusion within the oil sector, but also bring it to new levels and expand it to new institutions. As the following sections show, Maduro has applied function fusion to the military, organized civilian groups, a Constituent National Assembly (Asamblea Nacional Constituyente, CNA), judges, the ruling party, local neighborhood communities, and foreign armies.

The Military Gets Economic Functions

As the previous chapter showed, military support is the sine qua non of regime survival for any authoritarian regime, and Maduro has used classic coup-proofing strategies. But he has also innovated. Maduro's military entourage, in many respects, is more unconventional than not.

Maduro's military entourage is not characterized by a single professional, vertically organized actor. Instead, the military comprises at least five actors, each with its own interest in supporting Maduro.[3]

The first group is the *standard military establishment*, which in Venezuela consists of professional career soldiers as well as ideologized soldiers. Another group consists of *military politicians*. These are individuals who occupy civilian posts in government, either as cabinet members or governors. Under Maduro, the military presence in government posts increased dramatically (Gunson 2016). Yet another group consists of *bureaucrat generals*. These officials are aligned with Maduro because they have good jobs running at least seventy state-owned corporations (International Crisis Group 2019), including the state-owned oil company, PDVSA, from 2017 to 2020.

Still another group consists of *profit-seeking soldiers*. Maduro has given the military other functions not typically associated with the institution: access to legal and illegal economic activities. This has given rise to profit opportunities for soldiers. From the legal side, Maduro has expanded the number of businesses run by the military (International Crisis Group 2019). Between 2013 and 2019, Maduro established fourteen military-owned business firms. Chávez, in contrast, only created two military-business firms during his presidency. Before Chávez, the military controlled only three firms (Armas 2017). Maduro's military-business firms are involved in a large variety of industries: mining, construction, banking, farming, transportation, media, car dealerships, water distribution, clothing, printing, and even distribution of subsidized foods.

Finally, Venezuela under Maduro developed *mafia soldiers*. Maduro has allowed the military to become heavily involved in illicit economic activities (International Crisis Group 2019). These activities involve control of domestic informal markets; smuggling of consumer products, including gasoline, into Colombia and Brazil (Cardona 2018); collaboration with the drug trade that originates in the Andean countries—it is estimated that one-quarter of Colombia's drug exports pass through Venezuela; and more recently, the illegal export of gold (Cardona 2018, Alexander 2019, Casey 2019, Christofaro 2019, Delgado et al. 2019, Ebus 2019, Paton Walsh et al. 2019). While some analysts argue that charges coming from the United States on the military's involvement in the drug trade may be overstated (Ramsey et al. 2020), few disagree that the military is involved to some extent in a variety of illicit activities. Analysts disagree as to which of these activities is more central to the military and how organized its illicit businesses may be. But a consensus exists that the government rarely punishes any military official for participating in these activities.

In short, the latter three military actors described above fuse military with economic functions. They have become key bastions of support for the regime, perhaps more important than the standard military dedicated exclusively to professional security affairs.

Civilians Get Military- and Gangster-Like Functions

Another institution treated with function fusion are organized civilians, or more specifically, the colectivos. As mentioned in chapter 5, *colectivos* is the term used in Venezuela for civilians paid or encouraged by the government to terrorize political dissidents

The regime began using colectivos in the early 2000s, first as community-organized civilians. The colectivos, then known as Bolivarian Circles, were originally formed by Chávez to help implement government policy at the local level (Office of the United Nations High Commissioner for Human Rights 2017). However, their security-enhancing potential became obvious during the 2002 coup attempt: they helped counterbalance the military, which had refused to mobilize against protestors (Venezuela Investigative Unit 2018b). Chávez began funding and arming colectivos, turning them into informal militias, sometimes including reservists (Venezuela Investigative Unit 2018b).

Today, colectivos consist mostly of party followers, paid civilians, delinquents, thugs, and even former inmates (Vallejo 2019), hired informally by the state to execute some of the dirtiest forms of repression. Colectivos are distributed throughout the country, operating mostly in low-income neighborhoods, though they can be mobilized quickly throughout cities. Some estimates say that colectivos control 10 percent of cities (Torres and Casey 2017, Sheridan and Zúñiga 2019).

Colectivos are especially effective in intimidating small neighborhood protests and gatherings. In Venezuela, street protests have either been nationally organized and coordinated (as in 2014 and 2017) or small and dispersed, occurring in particular neighborhoods throughout the country and not necessarily coordinated by national-level politicians. These latter-type of protests include street meetings, marches, and labor strikes. In addition to using the traditional uniformed military officials like the Venezuelan National Guard (Guardia Nacional Bolivariana, GNB) and Venezuelan National Police (Policía Nacional Bolivariana, PNB), Maduro has opted to use colectivos to contain the spread of smaller protests. They show up unannounced and armed. They arrive driving motorcycles and their faces are often covered. Because they are not wearing uniforms, it is difficult for reporters to certify that they are government-supported operatives. Any violence generated by these colectivos cannot indisputably be classified as generated by state forces.

Colectivos have thus become the unofficial sheriffs or gangs in particular neighborhoods. They are therefore a bit different from their counterparts in Cuba, the Brigades for Rapid Action. Those brigades were established specifically as coercive civilians to attack protesters. Colectivos in Venezuela have more autonomy to engage in random crimes. In addition to containing political protests, they also have the freedom to engage in ordinary felonies and criminal activities, such as armed robberies, smuggling, burglaries, drug trafficking, and extortions of both private individuals and businesses (Venezuela Investigative Unit 2018b). In an economy where there is so much scarcity and so few business opportunities, the chance to engage in criminality with almost complete impunity is appealing to many civilians. All that colectivos need to do to earn their impunity is to do political jobs on behalf of the state.

Colectivos are allowed to be the regime's unofficial security forces. In the 2017 attack on the National Assembly, some sources report that security forces were given orders not to intervene against colectivos (Office of the United Nations High Commissioner for Human Rights 2017, Canton et al. 2018). A 2018 Organization of American States (OAS) report on violence during the protests essentially confirmed the coordination of tactics by security forces and colectivos as evidence of covert collaboration between the two groups (Canton et al. 2018).

The state gains much by giving civilians functions associated with the military and criminal syndicates. First, colectivos spare the government the embarrassing task of using uniformed personnel to practice repression. Colectivos allow the state to engage in plausible deniability of repression. In addition, colectivos can act more quickly than the uniformed military, making them especially effective at executing tasks like ambushing opposition lawmakers, as well as playing a supportive role to the PNB and GNB during large protests. It is also unclear whether ordinary soldiers in Venezuela are loyal enough to Maduro to engage in open repression of citizens. There are plenty of examples of ordinary GNB/PNB beating up protesters in recent years, but colectivos are used often enough (Sheridan and Zúñiga 2019). And because colectivos, unlike the official Armed Forces, do not control a large network of soldiers, infrastructure, and artillery, they are less likely to orchestrate a successful coup against the state on their own.

In fact, during recent years we have seen that colectivos who climb high enough up the ladder are integrated into official bodies, further legitimizing their role in the regime. For instance, in 2019 a notorious colectivo was appointed leader of the PNB's Special Action Forces (Fuerzas de Acciones Especiales de la Policía, FAES). FAES is known to hire colectivos into its ranks (InSight Crime 2019b).

Colectivos and paramilitaries solve a conundrum identified by the growing literature on coup-proofing. The conundrum is that states engaged in bad governance need a strong and well-endowed professional military apparatus to protect the regime from insurgents, but a strong and professional military can rise up and even stage its own coups—posing a threat to the state. This is one reason that leaders counterbalance that threat by "dividing the military into multiple rival forces," and "creating parallel militaries" (Sudduth 2017).

Judges as Vendors

A classic autocratic tool consists of undermining the independence of the judiciary. The previous chapter discussed how both Chávez and Maduro used this tactic promiscuously: packing the Supreme Court, keeping at least 75 percent of judges untenured, directly pressuring judges to rule along party lines, undermining the autonomy and funding for defense attorneys, and appointing loyalists to the top positions of the Ministry of Citizens Power, the equivalent of the U.S. Department of Justice, which included the Ombudsman, the Attorney General, and the Comptroller General (United Nations Human Rights Council 2020). This is the tactic that allowed both presidents to engage in autocratic legalism.

But judges and legal authorities in Venezuela have also been allowed to become state contractors. According to an investigative report (Poliszuk and Marcano 2019), 7.7 percent (461) of all active or retired judges under Chavismo (5,928) have been allowed to own corporations or be part of the board of directors of corporations that receive contracts with the state for private services. Most of these contracts involve construction work (23.0 percent), all-service operations (19.0 percent), and maintenance services (11.9 percent). In times of scarcity, these firms not only get contracts with the state but also manage to acquire scarce products like cement and bricks. They also have access to scarce dollars using preferential rates. Some judges have been found to have several contracts (through separate private firms). Most of these contracts are offered without public bidding. Of these 461 judges-vendors, 52.2 percent are also members of the ruling party. Judges who served on some of the most high-profile cases are listed as state contractors (e.g., María Verónica Emmanuelli, who served on the Walid Makled case in which the government was prosecuting a drug lord who once did business with the government but started supporting independent candidates for office; Pedro Alexander Lunar, who served on the Golpe Azul case, in which the state was accusing fifteen individuals of plotting a coup).

Venezuela's Constitution explicitly prohibits state employees from establishing contracts with the state (Article 145). The same article in the Constitution also prohibits the state from hiring or firing civil servants based on political affiliations. But it is clear that the state violates this constitutional norm as a form of compensation for their loyalty.

The Ruling Party Gets (Dictatorial) State Functions

Maduro not only merged state structures with ruling party structures, as the previous chapter explained, he also gave the leaders in the ruling party state functions, in particular, security functions and economic functions. Maduro has borrowed Cuba's concept of Committees for the Defense of the Revolution and expanded their functions so that parts of the ruling party can participate in the illegal economic activities that are more prevalent in Venezuela than in Cuba.

One of Maduro's most important transformations of the PSUV was to turn the base into spying cells. This can be appreciated by looking at the party's Bolívar Chávez Battle Units (Unidades de Batalla Bolívar Chávez). These units were given a number of official tasks: (1) ideological training; (2) mobilization; (3) propaganda, agitation, and communication; (4) liaisons with women's and youth movements; (5) support Maduro's "Street Government"; (6) comprehensive security; and (7) electoral techniques and logistics. Extra-officially, one of their key tasks was to keep a close watch on members: their voting behavior, their friendships, and even their discourse. By 2015, the party had activated 13,683 Battle Units, mostly located very close to voting centers. These Battle Units were asked to carry out their control functions during electoral campaigns but also during nonelectoral periods.

Additionally, in 2014, Battle Units were given the right to organize policy responses to any "conflicts or social problems" they would encounter. They were also allowed to register as "virtual soldiers," thus earning the right to exercise coercive functions, including the use of violence, in what was a novel adaptation of Chávez's famous concept of the civic-military model (von Bergen Granell 2017). Party-affiliated governors were given carte blanche within their states to rule by discretion, and even to engage in smuggling. In 2016, they were given the role of inspecting businesses to ensure compliance with rationing and price control regulations, to defeat the "economic warfare." They were allowed to set up CLAPs, receiving specific guidelines to privilege party members.

In 2019, Maduro announced that he would hand over an active gold mine to each and every "Bolivarian governor" so that they could generate foreign exchange for their needs. One analyst described this as a return to the early nineteenth century when there was no real national state (Benítez 2019). Another called it a sort of political vandalism (Pérez Vivas 2019).

Party subunits in many ways became mini-dictatorial units. Whether governors, community organizers, managers at state-owned companies, they obtained plenty of latitude to rule as they see fit, provided of course that their loyalty to Maduro remains unquestionable.

The Constituent Assembly Gets Legislative, Judicial, and Politburo Functions

The most autocratic mechanism for ending the problem of a legislature that refuses to go along with the executive branch is of course a self-coup (Cameron 1998). The problem with self-coups is that they receive immediate international condemnation. Maduro discovered an alternative to self-coups that accomplishes the same outcome: convene a Constituent National Assembly (CNA) that, once elected, would assume broad functions.

Maduro acquired the problem of a nonsubservient legislature after the 2015 legislative election in which the opposition took control of the legislature. After a period of tension between the branches, Maduro decided to solve this crisis in executive-legislative relations by invoking Article 347 of the Venezuelan Constitution, which grants the people the right to convene a Constituent National Assembly (Melimopoulos 2017). The decision to establish the CNA and the process of electing this body were highly irregular (Phippen 2017, Corrales 2020b):

- *No citizen consultation:* According to the Constitution, the people need to express whether they want a change of constitution or not. Voters were not consulted. According to some polls, 85 percent of citizens opposed this election (Milliken et al. 2017).

- *Violating the relationship between seats and population:* The government assigned one seat per district regardless of population size. This favored small and rural districts, where the ruling party was stronger. In capital cities, where the government was weaker, the government created two seats, with the rule that the second seat goes to the loser.

- *Violating the rule of one person, one vote:* The government created eight sectors that would elect their own representatives: Indigenous, students, peasants, fishermen, businesspeople, people with disabilities, communal councils, and communes and workers. Only voters deemed by the government to belong to those sectors could vote for those representatives.

- *Ban on parties:* The government barred candidates from running under the sponsorship of political parties.

- *Erosion of freedom to vote:* Venezuela's 2.8 million public sector employees were threatened with losing their jobs, and beneficiaries of government social programs, with losing their benefits, if they abstained (Chinea 2017).

- *No auditing:* Voting centers did not have auditors and witnesses from the opposition.

The results of the election were noncredible. When the government finally announced the results—claiming that 8,089,320 voters participated (41.53 percent of the electorate), which was almost the same number that voted for Chávez in 2012 (8.10 million) and 2.46 million more than voted for the PSUV in the 2015 legislative elections—no member of the opposition believed the results. The opposition claimed the real number was closer to 2.0 million. Torino Capital, a financial firm, spoke of 3.6 million. Smartmatic, the multinational that runs the electronic voting system employed in Venezuela's elections, claimed that "there was manipulation of participation data," with a difference of "at least" 1 million votes between the results reported by the CNE and Smartmatic's numbers (BBC Mundo 2017).

More than forty countries and several international organizations, such as the European Union, the Organization of American States, the Carter Center, and the Socialist International, condemned this election for violating so many electoral principles.

Once the CNA came into being, Maduro moved quickly to extend its powers to include the following:

- *Legislative functions:* The CNA was allowed to legislate on issues concerning "peace, security, sovereignty, and the socio-economic and financial system" (Bronstein and Symmes Cobb 2017).

- *Electoral functions:* The Constituent National Assembly (CNA) determined when and how to organize the 2017 regional elections for governors and mayors. It also decreed an electoral norm stating that those parties that decided to boycott mayoral elections had to reregister with the CNE, a highly bureaucratic process. Finally, the CNA determined the change of schedule for the 2018 presidential election.

- *Supreme Court functions:* Acting as a court, the CNA, for instance, barred opposition candidates from running for office based on legal charges (Osborne 2017), and removed parliamentary immunity for four deputies, including Juan Guaidó, president of the National Assembly (TeleSUR 2019). The government also required newly elected governors to swear allegiance to the CNA, just as one would have elected officials swear in before a judge.

- *Politburo functions:* The CNA became the leading body establishing political principles and policy directives for the entire ruling party, including both the rank and file and the country's leadership. For instance, the CNA fired a cabinet member (Attorney General Luisa Ortega Díaz) when she became critical of the administration (Brocchetto et al. 2017), created truth commissions to investigate human rights charges (TeleSUR 2017), and offered opinions on a number of policy issues such as taxation and military affairs.

In addition to the opportunity to carry out a self-coup through other means, the purpose of function fusion with regard to the CNA was to allow Maduro the chance to give a political fiefdom to one of the ruling party's most important leaders, Diosdado Cabello. Cabello has always been considered Maduro's most important potential rival within the ruling party (Lansberg-Rodríguez 2014). He was one of the top leaders whom Chávez had considered as a possible successor. He wields influence across various sectors of the military, crony capitalists, and ideologues. Within Venezuela he is known as a crime lord and smuggler, and in 2020 he was charged with narco-terrorism and drug trafficking by the United States along with several other high-ranking Chavistas, for his role within the Cartel of the Suns (Venezuela Investigative Unit 2018c, U.S. Department of Justice 2020).[4]

Function fusion allowed Maduro to keep Cabello within his fold. Cabello soon became president of the Constituent Assembly, obtaining a national-level political platform with superpowers (and his brother, José David Cabello, is the superintendent of the office in charge of customs and taxation, SENIAT (Servicio Nacional Integrado de Administración Aduanera y Tributaria [National Integrated Service for the Administration of Customs Duties and Taxes]), which is perhaps the office that has the greatest capacity to extort business firms in Venezuela).

In fact, the same logic applies to the ruling party as a whole. Through irregular electoral tricks, Maduro managed to populate this assembly with a ruling party majority that included some of the party's top leaders and even his wife, Cilia Flores.

The task of writing a new constitution seems to have been relegated to these other alternate functions. Finally, in September of 2020, Cabello announced that the CNA, ironically, would not be drafting a new constitution. Despite being in session for three years, there was no new Magna Carta. By comparison, in 1999, when Chávez was keen on having a new constitution, the Constituent Assembly drafted and approved a new text in less than a year.

Communal Councils Get to Weaponize Hunger

The Maduro administration also relied on function fusion to weaponize welfare assistance.[5] The government turned communal councils, an illiberal institution inherited from the Chávez era (López-Maya 2018), into a mechanism for ensuring discipline and loyalty among welfare recipients during the hunger years.

Communal councils were created by Chávez in 2007, when he realized his party, regardless of its electoral dominance, would never achieve full control of subnational offices. The Constitution ensured that officeholding in municipal and state governments would always be determined by political competition, and that, even in the best electoral years, the opposition was going to have the chance to win some seats, if not full control of some of these offices. So Chávez came up with the idea of creating the "Communal State," consisting of political bodies distributed throughout the territory with the authority to make decisions and set regulations about regional development.

Communal councils, therefore, were charged with functions already entrusted, by the Constitution, to local governments: budget powers to address local needs (García Marco 2017). Chávez added more functions. In 2010, he also created so called *comunas* as a "socialist space" for neighborhood associations. When favored politicians from the PSUV would lose power in local elections, they could be transferred to communal councils or comunas with new roles, thus turning these spaces into placeholders (and thus reward posts) for loyal actors voted out of office. None of the laws created to regulate communal councils ever introduced the concept of political competition, so councils were used to delimit deliberation (and thus, expand the government's anti-pluralist agenda). Furthermore, the councils would be managed by the executive branch directly, granting it a new way to control subnational affairs. These groups have thus been described as "controlled comptrollers" (Chaguaceda 2020:257). But they were more than that. Councils also enjoyed party, local government, and cabinet-level functions.

One of Maduro's key innovations was to link the provision of social assistance to communal councils, thus granting them yet another function. He did not think of this idea right away. Initially, Maduro's response to the economic crisis was to introduce a rationing system, essentially replicating a model drawn from the Soviet bloc. The government launched consumption quotas, giving people permission to buy certain quantities of certain products on certain days of the week, but no more. By 2017 Venezuelans were spending an average of eight hours a week shopping and standing in line. Food lines, however, led to discontent and hoarding. Polls revealed that even former supporters of the ruling party were intensely irritated with Maduro. This discontent led to more protests. Roughly five food-related protests were occurring in Venezuela every day, a total of 954 in the first half of 2016—27 percent of all street protests in the country.

Soon the government started to use food lines as a way to keep tabs on citizens, giving the government the chance to extend Orwellian supervision. Retailers were required to keep tabs on who bought what and how much. The government installed fingerprint scanners in grocery and drug stores. The government seized supplies from food firms and threatened to take over idle factories. Armed Forces were assigned to grocery stores to watch lines and control access. The military was also responsible for dispersing any food riots that might pop up.

But this system of societal control through militarized lines became too difficult to monitor and too full of holes. The lines gave the government the opportunity to keep tabs on people, but not exactly to make people feel like they depended on the government. Venezuelans were still relying on private and informal markets to survive. So the government came up with a new idea: the creation of Local Committees for Supply and Production (CLAPs).

CLAPs are government-run "committees" that distribute groceries at highly subsidized prices. This set-up solves the problem of scarcity (by providing basics), and the problem of inflation (by providing affordable prices). Maduro's big innovation was to add one more task to communal councils: he made them administrators of CLAP programs. Communal council members would meet to determine how many food boxes were needed per council.

They, therefore, determined eligibility. They would also determine the sales of boxes. As of September 2020, there were 3,230 communes and 45,095 communal councils. CLAPs create citizen dependence on the state (by 2017, 87.5 percent of households reported receiving help from CLAPs) (The Caracas Chronicles Team 2018), and communal councils ensure that the state has the ability to reach out into communities, that is, to extend its network of controls beyond mere urban centers (Trivella 2021).

Needless to say, CLAPS and communal councils provided yet another function: the opportunity for corruption. Two Colombian businessmen, Alex Saab and Álvaro Pulido, were granted business rights to import food into Venezuela to supply CLAPs. Investigations by the U.S. Treasury Department revealed that the manipulation of permits, exchange rate quotas, and invoicing to import food was used in large-scale schemes to divert resources and business opportunities to close friends and families of political leaders. The United States imposed sanctions against ten individuals and thirteen companies tied to Maduro's regime and the web of corruption that characterizes the purchase and distribution of food for the CLAPs (Soto 2019).

CLAPs do nothing to end Venezuela's food crisis, but they do wonders for the government: they force Venezuelans to demonstrate loyalty to the Maduro regime to qualify for the handouts. A United Nations Report condemned the CLAP program for the following reasons: (1) it provides very little assistance: protein- and vitamin-heavy foods are scarce; (2) it is run without clear mechanisms of accountability and there is no way to present complaints or hold officials accountable; and (3) it is used as an "instrument for political propaganda and social control" that includes supporting the PSUV elections (Oficina del Alto Comisionado de las Naciones Unidas para los Derechos Humanos 2018:56).

Sharing Sovereignty with Foreign Armies and Non-state Actors

It is not unusual for authoritarian regimes to host and support foreign armies within their territories. What is less common is for authoritarian regimes to *share sovereignty* with such armies. This has been Maduro's approach to two foreign armies, both guerrillas: the dissenting FARC and the National Liberation Army (Ejército de Liberación Nacional, ELN). These armies are waging wars in neighboring Colombia. Maduro and many subnational authorities have not only sheltered them in Venezuelan territory (Venezuela Investigative Unit 2018a), but also allowed them to exercise state-like powers within Venezuela.

This shared sovereignty is most visible in the running of the gold industry (figure 7-1). When Venezuela's oil industry collapsed at the end of the Chávez administration and the start of the Maduro administration—a combination of declining oil prices and production—the Venezuelan state turned to gold mining to compensate for declining exports (see Rosales 2019). In 2011, Chávez announced the start of a state project to exploit the so-called Arco Minero in Bolívar, the state with the third-largest population of Indigenous people in Venezuela (Instituto Nacional de Estadísticas 2013). In February 2016, Maduro decided to go full steam ahead, with a decree establishing the Arco Minero as a National Strategic Development Zone. Venezuela officially became a gold-centric country.

Focusing on gold made sense considering the scarcity of alternative exports. In November 2018, Maduro estimated that his "Gold Plan" could yield as much as US$5 billion in revenues (Cotovio et al. 2019). What was surprising were the facilities Maduro extended to dissident FARC and ELN groups to operate in the gold-mining regions, a territory covering more than 43,000 square miles (Ebus 2019). Soon these actors began to operate even

Figure 7-1. Mining Fields in Venezuela

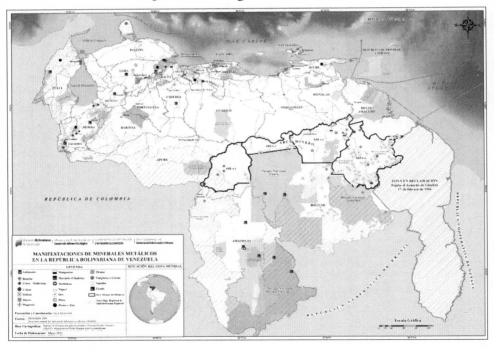

Source: Ministry of People's Power for the Ecological Development of Mining (n.d.), www.desarrollominero.gob.ve/coleccion-de-mapas-geologicos/.

outside this region, especially in border states. Maduro has been able to rely on these armies' illegal external ties to export some of this gold in defiance of U.S. sanctions (Martínez-Fernández 2019a, 2019b, Millan Lombrana 2019).

While the Arco Minero today may seem like a "no-go place" or an ungoverned space lacking state presence, it resembles what Clunan and Trinkunas (2010) label as "alternatively governed space." The state allows other actors to govern. Dissident FARC and ELN groups are not only allowed to conduct their own mining operations and to keep substantial revenues (a type of privatization) but also to control activities such as the commercialization of gold both within Venezuela and across borders, determining which other groups, legal or illegal, also get to participate in mining activities, and, most important, exercise control over the population. This latter point involves providing security (or not), controlling the borders of such territories, determining which individuals can be hired in the mining sector, and even providing social services to local citizens (InSight Crime 2020, Ellis 2021). Some reporters have documented similar state services provided by foreign guerrillas in the states of Apure, Táchira, and Amazonas (InSight Crime 2019a). Even before the pandemic, reports indicated that dissident FARC and ELN agents in border states recruited students for armed conflict or forced criminality (U.S. Department of State 2021). They do so by helping them with their school supplies, or if they have abandoned school, by offering gifts for them or their families. Some reports indicated that 75 percent of students not attending school in border states have had contact with dissident FARC and ELN actors (U.S. Department of State 2021). Since the pandemic, there are reports that ELN have taken on health-official duties: they have become enforcers of lockdown measures (Ellis 2021).

In controlling large portions of the nonoil extractive industries of Venezuela, these foreign armies (and by extension, the Venezuelan state) share sovereignty with criminal syndicates (Ebus and Martinelli 2021). These are armed gangs that also extract and commercialize gold for private gain. It is estimated that each mining town in the state of Bolívar has its own criminal syndicate (Kirschner 2020). Local citizens engaged in private mining have reported they prefer "to sell to the syndicates because the soldiers often take part or sometimes all of their gold" (López 2017).

The Venezuelan president has therefore agreed to share sovereignty in the extractive and border regions with both military and non-state actors. This presence of the military is extensive: the Armed Forces control twenty-five checkpoints along the highway that runs throughout the state of Bolívar from north to south, connecting the most important mines (Office of the United Nations High Commissioner for Human Rights 2020). Non-state actors include foreign armies and criminal syndicates—a concession to "private actors" that goes beyond what typical privatization would entail. These non-state actors have control of military, legal, and social policies in the territories they operate. They are quasi states operating within a nation-state. The president wins by expanding the number of groups co-opted, avoiding the need to patrol and provide services to these remote regions, and also bypassing U.S. sanctions. An added bonus is, of course, fortifying armies that are challenging the government of Colombia, which since 2016 has become an open critic of the Maduro administration.

The Ministry of Mining Development, as of 2020, was not reporting official figures, but research by journalists and anthropologists shows that the environmental and human costs of this form of mining are high. The mining boom has attracted workers to mining areas, leading to a remarkable population boom. Figure 7-2 shows the rapid expansion of mining-driven human settlements along the Chicanan River in the state of Bolívar. Reports indicate that most people in these new mining settlements have been exposed to mercury, malaria, crime, and abusive labor conditions (IPS 2020).

Whoever controls a given mine—a governor, a corporation, a guerrilla

Figure 7-2. Venezuela's Gold Rush

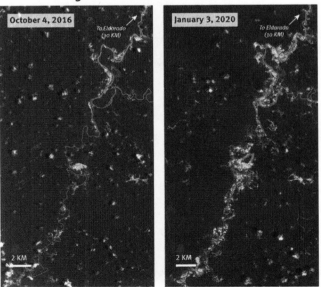

Notes: Mining-driven expansion of human settlements along the Chicanan River, Bolívar State.

Source: Planet Labs and IPS (2020).

force, a gang—can engage in all forms of labor exploitation: underpayment, trafficking, violence. Migrants are rushing to the Arco Minero looking for work. They typically get paid by getting to keep part of their extractions. They are often required to give up a large portion, ranging between 10 and 20 percent, just to have a license to work in the mine, and then 15 to 30 percent extra as a form of tax (Office of the United Nations High Commissioner for Human Rights 2020). Miners then need to exchange their gold for currency, which means that they need to transact with smugglers. Many miners are underage, and the new mining towns that have emerged attract young women for sex work. Sanitary conditions are dismal. The Pan American Health Organization (PAHO) has identified mining towns in Venezuela as hotspots for the spread of malaria. Chemical mercury, which is banned in most countries including Venezuela for its toxic and polluting effect, is common. Crime is high, and the mining municipalities of El Callao, Roscio, and Sifontes have registered homicide rates of 94, 109, and 64 homicides per 100,000 inhabitants, respectively (Office of the United Nations High Commissioner for Human Rights 2020), some of the highest rates in the world.

The literature on the resource curse is full of colorful adjectives to describe the damage that can result from mismanaged resource dependence: "Devil's excrement," "blood diamonds," "conflict minerals." We can now add a new term, "criminal gold." Gold mining in Venezuela relies on, and expands, crime—domestic as well as international, human as well as environmental, organized as well as random.

Making Nice with Crime

Many regimes become destabilized when they decide to wage war against organized crime. Because of its ties to lucrative drug trafficking, organized crime in Latin America has a remarkable ability to strike back hard at the state. Thus, wars on drugs generate significant violent clashes between states and criminal gangs. The Maduro regime has taken the opposite approach to organized crime. Instead of fighting crime, or even just tolerating some of it, it has decided to make nice with it. The state has allowed its top echelons to be fully involved in criminal activities.

We know that criminal syndicates have a particularly strong desire to co-opt the state, that is, to establish linkages with state actors (Sullivan 2013, Bagley and Rosen 2015). By corrupting the state, they gain room for maneuver. But this type of co-optation tends to be most insidious at subnational levels of government and in lower parts of the bureaucracy such as the police and lower level courts (Briscoe and Keseberg 2019).

The executive branch is typically torn about this form of state–drug lord co-optation. On the one hand, it finds that fighting drug lords may be counterproductive (too costly). On the other hand, it finds that when ties between the state and narco-groups become too extensive, those ties can become obstacles to effective governance, capable of turning states into failed states. Thus, presidents often feel it is in their interest to put some limits on state-capture by organized crimes. Their typical response is thus to tolerate some co-optation (i.e., accept some criminal activities that they cannot fight or which do not badly impair the state's ability to govern), while simultaneously fighting cartels in other dimensions. Wars on crime tend to be uneven: ferocious in some arenas and less intense in other areas.

In Venezuela, there is no war on crime, even or uneven. The linkages between the state and organized crime seem to be occurring at the deepest level, involving the top echelon of government. InSight Crime reported in 2018 that 123 high-level government officials have been involved in criminal activities (Venezuela Investigative Unit 2018d). This includes the Vice Presidency, the Ministries of the Interior, Defense, Agriculture, Education, Prison Service, Foreign Trade and Investment, and Electricity, the National Guard, the Armed Forces, the Bolivarian Intelligence Service, and PDVSA.

The starting point of these activities was the 2005 decision by Chávez to reduce the operations of the U.S. Drug Enforcement Administration in Venezuela. Chávez also allowed other branches of the military, not just the National Guard, to investigate crime, and this seems to have given them more opportunities to make deals with drug traffickers. Toward the end of the Chávez administration, there were some signs that the state had decided to stop some drug trafficking: there were several important Colombian drug traffickers arrested in Venezuela in 2011 and 2012. But under Maduro, there have been very few arrests of known criminal actors (Venezuela Investigative Unit 2018c). Less than a year into Maduro's presidency, France conducted a massive cocaine bust, discovering 1.3 tons of cocaine packed in thirty-one suitcases on an Air France plane that landed in Paris from Caracas. Twenty-eight arrests were made in Caracas, but there have been no more follow-ups since then.

The state has also allowed autonomous criminal organizations that are less transnational than drug lords to operate with impunity across the country. InSight Crime reports that in 2013 the government, led by José Vicente Rangel Ávalos, negotiated with a large criminal gang, or *megabandas*, "not to allow state security forces into designated zones without prior agreement" (Venezuela Investigative Unit 2018d). These zones were officially called "Peace Zones," but in reality they were impunity zones. This allowed these gangs to expand territorially and functionally. The Peace Zone policy was eventually abandoned by the government, but those areas still have some of the highest crime rates in the country. InSight Crime reports that twelve to sixteen megabandas operate in Venezuela as of 2018 in the states of Miranda, Guárico, Carabobo, Aragua, Zulia, Bolívar, Táchira, and in the capital Caracas. Megabandas are involved in kidnapping, extortion, drug dealing, and car and property theft.

Maduro has acquired the habit of actually promoting individuals sanctioned for corruption and links with drug trafficking (table 7-1). Although this could be seen as a form of defiance in foreign policy, it still sends a signal domestically that in Venezuela there can be political rewards for mixing crime and political loyalty.

Finally, the state allows the police force to engage in crime. Of the 26,615 crimes reported by Observatorio Venezolano de Violencia (OVV) in 2017, 5,535 occurred at the hands of security forces (Observatorio Venezolano de Conflictividad Social, various years). Citizens in Venezuela know that police officers have been instructed to "shoot first, ask questions later," which gives them ample powers to extort civilians.

Admittedly, there have been clashes between independent-minded community leaders and government forces. The case of Wilexis Acevedo, a warlord that Maduro's regime linked to Operation Gedeón, serves as an example. However, criminal syndicates in Venezuela generally do not see the state as their enemy. This has resulted in heightened insecurity for non-state actors and especially common citizens in Venezuela (in the form of escalating homicides), but some degree of security for the state.

Conclusion

In his ground-breaking book on the origins of early forms of democracy, Stasavage (2020) argues that premodern states were often compelled to engage in some form of collegial rule when they lacked (1) certainty about the sources of revenues, and (2) efficient bureaucracies. Rather than centralize power, the ruler in these contexts was forced to share power. Function fusion is a modern adaptation of this argument for authoritarian rulers. Under increasing economic travails and growing public sector incompetence (see Rosales 2019), Maduro was forced to give institutions and, by extension, the actors in charge of those institutions, additional powers.

Function fusion is perhaps Maduro's most important autocratic innovation. It was inspired by the Cuban model and relied on some of Chávez's policies, especially in the oil sector. But Maduro elevated the reach of function fusion and extended it to new sectors.

Function fusion helps authoritarian regimes in a number of ways. First, the executive branch engages in some form of power-sharing with other

Table 7-1. Venezuela: Ruling Party Leaders Sanctioned and Promoted

Leader	Sanction	Position before or at time of sanction	Promotion after sanction
Freddy Bernal	Sanctioned by the United States for involvement in drug trafficking (2017)	PSUV leader, member of the National Assembly (TeleSUR 2016), Chief of CLAP National Committee (El Estímulo 2016)	Named "Protector" of Táchira, an important border state, effectively displacing the opposition's governor in 2018 (Quintero 2018)
Carlos Osorio	Censure vote by the National Assembly for mismanagement of corruption (2016)	Chief Inspector of the National Guard, Chief of Strategic Integral Defense (Control Ciudadano 2018), Major General, Minister of Food (Dreier 2017)	Promoted as Minister of Transportation, then President of the Venezuelan Mining Corporation (Santistevan Gastelú 2019)
Mayor General Néstor Reverol	Sanctioned by the United States for drug trafficking (2018)	Minister for Interior Relations, Justice, and Peace (Torres 2020)	Named Sectorial Vice President for Public Works and Services (Rodríguez 2019)
Tareck El Aissami	Sanctioned by the United States, Canada, and the European Union for links with drug trafficking (2017–2018)	Governor of Aragua, recently appointed Vice President (Kurmanaev 2017)	Minister of Industries and National Production (2018) and Minister of Oil (April 2020) (Reuters 2020)
Tarek William Saab	Sanctioned for undermining democracy (2017)	Ombudsman	Prosecutor General, replacing defector Luisa Ortega in 2017 (Bronstein and Pons 2017)
Iris Varela	Sanctioned for undermining democracy (2017)	Member of Presidential Commission for the Constituent Assembly, Minister of Prisons	Stepped down as Minister of Prisons so she could be appointed Member of the National Constituent Assembly, then she was again appointed as Minister of Prisons (Párraga 2020)
Diosdado Cabello	Sanctioned for money laundering (2018)	Vice President of PSUV	President of the Constituent National Assembly (Soto and Laya 2018).

Notes: CLAP = Comités Locales de Abastecimiento y Producción (Local Committees for Supply and Production).

Source: As noted in table.

members of the ruling coalition, which thus expands the reach of the governing coalition. Second, function fusion allows the state to either save on the use of traditional authoritarian tools or at least deny involvement in traditional authoritarian practices such as outright repression (the role of colectivos), smuggling (the role of drug traffickers and foreign armies), and brutal environmental and labor practices (illegal mining by non-state actors). By multiplying the powers of authoritarian institutions, function fusion provides an autocratizing executive branch with a win-win situation. The executive gets to co-opt more actors while allowing it to contract out its most unsavory and illegal authoritarian practices.

Several aspects of function fusion require us to rethink some Weberian theories of the state. In the classic conception by Max Weber, the state seeks a monopoly on violence, always distrustful of private use and misuse of violence and the law. The Venezuelan case shows that one form of rule is for states to create ambiguity about the dividing line between public and private violence, official and nonofficial coercion, legal and illegal affairs. As long as the state gets assurances that private violence, nonofficial coercion, and illegal transactions will not be used against the state, state leaders will condone and even promote these activities. Research has shown that this blurriness between public and private uses of violence has existed in early-development democracies, such as the United States in the early nineteenth century (Obert 2018). It also exists in contemporary democracies facing serious forms of military challenges such as guerrillas or heavily armed drug lords.

The distinctiveness of the Maduro case is how extensively the regime has used function fusion. More than a new case, it is perhaps an extreme example of non-Weberian forms of governance. The Maduro case also challenges Mancur Olson's argument about the culmination of authoritarianism into a "stationary bandit." In Olson's analysis, autocracy takes two forms: roving banditry, where the autocrat faces much insecurity for his/her tenure in office and thus engages in maximum predatory behavior; and stationary bandit, where the autocrat neutralizes enemies, feels less fearful for his/her tenure, and can grant some forms of property rights for non-state actors. Venezuela shows that neither model truly captures a modern autocracy that is facing insecurity. The "Venezuelan bandit," to use Olson's terminology, does face insecurity and engages in predation (as you would expect a roving bandit to do), but also allows other bandits to do the same. In addition, it dispenses some property rights to non-state actors (as you would expect under conditions of stationary banditry), but also shares sovereignty with those other actors.

The way Maduro has used function fusion to survive in office—not by solving a national crisis, but by amplifying how his allies can profit from the crisis—has produced a worse version of Charles Tilly's (1985) argument about state-making as a racket.[6] Tilly argued that monarchical government emerged in Europe as a result of a racket: the monarch would fabricate threats against the population and then charge subjects (with taxes) for protection.

The Venezuelan government's system is more perverse. It creates (rather than merely fabricates) a threat against the population: economic collapse and hunger. It then blames the crisis on others—the private sector, citizens who overconsume, smugglers, the sanctions—and proceeds to charge citizens an extra premium: runaway inflation, scarcity, long lines, and informal markets. But instead of offering protection, the state redoubles threats by expanding state powers, as well as those of a number of ancillary actors, including some government-sanctioned criminal gangs.

In Venezuela, the state has created hunger games and these games have morphed into war games. There is a war of the state against citizens and a war of citizens against citizens. These war games, more so than the drop in the price of oil, are the essence of Venezuela's humanitarian crisis.

No doubt, function fusion is risky. Every time the executive branch shares powers and sovereignties with other state and non-state actors, these groups could potentially become powerful enough to challenge the president. In Venezuela, function fusion also encompassed non-state armed actors and extra-legal actors. This finding also updates Tilly's (1985) model of autocratic governance; the state not only bargains with legitimate subjects, as Tilly argues, but also with illicit actors. This can be rewarding for the state, but also risky, not to mention deleterious for institution building. The ruler accepts a political gain of loyalty in the context of declining revenues and governance capacity, in return for the political loss of centralized rule and pacts with hard-to-control actors. The Venezuelan case shows that an authoritarian president in constant danger of falling may conclude that the risks of function fusion, however serious, are less daunting than the risk of relying exclusively on conventional autocratic practices or standing idle in the face of resistance from below.

8

Conclusion

VULNERABLE AUTOCRACY, COLLAPSING NATION

We are living in the era of democratic backsliding. Since the early 2000s, democracies of all stripes have experienced declines in their democratic institutions through actions taken by the executive branch. They are experiencing executive aggrandizement and executive-led degradation of rights. This has occurred in both established as well as young democracies, in robust as well as weak ones. Some scholars refer to this phenomenon as the Third Wave of Autocratization (Lührmann and Lindberg 2019). This chapter summarizes the various contributions this book has made to our understanding of this Third Wave of Autocratization.

On Democratic Backsliding, Autocratic Legalism, and Its Initial Mixed Signals

Venezuela since the 2000s is both a typical and an atypical case of democratic backsliding. Venezuela is typical because in the early phases (under Hugo Chávez), backsliding proceeded in ways that are recognizable across the vast majority of cases of backsliding. A ruling party promises big policy change in a climate of social discontent, political gridlock, and policy atrophy. Although leadership characteristics matter (e.g., a president with a questionable commitment to liberal democracy seems to be a necessary condition), the first key factor in determining how far backsliding will go depends on the party system. The unifying element across these cases of significant backsliding is that the ruling party encounters an opposition that is weak electorally or too fragmented. I showed how this process also happened in Nicaragua, Colombia, and Ecuador. This weakening grants the ruling party plenty of room for maneuvering, even if the ruling party did not achieve an impressive electoral victory.

At first, the ruling party introduces several reforms that seem hard to classify because they contain measures that are both democratic and nondemocratic. For the opposition, however, there is no ambiguity. The opposition recognizes the process of executive aggrandizement that is underway for what it is: an effort to concentrate power. Autocratic legalism—the use, abuse, and lack of use of the law and the legal system to favor the executive branch and hurt opponents—becomes the predominant tool of action by the president. The opposition does what it can to denounce and stop autocratic legalism. However, for government supporters, changes appear to be enhancing aspects of democracy; the president is seen as merely empowering institutions to bring about needed reforms. The electorate becomes polarized.

In Venezuela, Nicaragua, and to a lesser extent Ecuador in the 2000s, the three fundamental pillars of democracy—electoral, liberal, and participatory features—were eventually degraded through actions taken by the executive branch. Democratic backsliding reached far, covering every aspect of the regime. In Colombia, backsliding did not reach the same level but it was proceeding in the same direction.

These cases also confirm the idea that modern-day populism lends itself comfortably to democratic backsliding. With its emphasis on dividing the political system into the "binary antagonism" of (deserving) people versus enemies of the people, its penchant for easing limits on executive power, and its disdain for pluralism and technocracy, a populist ideology offers a compatible justification for almost every form of executive aggrandizement, rights degradation, and autocratic legalism. In Venezuela, as was the case in Nicaragua and Ecuador, the regime used a leftist-populist discourse, with a heavy emphasis on distributionism and anti-capitalism, to justify backsliding. In Colombia, the regime invoked right-wing populism, with a heavy emphasis on lessening insecurity. Either way, populist rule and democratic backsliding proved compatible.

However, Venezuela's democratic backsliding is atypical in a number of ways as well. First, very few cases of democratic backsliding since the 2000s have experienced as steep a democratic decline as Venezuela. The regime went from democracy to semi-authoritarianism to full-fledged autocracy between 1999 and 2016. To aid in that transition, the regime was forced to change the focus of autocratic legalism: the new focus became to enable not just concentration of power by the executive, but also actual repression of opponents and even the disbanding of institutions of representation, such as parties, NGOs, and even the Congress. In the Americas since 2000, the only case that matches this intensification and re-purposing of autocratic legalism is Nicaragua.

Venezuela is atypical also in that, among those cases that have declined to such lows, very few started as high as Venezuela did, both in terms of income levels (middle income) and levels of democracy (relatively high). And within Latin America, a region where semi-authoritarian regimes are common, there are examples of reversals in which the regime actually breaks down or liberalizes. Venezuela and Nicaragua did not make that U-turn.

Backsliding in Venezuelan also displays some characteristics that may or may not be repeated in other cases of backsliding: a significant degree of protagonism by both military and non-state armed actors, a full revamping of the constitution, the full capturing of the judiciary and the electoral authorities, a strong array of policies designed to restrict market forces, an enormous electoral coalition built on both patronage and cronyism, and when the economy crashed, a full defense of ruinous economic policies for the sake of weakening civic groups. These features matter because what happens after backsliding depends in many ways on variations in party variables, but also in these institutional factors.

On the Causes of Backsliding and Autocratization

This book also contributes to the literature on the causes of democratic backsliding, and, especially, what comes next after semi-authoritarianism. Scholars have offered a variety of theories to explain the factors that cause democratic backsliding. In the case of Venezuela, the challenge has been to find an argument that explains democratic backsliding in its entire time dimension, from the very beginning, when the process gets underway and is somewhat ambiguous, to its later stages, when the regime transitions to full authoritarianism.

Without necessarily denying the importance of other possible causes, this book highlights a particular explanation: the combination of changes in the party system together with institutional capturing in the state and even outside the state. Asymmetrical party system fragmentation (APSF) occurs when the ruling party achieves internal unity while the opposition fragments into parties that are too small or too convulsed to compete. It is a permissive condition for democratic backsliding in the early stages.

However, APSF is not enough. Backsliding also requires an executive that is able to achieve some degree of institutional capturing, namely, destroying or colonizing political institutions that are supposed, in theory, to be independent of the executive branch—that is, liberal democratic institutions. If the president manages to control the judiciary and the electoral authorities, even if he or she lacks full control of the Congress, then the chances of profound democratic backsliding increase significantly, provided of course that APSF is in place. This happened in Nicaragua early on as well, and to a good degree in Ecuador.

At deeper stages of backsliding, when the regime is already an established semi-authoritarian regime, the same variables help explain whether the regime will transition to full-fledged authoritarianism or not. However, the causal mechanisms differ.

The first trigger is a flip in party system competition: an easing of APSF. This flip can be caused by policy mistakes by the government (in the case of Venezuela, economic mismanagement), but it is ultimately dependent on party-building and international-coalition strategies by the opposition. If the flip occurs, the party system, by definition, no longer empowers the executive branch to act the way an asymmetrically fragmented party system empowers the executive branch to act in the early stages of backsliding. What this new, more equally competitive party system does, at this stage of backsliding, is to give the executive branch the *urgent incentive* to take desperate measures to prevent a fall from power.

For the regime to survive, it must either negotiate with the opposition, change policy course, or harden the restrictions on the political system. And here is where the variable institutional capturing plays a central role.

The choice to harden the regime is more likely to materialize if the regime enjoys pre-acquired institutional reservoirs. If the state has at its disposal (1) full control of the courts and the electoral authorities, (2) sufficient autocratic laws and practices to draw from, and (3) a patrimonial military together with supportive paramilitary groups, a semi-authoritarian regime is more likely to choose autocratization in the context of easing APSF. Regime actors will be tempted to use those institutional reservoirs in response to crises. Autocratic legalism in conjunction with a two-tier coercive apparatus is deployed to suppress the challengers.

In other words, the costs of autocratization decline because the tools needed for the job do not need to be invented. This reduces the cost of turning autocratic. Regime actors turn easily into hard-liners because they have the tools to do so. At this point, the arsenal is already in place. All that is needed for the regime to survive is for the executive branch to redeploy, repurpose, escalate, and custom-tailor its arsenal of tools in response to emerging political crises.

The Maduro regime exemplified this response. Facing challenges from three angles—the opposition, foreign actors, and even from within its winning coalition—the regime redeployed autocratic practices from the past. Had these tools been unavailable, this book posits that the regime's response to declining competitiveness would have been less autocratic or less survivable.

I offered comparisons with Nicaragua (autocratization) and Colombia and Ecuador (liberalization) to demonstrate the applicability of this argument beyond Venezuela. In Nicaragua, the regime enjoyed similar autocratic tools; in Colombia and Ecuador, the tools were less available. A transition from semi-authoritarianism to authoritarianism in the latter two cases would have been too costly for the incumbents.

On Democratic Backsliding in the United States under Donald Trump

The argument that backsliding can be facilitated or contained by APSF and institutional reservoirs helps explain the evolution of democratic backsliding not just in Venezuela, Colombia, Ecuador, and Nicaragua, but also in the United States under President Donald Trump. While this book does not address the United States, I do not want to conclude this study without addressing it.

According to V-Dem, the United States during the Trump administration (2017–2021) experienced its steepest decline in liberal democracy since the 1950s. Many analysts contend that Trump, both as candidate and president, showed little respect for liberal democracy. In terms of discourse and policy preferences, he was seen as a high-profile example of a right-wing populist (Weyland and Madrid 2018), and thus, a likely embracer of democratic backsliding.

As is typical of efforts at democratic backsliding, Trump did try to govern using autocratic legalism. He was first impeached for trying to subvert foreign policy (aid to Ukraine), but the key story behind that imbroglio was Trump's intention to hurt his political adversary, Joe Biden. Trump also pressured the Justice Department to lower the scale of the sentence for key allies (e.g., Roger Stone) and to go harsh on civil servants who did not help him (e.g., former deputy F.B.I. director Andrew G. McCabe who investigated Russia's role in the 2016 election). Trump often engaged in tirades against liberal Justices Sonia Sotomayor and Ruth Bader Ginsburg. The use and lack of use of the law to help the president and hurt opponents was a feature of Trumpism in office.

Many analysts agree that, left to his own devices, Trump would have concentrated formal power far more than he achieved, eventually fully undermining the legal system to his advantage. In the end, however, democratic backsliding in the United States under Trump did not go far or continue in time. It was contained, both by institutions that resisted and by an opposition party that defeated him at the polls in 2020.

Part of the reason democratic backsliding under Trump was contained is that the case never exhibited APSF, in line with this book's argument. Trump did not come to office with his opposition in tatters or fragmented. On the contrary, the Democrats won the electoral vote in 2016 (despite losing the electoral college), stayed electorally united during all of Trump's term (despite multiple factions co-existing in the party), invested in electoral participation and mobilization (as well as some protest activity by the Black Lives Matter and Me Too movements). As a result, the opposition regained the House of Representative in 2018 and swept to victory in the 2020 presidential elections. If the opposition had been electorally weak or fragmented, Trump would have gone further with his legislative agenda, would have gotten re-elected in 2020, and the process of backsliding through autocratic legalism would have continued and even accelerated.

In addition, the case does not exhibit sufficient institutional capturing. Trump never achieved full control (and de-professionalization) of the Supreme Court, let alone, the entire justice system. He did not achieve full control of electoral authorities either, in part because in the United States the system is decentralized: each state has its own electoral authority. He also never managed to de-professionalize the armed forces.

That said, it is revealing that when Trump lost the 2020 election (a visible sign of declining electoral competitiveness), he engaged in a desperate last-ditch effort at institutional capturing. A 2021 investigation by the *New York Times* revealed that shortly after the election, between mid-November 2020 and January 2021, Trump began a relentless campaign to pressure the Department of Justice to declare the election in states he lost as corrupt (Benner 2021). He fired his attorney general, William P. Barr, for refusing to go along. Trump then pressured Barr's successor, acting attorney general Jeffrey A. Rosen, to also claim fraud and "leave the rest to me." He developed a plan to oust Rosen in favor of a loyalist who was willing to go along with his plan. He also pressured state electoral officials in the swing states that Biden won to "find votes" or denounce fraud within their states. Trump also ramped up pressure on the Supreme Court to dismiss the results in those swing states (Nakamura and Barnes 2020).

Then came the January 6, 2021, storming of the capitol. This was not only a direct assault against his cabinet (with an attack on Vice President Pence, who was presiding over the official ceremony in the Capitol), the key institution of minimal democracy (the certification of an election in which an incumbent loses), a key institution of liberal democracy (the autonomous functioning of the legislative branch), but also the use by the Executive branch of non-state armed actors to carry out an electoral irregularity. The assault included not just civilians but also retired military actors. An initial investigation of 140 individuals charged with participating in the assault revealed that 20 percent had served or were currently serving in the military (Dreisbach and Anderson 2021). The assault also included members of far-right armed groups such as Proud Boys and the Oath Keepers. In short, Trump tried to make use of autocratic legalism throughout his term and paramilitarism at the very end.

However, Trump never managed to gain full control of the key institutions needed for full autocratic legalism: the judicial system and the electoral system. He did achieve some institutional capturing of the Department of Justice, but his control remained partial. Consequently, democratic backsliding under Trump was contained. When he lost reelection, Trump responded as expected by the argument in this book: by trying to activate autocratic legalism. He even mobilized para-military forces to storm the capitol and block rotation of power. But it was too late and the arsenal was not fully developed. For that reason, democratic backsliding in the United States was contained this time.

On the Resurgence of the Opposition

This book also contributes to a subset of literature on democratic backsliding: conditions under which opposition parties may rise in the context of autocratization. One of the predicaments of democratic backsliding is that it occurs in tandem with (in fact, is facilitated by) an opposition that weakens, fragments, or collapses. As mentioned, this did not happen in the United States under Trump, but it did happen in Venezuela under Chávez and in most cases of advanced backsliding. Semi-authoritarianism is all about deploying autocratic legalism to impede the opposition's revival. How then can the opposition resuscitate under such disadvantages?

This book looks at two variables in particular: economic crises/mismanagement and party-building strategies. Regarding economic crises, the book's main argument is that the relationship with opposition revival is nonlinear. The onset of economic crises (late 2000s) did not immediately produce serious voter defection from the ruling party. In semi-authoritarian systems where the ruling party has strong linkages with voters and the system is polarized, the ruling party can afford some economic deterioration without suffering substantial electoral damage. However, once the crisis becomes severe enough, voter defection becomes a problem for the ruling party. This creates an obvious opportunity for the opposition. That said, if the crisis becomes too severe, with people suffering extreme hardship, the crisis is no longer automatically beneficial for the opposition. Severe crises produce exit options for the electorate: figuratively in terms of voters choosing not to participate in politics and literally in terms of migration. These exit options actually hurt the opposition.

Furthermore, even when economic crises produce voter defections from the ruling party, it is not a given that the opposition will attract those voters. To gain competitiveness, the opposition must engage in party-building strategies. This includes embracing elections even if elections are unfair, forming coalitions even with ideologically distant parties, upholding unity during election times by agreeing on united candidacies for available offices, fighting abstentionism, using pressure tactics including denunciation and street protests, guarding hard-won institutions, obtaining international allies, and renewing its leadership.

This book shows that the Venezuelan opposition achieved many of these party-building goals between 2006 and 2016, albeit not at all times or consistently well in all dimensions. Because it was nonetheless successful, at least for a decade, it placed the regime under duress—not a frivolous triumph.

Nevertheless, the opposition's victories came with negative side effects. Those victories prompted the state and the ruling party to counteract. A key message of this book is that the state was able to respond in kind to almost every victory achieved by the opposition. Every time the opposition learned to adapt to the new increasingly authoritarian rules established by the government (e.g., increasing electoral irregularities), the state would change the rules, usually in the direction of greater restrictions, repression, and incentives to encourage division.

This interactive give-and-take between a rising opposition and a threatened semi-authoritarian regime resulted in an expansion of autocratic responses and, thus, a transition to full-fledged authoritarianism. As the system became more restrictive, the chances of the opposition relying on moderate and institutional approaches became fewer. The problem was that the more radical and extra-institutional the opposition acted, the more the state repressed and the more moderate voters felt disenchanted, especially if victories continued to elude the radicalized opposition. Under autocracy, opposition moderation yields declining payoffs, while radicalization incentivizes the state to turn more autocratic. This is the fundamental predicament of the opposition in autocratizing contexts.

If the government is capable of counter-attacking, one could ask, Why then should the opposition engage in any of these tactics of contestation. The answer is that by counter-attacking, the government will commit more mistakes, and thus, acquire more vulnerabilities. Uncertainty therefore shifts. In a semi-authoritarian context, the uncertainty centers on whether the opposition will ever revive. Under an autocracy that is facing an active opposition, the uncertain shifts to whether the government will survive. My sense is that it is better for opposition parties in autocratizing contexts to live under the latter type of uncertainty. While the opposition may not prevail at every confrontation with the government, staying active contesting the regime electorally is one way to keep the ruling party from feeling too confident in office.

On Innovative Tools of Autocratization

In response to a rising opposition, economic collapse, and external sanctions, Maduro's regime not only engaged in autocratic redeployment but also autocratic innovation. The regime's most important innovation was function fusion: granting existing institutions a multitude of functions that typically belong to other institutions. The military became business actors, engaged in both legal and illegal profiteering. More civic groups became paramilitary actors, with autonomy to engage in all forms of coercive activities, including criminality. Judges became state contractors. Neighborhood groups were given the right to weaponize welfare provision. Members of the ruling party became mini-dictators within their fiefdoms. And gangs, criminal syndicates, mafias, smugglers, and even foreign armies were granted permission to perform some state functions. Many parts of Venezuela's territory, which looked from the outside as ungoverned, became "alternatively governed spaces," where state actors co-ruled with nonstate and extralegal actors.

While the redeployment, repurposing, and escalation of classic authoritarian tactics help the state contain the opposition, function fusion helps the ruler by rewarding the so-called winning coalition: the group of state and non-state actors that have the power to unseat a ruler. In a situation of economic scarcity and policy incompetence, such as the one that Venezuela experienced starting in 2010, function fusion served as a useful currency the state could distribute to reward loyalists and as a signal to allies with questionable loyalties that the regime was interested in power-sharing in exchange for loyalty.

Function fusion, therefore, is highly risky: it has the potential of empowering groups that at some point may challenge the executive branch. However, if enough autonomy is granted, together with enough punishments for internal dissent, function fusion can help the state keep most of its domestic allies content, at least for a while.

This way of ruling—giving institutions multiple, overlapping, and often extralegal and coercive functions—challenges Weberian notions of the state as an entity keen on preserving a monopoly of coercion. It also challenges the Hobbesian notion that states prefer the indivisibility of sovereignty. And finally, it also challenges Tilly's notion that states negotiate with mostly recognized legal groups. Venezuela's regime under Maduro shows that states may instead come to accept a social contract, not so much between the state and its people, but between the ruler and a small cadre of non-state armed groups and extralegal organizations. In this odd contract, the state actually cedes some functions to try to survive and keep the regime illiberal.

On the Political Economy of Development and Authoritarianism

This book also contributes to debates on the political economy of Latin America and, especially, resource dependence. Since the 1980s, scholars have been debating where to set the balance between states and markets to prompt pro-poor and sustainable development. Venezuela is a cautionary tale about the dangers of erring on either extreme.

On the one hand, it is clear that Hugo Chávez and Nicolás Maduro opted to set policy in favor of excessive statism, with very few controls on the state, if any. This was juxtaposed with excessive regulations on market forces in the form of onerous price controls, exchange rate controls, labor market controls, relentless audits, heavy taxation, and nationalizations that often seemed random.

This extreme imbalance of controls between states and markets is a type of socialism that produced epic failures across command economies during the Cold War. A similar, though less extreme, imbalance was also often present in many models of import substitution in Latin America, most of which ended up bankrupt in the 1980s. It was not shocking, therefore, for the Venezuelan economy, predicated on the same unevenness between states and markets, to collapse in the 2010s. The virtual extinction of the oil sector (in state hands) and in fact most of the domestic industry and agriculture (increasingly in state hands) stems from this imbalance.

Having said that, Maduro's political economy also showed the pitfalls of erring too much on the side of laissez-faire economics. When the economic crisis hit hard, Maduro supplemented his command-economy model with a sort of fend-for-yourself economic model. The state pursued indiscriminate social spending cutbacks, privileged foreign creditors (in the allocation of scarce foreign currency), and privatized many economic activities, including welfare provision, without any form of bidding. This is a form of "savage neoliberalism" far more extreme than any of the neoliberal models adopted in Latin America in the 1990s and which early *Chavismo* loudly denounced. Maduro's laissez-faire approach to crisis management, while at the same time upholding state overreach, not only failed to correct the economic crisis, but also yielded record-level immiseration.

And the state's response to the decline of its oil sector in the context of rising prices, rising demand, and rising reserves—unheard of among any contemporary oil states—was not to introduce corrective policy changes, but to actually transition to a new and more detrimental form of extractivist dependence: narco-mining. This mode of development is reminiscent of the neopatrimonial form of development typical of low-income sub-Saharan economies. It is a model that exacerbates rather than addresses resource curses. The state acts in collusion with, or at least with a blind eye toward, criminal syndicates, megabandas, paramilitaries, illegal miners, smugglers, drug dealers, foreign guerrillas, and foreign states that are mostly authoritarian. In addition to exacerbating inequalities, this form of neo-extractivism has wreaked havoc on labor standards, human security, and environmental sustainability.

Solving Venezuela's crisis will not be easy. The damage is so vast that the most extreme technical solutions—eliminating differential exchange rates, dollarization, competitive privatization, debt restructuring, broad opening to private investment in oil, boosting social spending, or a massive influx of humanitarian aid—may end up not working for years to come. The economic wounds are too severe to respond quickly to known treatments.

And yet, Venezuela requires more than just technical fixes. Recovery will require a fundamental overturning of the development model in place. The problem is not resource dependence, but rather institutional mismatch. Venezuela needs to introduce more controls on the state and more facilities and competition for the productive private sector.

Finally, a word on the absence of economic policy switch during most of Maduro's tenure. If Venezuela was on a precarious economic path since 2013, why didn't Maduro change paths? No doubt, for leftist-populist parties, policy switches involve a dilemma. Under economic crises resulting from excessive statism, if these parties stay the course, they risk losing votes. But this dilemma exists only if the party is committed to electoral democracy, or where a transition to authoritarianism is foreclosed because the ruling party does not want to turn autocratic or does not have the institutional reservoirs to take that route. In Venezuela, these two conditions were moot points. The ruling party was both comfortable going for authoritarianism as well as institutionally equipped to deliver it. So rather than policy switch, the government delivered regime hardening.

The Future of the Regime

The regime in Venezuela became more tyrannical not just because of need and incentive to survive (party system stimulus) but because of institutional inheritance: autocratic practices initiated by Chávez and intensified, redeployed, and reimagined by Maduro. Need and reservoirs—with a good amount of institutional innovation in the form of function fusion—allowed this semi-authoritarian regime to turn fully authoritarian.

What this book does not argue is that the Venezuelan regime, however autocratic, has become consolidated. No doubt, Maduro has been able to corner the opposition and neutralize its gains. As of this writing, in the context of strict COVID-19 lockdown measures extending into 2021, the government hardened its grip on power, manipulated (once again) electoral rules to disfavor the opposition, and succeeded at dividing its opponents.

But Maduro's survival tactics—letting the economy deteriorate to hurt the private sector and civil society, granting his close allies too many roles to appease their demands, constantly creating electoral instability to confuse the opposition—are risky strategies. Economic decline means that groups from within and outside the ruling coalition will always experience intense grievance. More significantly, function fusion means that groups in the government's inner circle are sufficiently autonomous to challenge Maduro. In 2021, there were reports of serious government clashes with many of these former allies in some border states. Clashes with so many power-holders is one of the regime's central vulnerabilities.

After rising for so many years, the opposition to Maduro is no doubt in a precarious condition as of this writing. And yet, Maduro's stranglehold on power does not look that firmly secured either. Maduro has transitioned to authoritarianism not by building institutions, but by wrecking them. Function fusion has granted him important allies, but also, institutional distortions as well as political debts. These are serious vulnerabilities. The regime appears powerful, but its foundations are tenuous. Just as in retrospect it never made sense to speak of democratic consolidation in Venezuela, even during the heyday of democracy, eight years into the Maduro era it probably makes no sense to speak of autocratic consolidation either, at least for as long as the model of governance discussed in this book stays in place.

Notes

Chapter 1

1. The only three presidents who have been defeated are Daniel Ortega in Nicaragua, Hipólito Mejía in the Dominican Republic, and Mauricio Macri in Argentina.

2. For the importance of focusing on states and markets to study Latin America's political economy, see Kingstone (2018), Edwards (2012), and Corrales (2012).

Chapter 2

1. On the distinction between being an oil-dependent country and a petro-state, see Ross (2012).

2. In addition to popular sectors and leftist parties, Chávez also received support from business elite outliers who feared that a right-wing president would deny them access to business deals with the state (see Gates 2010).

3. This section draws from Corrales (forthcoming).

4. In the case of Chávez, see Kronick, Plunkett, and Rodríguez (2021).

5. V-Dem defines the participatory principle of democracy as a measure of "active participation by citizens in all political processes, electoral and non-electoral. It is motivated by uneasiness about a bedrock practice of electoral democracy: delegating authority to representatives. Thus, direct rule by citizens is preferred, wherever practicable. This model of democracy thus takes suffrage for granted, emphasizing engagement in civil society organizations, direct democracy, and subnational elected bodies."

6. In the mid-1990s, Venezuela had one of the smallest armed forces in Latin America in terms of size of personnel per capita: 346 active personnel per 100,000 inhabitants. This was position number 17 of 20 Latin American countries. The top position was held by Uruguay (875), and the lowest by Jamaica (142). See Arcenaux (1999).

Chapter 3

1. When asked, "Which of the following causes do you think best explains why there are shortages/inflation?" only 23 to 25 percent of Venezuelans stated "economic war" or "the private sector" (Alfredo Keller y Asociados 2016).

2. For a review of these arguments, see Sinnot, Nash, and de la Torre (2010), Ross (2012), Mazzuca (2013), and Moses and Letnes (2017).

3. This section draws from Corrales, Hernández, and Salgado (2020).

4. Humorist José Rafael Briceño's "Reporte Semanal" (Weekly Report) on YouTube: https://youtu.be/hJcEH3Kdz_4.

Chapter 4

1. This section draws from Corrales (2020b).

2. Center-right parties included Vente Venezuela (led by María Corina Machado) and Proyecto Venezuela; center-left parties included Acción Democrática, Primero Justicia, Voluntad Popular, Un Nuevo Tiempo, and Avanzada Progresista; and leftist and extreme-left parties included Bandera Roja, Movimiento Amplio Venezuela Democrática, Patria Para Todos, and PODEMOS (Por la Democracia Social).

3. This section draws from Corrales (2019b).

Chapter 5

1. For more on opposition deputy Juan Requesens's arrest and imprisonment, see Laya (2020).

2. This section is based on Corrales (2020b).

3. This section draws from Corrales (2020b).

4. This section draws from Corrales (2020a).

5. In terms of injuries rather than deaths, Chile's repression was probably harsher: According to the Chilean Health Ministry, emergency services helped 11,564 people with injuries sustained from the protests, just between October 18 and November 22, with the most egregious injuries including lost eyes from the police's use of pellet shotguns to indiscriminately fire into the crowds. There are also reports during this period of over 15,000 detentions (Human Rights Watch 2020b).

6. This section draws from Corrales (2018b).

Chapter 6

1. This chapter draws significantly from a number of undergraduate students who either wrote supporting research papers or served as research assistants. Gordon Powers and Martín Wilkinson helped with the Nicaragua case. Alexandre Jabor and Conner Glynn helped with Ecuador. Jack Elvekrog, Jack Vander Vort, and Bayard DeMallie helped with Colombia and Ecuador. Scott Brasesco helped with all cases.

2. According to some polls, the MRS's expected vote before Lewites's death was 21.5 percent.

3. It was also important that Ortega had prior experience in the 1980s as a president who lost power after liberalizing, which probably taught him not to take that route ever again (see Corrales 2018a).

4. In fact, in 2003, Alemán was sentenced to a twenty-year prison term for several crimes, including money laundering and embezzlement of up to $100 million during his tenure in office. Shortly after his conviction, Sandinista-controlled courts gradually reduced these charges and released him from jail, placing him under house arrest instead. See Bruntel (2009).

5. This section draws from Bruntel (2009).

6. One reason for the weakness of party-based opposition in Nicaragua is that Ortega continued to repress party-based challenges as soon as they arose. In 2016, for instance, the Ortega-controlled Supreme Court removed PLI leader Eduardo Montealegre from his post, replacing him with the more Ortega-friendly Pedro Reyes Vallejos. Montealegre was the opposition leader with the strongest chances of defeating Ortega, and had recently signed a pact with the PLC to challenge Ortega. The Supreme Electoral Council (Consejo Supremo Electoral, CSE) forced sixteen opposition members of the National Assembly to resign for refusing to recognize the court's ruling.

7. The regime also used other autocratic tools at its disposal. Because it controlled the media, it was able to launch a massive social media campaign to identify and discredit protesters.

Chapter 7

1. This chapter draws extensively from Corrales (2020a).

2. The Trump Administration imposed targeted financial sanctions on high-level officials and organizations, including Vice President and First Lady Rosario Murillo, three of the president's sons, and the Nicaraguan National Police, for corruption and serious human rights abuses, but it never imposed financial and trade sanctions as it did with Venezuela.

3. This section draws from Corrales (2019a).

4. According to the U.S. Department of Justice, the cartel's name refers to the sun insignias affixed to the uniforms of high-ranking military officials. The United States argued that the cartel, in collaboration with Revolutionary Armed Forces of Colombia (Fuerzas Armadas Revolucionarias de Colombia, FARC),

aimed not only to "enrich its members and enhance their power" but also to "flood the United States with cocaine" (U.S. Department of Justice 2020). It is worth mentioning that as of 2020, there wasn't much evidence on behalf of a single organized "cartel." More likely, Venezuela has many different organized crime groups involved in drug trafficking that control different territories and are often tied to local officials. There does, however, appear to be a government strategy to turn a blind eye to drug trafficking, as long as officials are paid off (Berwick and Spetalnick 2020).

5. This section draws from Corrales (2017).

6. Tilly, Charles. 1985. "Warmaking and State Making as Organized Crime." In *Bringing the State Back In*. Peter P. Evans, Dietrich Rueschemeyer, and Theda Skocpol (eds.), Cambridge University Press, 169–191.

References

Abuelafia, E., and J. L. Saboin. 2020. *A Look to the Future for Venezuela*. Inter-American Development Bank.

Acemoglu, D., and J. A. Robinson. 2006. *Economic Origins of Dictatorship and Democracy*. Cambridge University Press.

Adler, G., and N. Magud. 2013. "Four Decades of Terms-of-Trade Booms." VoxEU, July 4.

Agencia EFE. 2015. "Venezuelan Opposition Candidate Barred 10 Years from Public Office," July 18.

Al Jazeera News. 2017. "Venezuela: Mixed Reaction Online after Election Results," October 16.

Albertus, M. 2015. "The Role of Subnational Politicians in Distributive Politics: Political Bias in Venezuela's Land Reform under Chávez." *Comparative Political Studies* 48 (13): 1667–710.

Alexander, H. 2019. "The Dirty Money and Drugs Keeping Venezuela's Nicolas Maduro in Power." *The Telegraph*, August 15.

Alfredo Keller y Asociados. 2016. *Estudio de la opinión pública nacional. 4to trimestre de 2016*. Alfredo Keller y Asociados.

Alonso, J. F. 2017. "Solo cinco de los 13 magistrados principales aprobaron el baremo del Consejo Moral." *Crónica Uno*, June 14.

Alpert, M. 2015. "Correa's Gamble." *Foreign Policy*, December 14.

Altman, D., and A. Pérez-Liñán. 2002. "Assessing the Quality of Democracy: Freedom, Competitiveness and Participation in Eighteen Latin American Countries." *Democratization* 9 (2): 85–100.

Álvarez, Á. E. 2009. "El Consejo Nacional Electoral y los dilemas de la competencia electoral en Venezuela." *América Latina Hoy* 51: 61–76.

Álvarez, Á. E., and M. Hidalgo. 2020. "Fragmentación de la oposición y persistencia del autoritarismo en Venezuela."

Alvarez, R. M., T. E. Hall, and S. D. Hyde (eds.). 2008. "Introduction: Studying Election Fraud." In *Election Fraud: Detecting and Deterring Electoral Manipulation*. Brookings Institution Press.

Amaya, V. 2017. "Pedido de elecciones en Venezuela acumula represión y muerte." *Semana.*

Amnesty International. 2016. "Brazil: Surge in Killings by Police Sparks Fear in Favelas Ahead of Rio Olympics," April 27. www.amnesty.org/en/latest/press-release/2016/04/brazil-surge-in-killings-by-police-sparks-fear-in-favelas-ahead-of-rio-olympics/.

Amnesty International. 2019. "Venezuela: Crimes against Humanity Require a Vigorous Response from the International Justice System." May 14.

Anderson, L. E., et al. 2021. "Aquiescencia y resistencia: el régimen de Ortega en Nicaragua." *América Latina Hoy* 87: 151–70.

Angelo, P. J., and O. L. Ilera Correal. 2020. "Colombian Military Culture." Military Culture Series. Jack D. Gordon Institute for Public Policy, Florida International University.

Angulo, N., and C. Batiz. 2019. "¿Por qué ocurrió el apagón nacional que provocó el caos en Venezuela? Los expertos explican." Univision, March 10.

Anzola, V. 2018. "Venezuelan Crisis Is Closely Related to Corruption and Poor Performance of the 576 State-Owned Enterprises." Transparencia Venezuela, November 20. https://transparencia.org.ve/Venezuelan-crisis-is-closely-related-to-corruption-and-poor-performance-of-the-576-state-owned-enterprises/.

Arcenaux, C. L. 1999. "The Military in Latin America: Defining the Road Ahead." In *Developments in Latin American Political Economy: States, Markets and Actors*, edited by J. Buxton and N. Phillips. Manchester University Press.

Armas, M. 2017. "Con 20 empresas la FANB acapara el poder económico." *Crónica Uno*, August 20.

Arnson, C. J. 2007. "La Agonía de Álvaro Uribe." *Foreign Affairs en Español* 7 (4): 51–60.

Associated Press. 2019. "Venezuela's Guaido Takes to Streets in Military Uprising." Politico, April 30.

Auty, R. M. 1993. *Sustaining Development in Mineral Economies: The Resource Curse Thesis*. Routledge.

Aveledo Coll, G. 2021. "Notas sobre los partidos políticos bajo un sistema autoritario: el caso venezolano." *Democratización* 3 (11): 47–58.

Bagley, B. M., and J. D. Rosen. 2015. *Drug Trafficking, Organized Crime, and Violence in the Americas Today*. University Press of Florida.

Baptista, A. 2003. "Las crisis económicas del siglo XX venezolano." In *En esta*

Venezuela: Realidades y nuevos caminos, edited by P. Márquez and R. Piñango. Ediciones IESA.

Barany, Z. 2011. "Comparing the Arab Revolts: The Role of the Military." *Journal of Democracy* 22 (4): 24–35.

Basabe-Serrano, S., and S. Llanos Escobar. 2014. "La Corte Suprema del Ecuador en el período democrático (1979–2013): Entre la inestabilidad institucional y la influencia partidista." *América Latina Hoy* 67: 15–63.

Baustista de Alemán, P. 2021. "Notas sobre al oposición venezolana después de 22 años de revolución chavista." *La Gran Aldea*, September 27. www.lagran aldea.com/2021/09/27/notas-sobre-la-oposicion-venezolana-despues-de-22 -anos-de-revolucion-chavista/.

BBC Mundo. 2017. "Smartmatic, la empresa a cargo del sistema de votación en Venezuela, denuncia 'manipulación' en la elección de la Constituyente y el CNE lo niega." August 2.

BBC News. 2015. "Venezuela Parliament DEFENDS Speaker Diosdado Cabello," May 20.

BBC News. 2018. "Ecuador 'Rejects Unlimited Election Terms', Blocking Correa Return," February 5.

BBC News. 2020a. "Juan Guaidó: The Man Who Wants to Oust Maduro," January 23.

BBC News. 2020b. "Venezuela's Maduro Urges Women to Have Six Children," March 4.

Becker, M. 2013. "The Stormy Relations between Rafael Correa and Social Movements in Ecuador." *Latin American Perspectives* 40 (3): 43–62.

Beittel, J. 2018. "Ecuador: In Brief." Congressional Research Service, February 18.

Beittel, J. 2021. "Ecuador: An Overview." Congressional Research Service, September 8.

Bell, C. 2016. "Coup d'État and Democracy." *Comparative Political Studies* 49 (9): 1167–200.

Bellin, E. 2012. "Reconsidering the Robustness of Authoritarianism in the Middle East: Lessons from the Arab Spring." *Comparative Politics* 44 (2): 127–49.

Benítez, P. 2019. "La Operación Oro con la que el régimen de Maduro compra a civiles y militares." *Alnavío*, October 23.

Bennaim, A. 2020. "The Death of the Autonomous Venezuelan Judiciary." *University of Miami Inter-American Law Review* 51 (2): 137–179.

Benner, K. 2021. "Trump Pressed Justice Dept. to Declare Election Results Corrupt, Notes Show." *The New York Times*, July 30.

Bermeo, N. 2016. "On Democratic Backsliding." *Journal of Democracy* 27 (1): 5–19.

Bernardoni de Govea, M. 2011. "El Proyecto de Reforma de la Ley Orgánica del Trabajo. Consideraciones generales sobre la LOT a 20 años de su promulgación." *Gaceta Laboral* 17 (1): 97–123.

Bernhard, M., et al. 2020. "Parties, Civil Society, and the Deterrence of Democratic Defection." *Studies in Comparative International Development* 55 (1): 1–26.

Berwick, A. 2018. "How ZTE Helps Venezuela Create China-Style Social Control." Reuters, November 14.

Berwick, A. 2019. "Imported Repression: How Cuba Taught Venezuela to Quash Military Dissent." Reuters, August 22.

Berwick, A., and M. Guanipa. 2019. "Disappointed Venezuelans Lose Patience with Guaido as Maduro Hangs On." Reuters, July 1.

Berwick, A., and M. Spetalnick. 2020. "Exclusive: U.S. Preparing Criminal Indictment against Wife of Venezuela's Maduro." Reuters, May 27.

Booth, J. A., et al. 2015. *Understanding Central America: Global Forces, Rebellion, and Change.* Sixth edition. Westview Press.

Borges, B. 2020. "How Maduro Is Using COVID-19 to Silence His Opponents Even Further." CEPAZ, July 21. https://cepaz.org/articulos/how-Maduro-is -using-covid-19-to-silence-his-opponents-even-further/.

Botero, F., et al. 2010. "Sobre forma y sustancia: Una evaluación de la democracia electoral en Colombia." *Revista de Ciencia Política* 30: 41–64.

Botero, S. 2017. "El plebiscito y los desafíos políticos de consolidar la paz negociada en Colombia." *Revista de Ciencia Política* 37 (2): 369–88.

Bowen, J. D. 2015. "Rethinking Democratic Governance: State Building, Autonomy, and Accountability in Correa's Ecuador." *Journal of Politics in Latin America* 7 (1): 83–110.

Bracho, Y., and V. Zubillaga. 2021. "The Experience of Armed Violence in the Barrios of Caracas." Interview with Verónica Zubillaga. In *When Exception Becomes the Norm: Crisis as an Ordinary Experience in Venezuela,* edited by F. Andréani and Y. Bracho. Noria Research.

Brennan, D. 2018. "Venezuela Army Sent to Enforce Food Prices as Currency Crashes." *Newsweek,* June 21.

Brewer-Carías, A. R. 2010. *Dismantling Democracy in Venezuela: The Chávez Authoritarian Experiment.* Cambridge University Press.

Briceño, H. 2021. "Sociedad, partidos y elecciones ¿cómo reconstruir la representación política?" *Democratización* 3 (11): 27–46.

Briceno Perez, I. 2015. "MUD ganó hasta donde votaba Chávez, donde vota Maduro y en varios bastiones rojos." Efecto Cocuyo, December 8.

Briscoe, I., and D. Keseberg. 2019. "Only Connect: The Survival and Spread of Organized Crime in Latin America." *PRISM* 8 (1): 114–31.

Brocchetto, M., F. Charner, L. Santiago, and J. Hanna. 2017. "New Venezuelan Assembly Ousts Attorney General Ortega." CNN, August 5.

Bronstein, H., and C. Pons. 2017. "Venezuela's Pro-Government Assembly Fires Dissident Prosecutor." Reuters, August 5.

Bronstein, H., and J. Symmes Cobb. 2017. "Venezuela Faces Outrage after New Assembly Takes Legislative Power." Reuters, August 18.

Brown, J. 2018. "Escaping the Confines of Market Democracy: Lessons from Venezuela." *Socialism and Democracy* 32 (2): 14–31.

Bruntel, E. 2009. "Rule of Law in Nicaragua: The Consequences of Governing by 'El Pacto.'" SSRN, April 1. https://papers.ssrn.com/sol3/papers.cfm?abstract_id=1440944.

Bueno de Mesquita, B., and A. Smith. 2011. *The Dictator's Handbook: Why Bad Behavior Is Almost Always Good Politics.* PublicAffairs.

Bull, B., and A. Rosales. 2020. "The Crisis in Venezuela: Drivers, Transitions, and Pathways." *European Review of Latin American and Caribbean Studies* 109: 1–20.

Bunce, V. J., and S. L. Wolchik. 2010. "Defeating Dictators: Electoral Change and Stability in Competitive Authoritarian Regimes." *World Politics* 62 (1): 43–86.

Bunce, V. J., and S. L. Wolchik. 2011. *Defeating Authoritarian Leaders in Post-communist Countries.* Cambridge University Press.

Burbach, R. 2009. "The Betrayal of the Sandinista Revolution." CounterPunch, March 1.

Burbach, R., and C. Piñeiro. 2007. "Venezuela's Participatory Socialism." *Socialism and Democracy* 21 (3): 181–200.

Burbano de Lara, F. 2017. "Parricidas, leales y traidores: La dramática transición ecuatoriana hacia el poscorreísmo." *Ecuador Debate* (102): 9–26.

Burbano de Lara, F., and C. de la Torre. 2020. "The Pushback against Populism: Why Ecuador's Referendums Backfired." *Journal of Democracy* 31 (2): 69–80.

Buxton, J. 2003. "Economic Policy and the Rise of Hugo Chávez." In *Venezuelan Politics in the Chávez Era,* edited by S. Ellner and D. Hellinger, 113–30. Lynne Rienner.

Buxton, J. 2011. "Foreword: Venezuela's Bolivarian Democracy." In *Venezuela's Bolivarian Democracy: Participation, Politics, and Culture under Chávez,* edited by D. Smilde and D. Hellinger. Duke University Press.

Caballero Argáez, C., and S. Bitar. 2016. "The Liberal Rarity of South America: Oil and Mining Policy Reform in Colombia in the 2000s." In *The Political Economy of Natural Resources and Development: From Neoliberalism to Resource Nationalism,* edited by P. A. Haslam and P. Heidrich, 121–40. Routledge.

Campbell, M. 2012. "Venezuela's Private Media Wither under Chávez." Committee to Protect Journalists, August 29.

Cameron, M. A. 1998. "Self-Coups: Peru, Guatemala, and Russia." *Journal of Democracy* 9 (1): 125–39.

Cañizález, A. 2021. "Censura bajo el régimen de Maduro (V): Fuera CNN de Venezuela." *El Estímulo,* February 12.

Cannon, B. 2009. *Hugo Chávez and the Bolivarian Revolution: Populism and Democracy in a Globalised Age.* Manchester University Press.

Canton, S., et al. 2018. "Report of the General Secretariat of the Organization of American States and the Panel of Independent Experts on the Possible

Commission of Crimes against Humanity in Venezuela." Organization of American States.

Caracas Chronicles. 2018. "ENCOVI 2017: A Staggering Hunger Crisis, in Cold, Hard Numbers." Caracas Chronicles, February 21.

Cardona, F. 2018. "Venezuela Asks Colombia to Help Combat Gasoline Smuggling." *Colombia Reports*, September 11.

Carey, S. C., and N. J. Mitchell. 2016. "Pro-Government Militias and Conflict." *Oxford Research Encyclopedia*. Oxford University Press.

Carrión, J. F. 2021. *A Dynamic Theory of Populism in Power: The Andes in Comparative Perspective*. Oxford University Press.

Casal Bértoa, F., and J. Rama. 2020. "Party Decline or Social Transformation? Economic, Institutional and Sociological Change and the Rise of Anti-Political-Establishment Parties in Western Europe." *European Political Science Review* 12 (4): 503–23.

Casey, N. 2017. "Venezuela Blocks CNN en Español over Report on Passport Fraud." *New York Times*, February 15.

Casey, N. 2019. "Within Venezuelan Military Ranks, A Struggle over What Leader to Back." *New York Times*, January 25.

Castañeda, J. G. 2021. "Cuba: las protestas y los tontos útiles." *Nexos*, July 12.

Castillejo, C. 2015. "Explainer: All about Venezuela's Upcoming Elections and New Gender Quota." AS/COA (Americas Society/Council of the America), July 15. www.as-coa.org/articles/explainer-all-about-Venezuelas-upcoming-elections-and-new-gender-quota.

Castillo, E. 2018. "Resultados ENCOVI 2017: Radiografía de la crisis Venezolana." *El Ucabista*, February 21.

CBS News. 2019. "Ecuador President, Indigenous Leaders Reach Deal to End Protests That Left 7 Dead." October 14.

Chaguaceda, A. 2012. "Régimen político y estado de la democracia en Nicaragua. Procesos en desarrollo y conflictos recientes." *Nueva Sociedad* 240.

Chaguaceda, A. 2020. *La otra hegemonía: Autoritarismo y resistencia en Nicaragua y Venezuela*. Editorial Hypermedia.

Chávez, H., et al. 2005. *Understanding the Venezuelan Revolution: Hugo Chavez Talks to Marta Harnecker*. Monthly Review Press.

Chinea, E. 2017. "Presidente de Venezuela ordena a trabajadores públicos votar en elección de Asamblea Constituyente." Reuters, July 7.

Christofaro, B. 2019. "Venezuela's Booming Drugs Trade Is So Lucrative That Traffickers Reportedly Burn Smuggling Planes after Using Them Just Once." *Insider*, April 17.

Cianetti, L., and S. Hanley. 2021. "The End of the Backsliding Paradigm." *Journal of Democracy* 32 (1): 66–80.

Ciccariello-Maher, G. 2013. *We Created Chávez: A People's History of the Venezuelan Revolution*. Duke University Press.

Cleary, M. R., and A. Öztürk. 2020. "When Does Backsliding Lead to

Breakdown? Uncertainty and Opposition Strategies in Democracies at Risk." *Perspectives on Politics*, 1–17.

Clunan, A. L., and H. Trinkunas. 2010. "Conceptualizing Ungoverned Spaces: Territorial Statehood, Contested Authority, and Softened Sovereignty." In *Ungoverned Spaces: Alternatives to State Authority in an Era of Softened Sovereignty*, edited by A. L. Clunan and H. Trinkunas, 17–33. Stanford University Press.

CNE (Consejo Nacional Electoral). Various Years. Resultados Electorales. www .cne.gob.ve/web/estadisticas/index_resultados_elecciones.php.

Collier, P. 2011. *The Plundered Planet: Why We Must—and How We Can—Manage Nature for Global Prosperity*. Oxford University Press.

Collier, R. B. 2001. "Populism." In *International Encyclopedia of Social and Behavioral Sciences*, edited by N. J. Smelser and P. B. Baltes, 11813–16. Elsevier.

Colombia Reports. 2018. "Alejandro Ordóñez," January 22.

Control Ciudadano. 2018. "Carlos Alberto Osorio Zambrano." Control Ciudadano, June 30. www.controlciudadano.org/fanb-y-poder/carlos-alberto-osorio-zambrano/.

Confidencial. 2020. "FSLN alista un movimiento de "fichas" en cúpulas CSJ y CSE." *Confidencial*, November 20.

Confidencial. 2021. "Ortega y Murillo dirigen 'cadena de mando' de jueces y Policía, confirma Rafael Solís." *Confidencial*, April 21.

Conaghan, C. C. 2016. "Delegative Democracy Revisited: Ecuador under Correa." *Journal of Democracy* 27 (3): 109–18.

Connectas/El Pitazo. 2018. "La generación del hambre." www.connectas.org/especiales/la-generacion-del-hambre/.

Consejo Nacional Electoral (Venezuela). 2021. Resultados Electorales. http://www.cne.gob.ve/web/index.php.

Consejo Supremo Electoral (Nicaragua). 2021. Elecciones generales. https://www.cse.gob.ni/.

Consultores 21. 2018. Agrado de Políticos. PowerPoint Presentation.

Consultores 21. 2020. "Perfil 21: Servicio de análisis de entorno." No. 164.

Coppedge, M. 2005. Explaining Democratic Deterioration in Venezuela through Nested Inference. In *The Third Wave of Democratization in Latin America: Advances and Setbacks*, edited by F. Hagopian and S. P. Mainwaring, 289–316. Cambridge University Press.

Coronil, F. 1997. *The Magical State: Nature, Money, and Modernity in Venezuela*. University of Chicago Press.

Coronil, F. 2005. "Estado y nación durante el golpe contra Hugo Chávez." *Anuario de Estudios Americanos* 62 (1): 87–112.

Corrales, J. 2002. *Presidents without Parties: The Politics of Economic Reform in Argentina and Venezuela in the 1990s*. Penn State University Press.

Corrales, J. 2005. "In Search of a Theory of Polarization." *European Review of Latin American and Caribbean Studies* 79: 105–18.

Corrales, J. 2006. "Cuba's New Daddy." *Hemisphere. A Magazine of the Americas* 17: 24–29.

Corrales, J. 2009. "Using Social Power to Balance Soft Power: Venezuela's Foreign Policy." *Washington Quarterly* 32 (4): 97–114.

Corrales, J. 2010. "The Repeating Revolution: Chávez's New Politics and Old Economics." In *Leftist Governments in Latin America,* edited by K. Weyland, R. Madrid, and W. Hunter, 27–56. Cambridge University Press.

Corrales, J. 2011. "Why Polarize? Advantages and Disadvantages of a Rational-Choice Analysis of Government-Opposition Relations under Hugo Chávez." In *The Revolution in Venezuela: Social and Political Change under Chávez*, edited by T. Ponniah and J. Eastwood. DRCLAS/Harvard University Press.

Corrales, J. 2012. "Neoliberalism and Its Discontents." In *Routledge Handbook of Comparative Politics of Latin America*, edited by P. Kingstone and D. Yashar. Routledge.

Corrales, J. 2014. "Explaining Chavismo." In *Venezuela before Chávez: Anatomy of a Collapse,* edited by R. Hausmann and F. Rodríguez. Penn State University Press.

Corrales, J. 2015. "The Authoritarian Resurgence: Autocratic Legalism in Venezuela." *Journal of Democracy* 2: 37–51.

Corrales, J. 2017. "¿Cómo explicar la crisis económica en Venezuela?" *Tribuna: Revista de Asuntos Públicos* 14: 30–34.

Corrales, J. 2018a. *Fixing Democracy: Why Constitutional Change Often Fails to Enhance Democracy in Latin America.* Oxford University Press.

Corrales, J. 2018b. "The Venezuelan Crisis Is Part of Maduro's Plan." *New York Times*, September 25.

Corrales, J. 2019a. "How to Tackle Venezuela's Military Problem." *New York Times*, March 4.

Corrales, J. 2019b. "Opinion: Foreign Forces Did Not Start Venezuela's Transition. Venezuela Did." NPR, January 30.

Corrales, J. 2020a. "Authoritarian Survival: Why Maduro Hasn't Fallen." *Journal of Democracy* 31 (3): 39–53.

Corrales, J. 2020b. "Democratic Backsliding through Electoral Irregularities: Venezuela, 1999–2019." *European Review of Latin American and Caribbean Studies* (109), 41–65.

Corrales, J. 2021. "Latin America's Former Presidents Have Way Too Much Power." *New York Times*, April 14.

Corrales, J. Forthcoming. "Venezuela's Democratic Backsliding, 1999–2021." In *When Democracy Breaks Down*, edited by A. Fung and D. Moss.

Corrales, J., G. Hernández Jiménez, and J. C. Salgado. 2020. "Oil and Regime Type in Latin America: Reversing the Line of Causality." *Energy Policy* 142: 111347.

Corrales, J., and M. Hidalgo. 2013. "El régimen híbrido de Hugo Chávez en transición (2009–2013)." *Desafíos* 25: 45–84.

Corrales, J., and M. Penfold. 2015. *Dragon in the Tropics: Venezuela and the Legacy of Hugo Chávez*, 2nd edition. Brookings Institution Press.

Corrales, J., and C. A. Romero. 2012. *U.S.-Venezuela Relations since the 1990s: Coping with Midlevel Security Threats.* Routledge.

Corrales, J., and F. von Bergen. 2015. "Venezuela's Media Isn't Smearing the Opposition; It's Making Them Invisible." *Americas Quarterly.*

Cotovio, V., I. Soares, and W. Bonnett. 2019. "A Trail of 'Bloody Gold' Leads to Venezuela's Government." CNN, August 23.

Council on Hemispheric Affairs. 2004. "An Unjust Attack on Nicaraguan President Enrique Bolaños," November 19.

Crisp, B. 2000. *Democratic Institutional Design: The Powers and Incentives of Venezuelan Politicians and Interest Groups.* Stanford University Press.

Crisp, B. F., D. H. Levine, and J. E. Molina. 2003. "The Rise and Decline of COPEI in Venezuela." In *Christian Democracy in Latin America*, edited by S. Mainwaring and T. R. Scully. Stanford University Press.

Cruz, C., and R. Diamint. 1998. "The New Military Autonomy in Latin America." *Journal of Democracy* 9 (4): 115–27.

Cuzán, A. G. 2015. "Five Laws of Politics." *Political Science and Politics* 48 (3): 415–19.

Cyr, J. 2017. *The Fates of Political Parties.* Cambridge University Press.

Cyr, J. 2019. "Normal Parties in Extraordinary Times: The Case of Primero Justicia and Voluntad Popular in Venezuela." Unpublished paper.

Dahl, R. A. 1971. *Polyarchy: Participation and Opposition.* Yale University Press.

De Freitas, M., M. Arévalo, and F. Martínez. 2019. "Manual contra la corrupción: 12 acciones y un madato." Trasparencia Venezuela.

de la Torre, C. 2013. "In the Name of the People: Democratization, Popular Organizations, and Populism in Venezuela, Bolivia, and Ecuador." *European Review of Latin American and Caribbean Studies* (95): 27–48.

de la Torre, C. 2014. "The People, Democracy, and Authoritarianism in Rafael Correa's Ecuador." *Constellations* 21 (4): 457–66.

de la Torre, C. 2020. "Rafael Correa's Technopopulism in Comparative Perspective." In *Assessing the Left Turn in Ecuador.* Edited by F. Sánchez and S. Pachano, 91–114. Springer Nature.

de Sa e Silva, F. 2021. "Law and Illiberalism: A Sociolegal Review and Research Roadmap." Law and Society Association Meeting, May 26–31.

de Waal, A. 2015. *The Real Politics of the Horn of Africa: Money, War and the Business of Power.* Polity.

Delgado, A. M. 2019. "Is the Military Really Loyal to Maduro—or Its Own Survival?" *Miami Herald*, May 6.

Delgado, A. M., B. Ebus, K. Gourney, J. Weaver, N. Nehamas, and J. Wyss. 2019. "How Miami, a Major Destination for Venezuelan Gold, Is Helping Prop Up Maduro's Regime." *Miami Herald*, July 23.

Demarest, G. L. C. 2018. "The Cubazuela Problem." *Military Review,*

November–December 2018. www.armyupress.army.mil/journals/military-re view/english-edition-archives/november-december-2018/demarest-cubazuela/.

DeShazo, P., T. Primiani, and P. McLean. 2007. "Back from the Brink: Evaluating Progress in Colombia, 1999–2007." Center for Strategic and International Studies.

Desilver, D. 2019. "Fewer Than a Third of Countries Currently Have a Military Draft; Most Exclude Women." Pew Research Center, April 23. www.pewre search.org/fact-tank/2019/04/23/fewer-than-a-third-of-countries-currently -have-a-military-draft-most-exclude-women/ft_19-04-11_militarydraftmap/.

Deutsche Welle. 2017. "Ecuador's President Strips Vice President of All Functions." August 4.

Diamond, L., and L. Morlino. 2004. "An Overview: The Quality of Democracy." *Journal of Democracy* 15 (4): 20–31.

Di John, J. 2004. "The Political Economy of Economic Liberalisation in Venezuela." Crisis States Programme Working Paper Series 1. London School of Economics.

Di John, J. 2009. *From Windfall to Curse? Oil and Industrialization in Venezuela, 1920 to the Present.* Penn State University Press.

Diamond, L. 2015. "Facing Up to the Democratic Recession." *Journal of Democracy* 26 (1): 141–55.

Diamond, L. 2019. *Ill Winds: Democracy from Russian Rage, Chinese Ambition, and American Complacency.* Penguin Press.

Dickovick, J. T. 2011. *Decentralization and Recentralization in the Developing World: Comparative Studies from Africa and Latin America.* Pennsylvania State University Press.

Doocy, S., K. Page, and T. Taraciuk Broner. 2019. "Venezuela's Humanitarian Emergency: Large-Scale UN Response Needed to Address Health and Food Crises." Human Rights Watch.

Dosh, P., and N. Kligerman. 2009. "Correa vs. Social Movements: Showdown in Ecuador." *NACLA Report on the Americas* 42 (5): 21–24.

Dreier, H. 2017. "U.S. Lawmakers Propose Sanctions for Venezuela Food Corruption." Associated Press, January 23.

Dreisbach, T., and M. Anderson. 2021. "Nearly 1 in 5 Defendants in Capitol Riot Cases Served in the Military." NPR, January 21.

Dunning, T. 2008. *Crude Democracy: Natural Resource Wealth and Political Regimes.* Cambridge University Press.

Ebus, B. 2019. "Venezuela's Mining Arc: A Legal Veneer for Armed Groups to Plunder." *The Guardian*, June 8.

Ebus, B., and T. Martinelli. 2021. "Venezuela's Gold Heist: The Symbiotic Relationship between the State, Criminal Networks and Resource Extraction." *Bulletin of Latin American Research*, May 26.

Edwards, S. 2012. *Left Behind: Latin America and the False Promise of Populism.* University of Chicago Press.

El Estímulo. 2015. "Anulan candidatura de Nicmer Evans y otros postulados por Marea Socialista." *El Estímulo*, August 25.

El Estímulo. 2016. "Bernal: Defenderé Los Clap De Los Ataques De La Asamblea Nacional." *El Estímulo*, July 7.

El Estímulo. 2020. "Diputados exiliados: Maduro tiene miedo a la AN." *El Estímulo*, August 28.

El Nacional. 2017. "El país gritó: 'Maduro, no to queremos.'" *El Nacional*, April 20.

El Nacional. 2020. "Desconexión y censura: el reporte del Ipys Venezuela." *El Nacional*, May 21.

Ellis, R. E. 2021. The Reinforcing Activities of the ELN (National Liberation Army) in Colombia and Venezuela. *USAF Journal of the Americas* 3(2): 194–213.

Ellner, S. 2003. "Introduction: The Search for Explanations." In *Venezuelan Politics in the Chávez Era: Class, Polarization, and Conflict*, edited by S. Ellner and D. Hellinger, 7–25. Lynne Rienner.

Ellner, S. 2008. *Rethinking Venezuelan Politics: Class, Conflict and the Chávez Phenomenon*. Lynne Rienner.

Ellner, S., and D. Hellinger (eds.). 2003. *Venezuelan Politics in the Chávez Era: Class, Polarization, and Conflict*. Lynne Rienners.

ENCOVI. 2020. "Encuesta nacional de condiciones de vida." Universidad Católica Andrés Bello. www.proyectoencovi.com/encovi-2019.

Empresas Polar. 2015. "Lorenzo Mendoza: 'Siempre respondemos los ataques con más trabajo y compromiso,'" October 27. https://empresaspolar.com/sala-de -prensa/lorenzo-mendoza-siempre-respondemos-los-ataques-con-mas-trabajo -y-compromiso.

Enyedi, Z. 2016. "Populist Polarization and Party System Institutionalization." *Problems of Post-Communism* 63 (4): 210–20.

Ermakoff, I. 2020. "Law against the Rule of Law: Assaulting Democracy." *Journal of Law and Society* 47 (S1): 164–86.

Escalona, J. 2019. "173 agresiones a trabajadores de la prensa contabiliza Comisión de Medios de la Asamblea Nacional." *El Impulso*, March 13. www.elimpulso .com/2019/03/13/173-agresiones-a-trabajadores-de-la-prensa-contabiliza -comision-de-medios-de-la-asamblea-nacional-13mar/.

Espacio Público. 2021. "Situación general del derecho a la libertad de expresión en Venezuela enero – diciembre 2020." Espacio Público, January 30. http:/ /espaciopublico.org/situacion-general-del-derecho-a-la-libertad-de-expresion -en-Venezuela-enero-diciembre-2020/.

Fagen, R. 1969. *The Transformation of Political Culture in Cuba*. Stanford University Press.

Faiola, A. 2017. "Sickness and HIV Drug Shortages Rise as Venezuela's Economy Crumbles." *The Independent*, September 8.

Faiola, A., and R. Krygier. 2017. "A Venezuelan Woman Had Grown Used to Shortages. Then Her HIV Drugs Ran Out." *Washington Post*, September 6.

Faiola, A., and R. Krygier. 2019. "During Secret Venezuela Talks, Maduro Offered New Elections. Is It a Real Breakthrough or a Stall?" *Washington Post*, August 16.

Falleti, T. 2011. "Varieties of Authoritarianism: The Organization of the Military State and Its Effects on Federalism in Argentina and Brazil." *Studies in Comparative International Development* 46: 137–62.

Feinberg, R., and D. Kurtz-Phelan. 2006. "Nicaragua between 'Caudillismo' and Modernity: The Sandinistas Redux?" *World Policy Journal* 23 (2): 76–84.

Fermín Kancev, M. V. 2020. "Petróleo avanza a playa de Río Seco, advierte pescador sobre nuevo derrame en Falcón." *Efecto Cocuyo*, September 17.

Fernandes, S. 2010. *Who Can Stop the Drums? Urban Social Movements in Chávez's Venezuela*. Duke University Press.

FIDH and CENIDH. 2021. "¡Basta ya de impunidad! Ejecuciones extrajudiciales y represión en Nicaragua, hasta cuándo?" Managua: International Federation for Human Rights and Centro Nicaraguense de Derechos Humanos, Report No. 764e, February.

Fierro, M. I. 2014. "Álvaro Uribe Vélez Populismo y Neopopulismo." *Análisis Político* 27 (81): 127–47.

Flores-Macías, G. A. 2014. "Financing Security through Elite Taxation: The Case of Colombia's 'Democratic Security Taxes.'" *Studies in Comparative International Development* 49: 477–500.

Foro Penal Venezolano. 2014. "Venezuela 2014: Protestas y Derechos Humanos." PROVEA, June 24. https://issuu.com/proveaong/docs/informe-final-protes tas2.

Frantz, E. 2018. *Authoritarianism: What Everyone Needs to Know*. Oxford University Press.

Frantz, E., and L. Mogenbesser. 2017. "'Smarter' Authoritarianism: The Survival Tools of Dictators." Southern Political Science Association Annual Meeting. New Orleans, January 12–14.

Freden, B. A. 2021. OAS Resolution Condemns Ortega Regime in Nicaragua. U.S. Mission to the Organization of American States, June 15. https://usoas .usmission.gov/oas-resolution-condemns-ortega-regime-in-nicaragua/.

Freedom House. 2010. "Freedom in the World 2010: Ecuador." www.refworld .org/docid/4c1a1eaac.html.

Freedom House. 2019. "Freedom in the World 2019: Nicaragua." https://free domhouse.org/country/nicaragua/freedom-world/2019.

Freedom House. 2020. "Freedom in the World 2020: Nicaragua." https://free domhouse.org/country/nicaragua/freedom-world/2020.

Freedom House. 2021. "Freedom in the World 2021: Ecuador." https://freedom house.org/country/ecuador/freedom-world/2021.

Freedom House. 2021. *Freedom in the World* (dataset). https://freedomhouse.org/ report/freedom-world.

Freeman, W. 2018. "Colonization, Duplication, Evasion: The Institutional

Strategies of Autocratic Legalism," March 18. https://papers.ssrn.com/sol3/papers.cfm?abstract_id=3210488.

Freeman, W. 2020. "Sidestepping the Constitution: Executive Aggrandizement in Latin America and East Central Europe." *Constitutional Studies* 6 (1): 35–58.

Fuente, Á. 2018. "La escasez de medicinas mata en Venezuela." *El País*, May 7.

Fundación Váyalo. 2018. "Informe sobre la emergencia humanitarian en Venezuela." Fundación Váyalo, August 13. www.fundacionreflejosdeVenezuela.com/hagamos-un-hecho/emergencia-humanitaria-en-Venezuela/.

Galíndez, Y. S. 2016. "Rodríguez: Unasur planteó al Gobierno sincerar los previos de electricidad y gasolina." Globovisión, September 7.

Gallegos, R. 2016. *Crude Nation: How Oil Riches Ruined Venezuela.* Potomac Books.

Galston, W. A., J. D. Hunter, and J. M. Owen. 2018. *Anti-Pluralism: The Populist Threat to Liberal Democracy.* Yale University Press.

Gamboa, L. 2017. "Opposition at the Margins: Strategies against the Erosion of Democracy in Colombia and Venezuela." *Comparative Politics* 49 (4): 457–77.

García, J., G. Correa, and B. Rousset. 2019. "Trends in Infant Mortality in Venezuela between 1985 and 2016: A Systematic Analysis of Demographic Data." *Lancet Global Health* 7 (3): e331–36.

García Marco, D. 2016. " 'Hay más fortalezas en la economía que debilidades': La visión sobre Venezuela del español Alfredo Serrano, el 'Jesucristo de la Economía' según Nicolás Maduro." BBC Mundo Caracas, October 13.

García Marco, D. 2017. "Qué son los consejos comunales de Venezuela y por qué son tan importantes para la Asamblea Nacional Constituyente que convocó Nicolás Maduro." BBC Mundo Caracas, May 2.

García-Guadilla, M. P. 2007. "Social Movements in a Polarized Setting: Myths of Venezuelan Civil Society." In *Venezuela: Hugo Chávez and the Decline of an Exceptional Democracy*, edited by S. Ellner and M. Tinker-Salas, 140–54. Rowan & Littlefield.

García Villegas, M., and J. E. Revelo Rebolledo. 2009. *Mayorías sin democracia: Desequilibrio de poderes y Estado de derecho en Colombia, 2002–2009.* Bogotá, Dejusticia.

Gates, L. C. 2010. *Electing Chávez: The Business of Anti-Neoliberalism Politics in Venezuela.* Pittsburgh University Press.

Geddes, B. 1999. "What Do We Know about Democratization after Twenty Years." *Annual Review of Political Science* 2: 115–44.

Geddes, B., J. Wright, and F. Erica. 2018. *How Dictatorships Work: Power, Personalization, and Collapse.* Cambridge University Press.

Gerschewski, J. 2021. "Erosion or Decay? Conceptualizing Causes and Mechanisms of Democratic Regression." *Democratization* 28 (1): 43–62.

Gandhi, J., and E. Lust-Okar. 2009. Elections Under Authoritarianism. *Annual Review of Political Science* 12 (1): 403–22.

Ghitis, F. 2016. "How Ortega Took the Suspense Out of Nicaragua's Presidential Election." *World Politics Review*, November 3.

Gibler, D. M., and K. A. Randazzo. 2011. "Testing the Effects of Independent Judiciaries on the Likelihood of Democratic Backsliding." *American Journal of Political Science* 55 (3): 696–709.

Gill, T. M. 2018. "The Possibilities and Pitfalls of Left-Wing Populism in Socialist Venezuela." *Journal of World-Systems Research* 24 (2): 304–13.

Giugale, M. M. 2017. *Economic Development: What Everyone Needs to Know*, 2nd edition. Oxford University Press.

GlobalSecurity.org. n.d. "Rafael Correa." www.globalsecurity.org/military/world /ecuador/president-correa.htm.

Globovisión. 2020. "Datanálisis: Popularidad de Guaidó está por el suelo," July 21. www.globovision.com/article/datanalisis-popularidad-de-guaido-esta-por -el-suelo.

Goodman, J., L. Alonso Lugo, and R. Gillies. 2019. "AP Exclusive: Anti-Maduro Coalition Grew from Secret Talks." Associated Press, January 25.

Grandin, G. 2016. "Christmas in Caracas? Worse Than the Grinch. A Conversation with Alejandro Velasco." *The Nation*, December 16.

Gratius, S., and A. Ayuso Pozo. 2020. "Sanciones como instrumento de coerción: ¿cuán similares son las políticas de Estados Unidos y la Unión Europea hacia Venezuela?" *América Latina Hoy* 85: 31–53.

Grier, K., and N. Maynard. 2016. "The Economic Consequences of Hugo Chavez: A Synthetic Control Analysis." *Journal of Economic Behavior & Organization* 125: 1–21.

Gunson, P. 2016. "Slow-Motion Coup in Venezuela?" International Crisis Group, August 5. www.crisisgroup.org/latin-america-caribbean/andes/Vene zuela/slow-motion-coup-Venezuela.

Gunson, P. 2019. "In Venezuela, a High-stakes Gambit." International Crisis Group, January 24. www.crisisgroup.org/latin-america-caribbean/andes/vene zuela/venezuela-high-stakes-gambit.

Gupta, G., and A. Ulmer. 2017. "Venezuela Quells Attack on Military Base, Two Killed." Reuters, August 6.

Guriev, S., and D. Treisman. Forthcoming. "Discourse Dictators: How Today's Strongmen Rule by Distorting the News."

Haggard, S., and R. Kaufman. 2021. *Backsliding: Democratic Regress in the Contemporary World*. Cambridge University Press.

Haggard, S., and R. R. Kaufman. 1995. *The Political Economy of Democratic Transitions*. Princeton University Press.

Haggard, S., and R. R. Kaufman. 1997. "The Political Economy of Democratic Transitions." *Comparative Politics* 29 (3): 263–83.

Hall, T. E., and T. A. Wang. 2008. "International Principles for Election Integrity." In *Election Fraud: Detecting and Deterring Electoral Manipulation*, edited by R. M. Alvarez, T. E. Hall, and S. D. Hyde. Brookings Institution Press.

Hanke, S. H. 2016. "Venezuela Enters the Record Book, Officially Hyperinflates." Cato Institute.

Hausmann, R. 2018. "The Venality of Evil." Project Syndicate, July 31.

Hausmann, R., and F. Rodríguez. 2013. "Why Did Venezuelan Growth Collapse?" In *Venezuela: Anatomy of a Collapse*, edited by R. Hausmann and F. Rodríguez. Penn State University Press.

Hawkins, D. 2011. "The Influence of Organized Labour in the Rise to Power of Lula in Brazil and Correa in Ecuador." *Labour, Capital and Society* 44 (2): 26–55.

Hawkins, K. A. 2003. "Populism in Venezuela: The Rise of Chavismo." *Third World Quarterly* 24 (6): 1137–60.

Hawkins, K. A. 2010a. *Venezuela's Chavismo and Populism in Comparative Perspective.* Cambridge University Press.

Hawkins, K. A. 2010b. "Who Mobilizes? Participatory Democracy in Chávez's Bolivarian Revolution." *Latin American Politics and Society* 52 (3): 31–66.

Hawkins, K. A., and C. Rovira Kaltwasser. 2017. "The Ideational Approach to Populism." *Latin American Research Review* 52 (4): 513–28.

Hellinger, D. 2003. "Political Overview: The Breakdown of Puntofijismo and the Rise of Chavismo." In *Venezuelan Politics in the Chávez Era: Class, Polarization, and Conflict*, edited by S. Ellner and D. Hellinger, 27–54. Lynne Rienner.

Hellinger, D. 2011. "Afterword: Chavismo and Venezuelan Democracy in a New Decade." In *Venezuela's Bolivarian Democracy: Participation, Politics, and Culture under Chávez*, edited by D. Smilde and D. Hellinger. Duke University Press.

Hellinger, D., and A. P. Spanakos. 2017. "The Legacy of Hugo Chávez." *Latin American Perspectives* 44 (1): 4–16.

Helmke, G. 2017. *Institutions on the Edge: The Origins and Consequences of Inter-Branch Crises in Latin America.* Cambridge University Press.

Henderson, J. D. 2011. "Plan Colombia's Place in the Democratic Security Program of Alvaro Uribe Vélez." *The Latin Americanist* 55 (1): 3–15.

Heritage Foundation. 2021. "Index of Economic Freedom." www.heritage.org/index/about.

Hernández, J. I. 2015. "5 violaciones cometidas durante la designación de los magistrados del TSJ." Prodavinci, December 23.

Hetland, G. 2017. "From System Collapse to Chavista Hegemony: The Party Question in Bolivarian Venezuela." *Latin American Perspectives* 44 (1): 17–36.

Hogenboom, B. 2012. "Depoliticized and Repoliticized Minerals in Latin America." *Journal of Developing Societies* 28 (2): 133–58.

Hovi, J., R. Huseby, and D. F. Sprinz. 2005. "When Do (Imposed) Economic Sanctions Work." *World Politics* 57 (4): 481.

Howard, M. M., and P. G. Roessler. 2006. "Liberalizing Electoral Outcomes in Competitive Authoritarian Regimes." *American Journal of Political Science* 50 (2): 365–81.

Human Rights Watch. 2004. "Rigging the Rule of Law: Judicial Independence under Siege in Venezuela." https://books.google.se/books/about/Rigging_the_Rule_of_Law.html?id=IR02s7D3OgUC&redir_esc=y.

Human Rights Watch. 2019a. "Nicaragua: Events of 2018." www.hrw.org/world-report/2019/country-chapters/nicaragua.

Human Rights Watch. 2019b. "Nicaragua: Events of 2019." www.hrw.org/world-report/2019/country-chapters/nicaragua#.

Human Rights Watch. 2020a. "Ecuador: Events of 2019." www.hrw.org/world-report/2020/country-chapters/ecuador#.

Human Rights Watch. 2020b. "Chile: Events of 2019." www.hrw.org/world-report/2020/country-chapters/chile#.

Huntington, S. P. 1957. *The Soldier and the State.* Harvard University Press.

Huq, A., and T. Ginsburg. 2018. "How to Lose a Constitutional Democracy." *UCLA Law Review* 78.

InSight Crime. 2019a. "FARC in Venezuela." June 27. https://insightcrime.org/Venezuela-organized-crime-news/farc-in-Venezuela/.

InSight Crime. 2019b. "The Armed Groups Propping Up Venezuela's Government." March 1. https://insightcrime.org/news/analysis/armed-groups-propping-Venezuelas-government/.

InSight Crime. 2019c. "Ex-FARC Mafia, Venezuela and the Current International Climate." November 11. insightcrime.org/investigations/ex-farc-mafia-Venezuela-international-climate/.

InSight Crime. 2020. "ELN in Venezuela." January 28. https://insightcrime.org/Venezuela-organized-crime-news/eln-in-Venezuela/.

InSight Crime. 2021. "ELN Now Present in Half of Venezuela." February 3. insightcrime.org/news/analysis/eln-present-half-Venezuela/.

Instituto Nacional de Estadísticas. 2013. "La población indígena de Venezuela: Censo 2011." www.ine.gov.ve/documentos/SEN/menuSEN/pdf/subcomitedemografica/Indigena/BoletinPoblacionIndigena.pdf.

Inter-American Commission on Human Rights. 2020. "Persons Deprived of Liberty in Nicaragua in Connection with the Human Rights Crisis That Began on April 18, 2018." Organization of American States.

International Commission of Jurists. 2014. "Strengthening the Rule of Law in Venezuela." Geneva. www.icj.org/wp-content/uploads/2014/11/Venezuela-Strengthening-the-RoL-Publications-Reports-2014-Eng.pdf.

International Commission of Jurists. 2017. "Achieving Justice for Gross Huan Rights Violations in Venezuela, Baseline Study." Geneva. www.icj.org/wp-content/uploads/2017/08/Venezuela-GRA-Baseline-Study-Publications-Reports-Thematic-reports-2017-ENG.pdf.

International Crisis Group. 2018. "Friendly Fire: Venezuela's Opposition Turmoil." Caracas. www.crisisgroup.org/latin-america-caribbean/andes/Venezuela/71-friendly-fire-Venezuelas-opposition-turmoil.

International Crisis Group. 2019. "Venezuela's Military Enigma." Briefing 39. Caracas. www.crisisgroup.org/latin-america-caribbean/andes/Venezuela/039 -Venezuelas-military-enigma.

IMF (International Monetary Fund). 2019. "GDP Growth (Annual %)." http: //datatopics.worldbank.org/world-development-indicators/themes/economy .html#growth-and-structure.

IPADE. 2008. "Catálogo Estadístico de Elecciones en Nicaragua, 1990–2006." Managua, IPADE (Instituto para el Desarrollo y la Democracia). www.enri quebolanos.org/data/docs/Eleccion%20de%20Nicaragua.pdf.

IPS (Inter Press Service). 2020. "Venezuela: Violent Abuses in Illegal Gold Mines," February 5.

Jácome, F. 2018. "Los militares en la política y la economía de Venezuela." *Nueva Sociedad* 274.

Jaskoski, M. 2020. "Ecuador: Military Autonomy under Democratic Rule." *Oxford Research Encyclopedia of Politics.* Oxford University Press.

Jiménez, M. 2021. "Contesting Autocracy: Repression and Opposition Coordination in Venezuela." *Political Studies* (May 21).

Jones, M. P. 2010. "Beyond the Electoral Connection: The Effect of Political Parties on the Policymaking Process." In *How Democracy Works: Political Institutions, Actors, and Arenas in Latin American Policymaking*, edited by C. Scartascini, E. Stein, and M. Tommasi, 19–46. Inter-American Development Bank and David Rockefeller Center for Latin American Studies, Harvard University.

Kaplan, S. B. 2013. *Globalization and Austerity Politics in Latin America.* Cambridge University Press.

Karl, T. L. 1987. "Petroleum and Political Pacts: The Transition to Democracy in Venezuela." *Latin American Research Review* 22 (1): 61–94.

Karl, T. L. 1997. *The Paradox of Plenty: Oil Booms and Petro States.* University of California Press.

Kaufman, C. 2008. "The Ortega Government and Opposition from within Sandinismo." *The Marxist-Leninist* (November 23). https://marxistleninist .wordpress.com/2008/11/23/the-ortega-government-and-opposition-from -within-sandinismo/.

Kaufman, R. R., and B. Stallings. 1991. "The Political Economy of Latin American Populism." In *The Macroeconomics of Populism in Latin America*, edited by R. Dornbusch and S. Edwards. University of Chicago Press.

Kelly, J., and P. A. Palma. 2004. "The Syndrome of Economic Decline and the Quest for Change." In *The Unraveling of Representative Democracy in Venezuela*, edited by J. L. McCoy and D. J. Myers. Johns Hopkins University Press.

Kingstone, P. 2018. *The Political Economy of Latin America: Reflections on Neoliberalism and Development*, 2nd edition. Routledge.

Kirschner, N. 2020. "Gold Mining in Venezuela Rampant with Human Rights Abuse." Share America, March 9.

Klein, E. 2021. "2021: A Black Year for the Caribbean: Oil Spills in Venezuela." Remote Sensing Laboratory, Simón Bolívar University. https://docs.google.com/presentation/d/1oSMXLXP7vsPaxOJcumNZ_OdGcLj_r9wpbbMIrZf-dfA/edit#slide=id.p.

Kneuer, M. 2021. "Unravelling Democratic Erosion: Who Drives the Slow Death of Democracy, and How?" *Democratization* 28 (8): 1442–62.

Kornblith, M. 1997. *Las crisis de la democracia*. Ediciones IESA (Instituto de Estudios Superiores de Administración).

Kornblith, M. 2007a. "Venezuela: Calidad de las elecciones y calidad de la democracia." *América Latina Hoy* 45: 109–24.

Kornblith, M. 2007b. "Venezuela: De la democracia representativa al socialismo del siglo XXI. La nueva encrucijada en los países andinos." In *Política y sociedad a inicios del siglo XXI*, edited by M. Tanaka. Instituto de Estudios Peruanos.

Kozloff, N. 2007. *Hugo Chavez: Oil, Politics, and the Challenge to the U.S.* St. Martin's Griffin.

Kronick, D., B. Plunkett, and P. Rodríguez. 2021. "Backsliding by Surprise: The Rise of Chavismo." https://ssrn.com/abstract=3810203 or http://dx.doi.org/10.2139/ssrn.3810203.

Krygier, R., M. B. Sheridan, and A. Gearan. 2019. "The Accidental Leader: How Juan Guaidó Became the Face of Venezuela's Uprising." *Washington Post*, February 9.

Kulisheck, M., and B. F. Crisp. 2003. "The Legislative Consequences of MMP Electoral Rules in Venezuela." In *Mixed-Member Electoral Systems: The Best of Both Worlds?*, edited by M. S. Shugart and M. P. Wattenberg. Oxford University Press.

Kurmanaev, A. 2017. "Tareck El Aissami, Sanctioned Venezuelan Vice President, Had Ruthless Rise." *Wall Street Journal*, February 14.

Kurmanaev, A. 2019. "Venezuela's Collapse Is the Worst Outside of War in Decades, Economists Say." *New York Times*, May 17.

Kurmanaev, A., and I. Herrera. 2019. "Venezuela's Maduro Cracks Down on His Own Military in Bid to Retain Power." *New York Times*, August 13.

Kutner, J. 2011. "How Colombia's President Santos Made Peace with the Judiciary." *The Christian Science Monitor*, April 7.

Laebens, M. G., and A. Lührmann. 2021. "What Halts Democratic Erosion? The Changing Role of Accountability." *Democratization* 28 (5): 908–28.

Lamas, J. C. 2017. "Venezuela's Economic Crisis Exacerbates Deadly Shortage of HIV Medicines." CGTN America, December 1. www.youtube.com/watch?v=NUj-HMcoQcw.

Lansberg-Rodríguez, D. 2014. "The Frank Underwood of Venezuela." *The Atlantic*, March 6.

Lares Martiz, V. 2019. "Así se fraguó plan que consolidó opción de Guaidó como presidente (e)." *El Tiempo*, January 28.

Larrea, S., and J. D. Montalvo. 2017. "Can Presidential Popularity Decrease Public Perceptions of Political Corruption? The Case of Ecuador under Rafael Correa." LAPOP's AmericasBarometer, Vanderbilt University.

LatinNews. Various Years. *LatinNews Daily* and *Latin America Weekly Reports*. www.latinnews.com/about-us.html.

Lavallee, G. 2018. "Venezuela Authorities Detained 131 Accused of Economic Sabotage." Agence France Presse, August 31.

Laya, P. 2020. "Venezuelan Opposition Lawmaker Released from House Arrest." Bloomberg, August 28.

Leon, I. 2018. "Designación de nuevo Contralor evidencia 'partidización' de Poderes Públicos, señalan analistas." *Efecto Cocuyo*, October 25.

Levine, D. H. 1973. *Conflict and Political Change in Venezuela*. Princeton University Press.

Levine, D. H. 1998. "Beyond the Exhaustion of the Model: Survival and Transformation in Venezuela." In *Reinventing Legitimacy: Democracy and Political Change in Venezuela*, edited by D. Canache and M. R. Kulisheck. Greenwood Press.

Levitsky, S., J. Loxton, and B. Van Dyck. 2016. "Introduction: Challenges of Party-Building in Latin America." In *Challenges of Party-Building in Latin America,* edited by S. Levitsky, J. Loxton, B. Van Dyck, and J. I. Domínguez, 1–48. Cambridge University Press.

Levitsky, S., and L. A. Way. 2002. "The Rise of Competitive Authoritarianism." *Journal of Democracy* 13 (2): 51–65.

Levitsky, S., and L. A. Way. 2020. "The New Competitive Authoritarianism." *Journal of Democracy* 31 (1): 51–65.

Lewis, P., C. Barr, S. Clarke, A. Voce, C. Levett, and P. Gutiérrez. 2019. "Revealed: The Rise and Rise of Populist Rhetoric." *The Guardian,* March 6.

Liendo, N., and R. Losada. 2015. "The Weight of New Political Parties in the Colombian Party System, 1986–2010." *Papel Político* 20 (1): 35–62.

Linz, J. J. 1964. "An Authoritarian Regime: Spain." In *Cleavages, Ideologies and Party Systems: Contributions to Comparative Political Sociology*, edited by E. Allardt and Y. Littunen, 291–342. Transactions of the Westermarck Society.

Linz, J. J. 1975. "Totalitarian and Authoritarian Regimes." In *Handbook of Political Science*. Vol. 3 of Macropolitical Theory, edited by F. I. Greenstein and N. W. Polsby. Addison-Wesley.

Llanos, M., and L. Marsteintredet. 2010. "Introduction: Presidentialism and Presidential Breakdowns in Latin America." In *Presidential Breakdowns in Latin America. Causes and Outcomes of Executive Instability in Developing Democracies*, edited by M. Llanos and L. Marsteintredet. Palgrave/Macmillan.

Long, T. 2017. *Latin America Confronts the United States*. Cambridge University Press.

López, É. 2017. "Gang Lords Rule the Orinoco Mining Arc." OCCRP (Organized Crime and Corruption Reporting Project). www.occrp.org/en/goldandchaos/gang-lords-rule-the-orinoco-mining-arc.

López Hernández, C. 2010. "La refundación de la patria: De la teoría a la evidencia." In *Y refundaron la patria: de cómo mafiosos y políticos reconfiguraron el estado colombiano*, edited by C. N. López Hernández and A. F. Ávila Martínez. Corporación Nuevo Arco Iris.

López-Maya, M. 2002. "Venezuela after the Caracazo: Forms of Protest in a Deinstitutionalized Context." *Bulletin of Latin American Research* 21 (2): 199–218.

López-Maya, M. 2003. "Hugo Chávez Frías: His Movement and His Presidency." In *Venezuelan Politics in the Chávez Era*, edited by S. Ellner and D. H. Hellinger, 73–92. Lynne Rienner.

López-Maya, M. 2016. *El ocaso del chavismo: Venezuela 2005–2015*. Editorial Alfa.

López-Maya, M. 2018. "Socialismo y comunas en Venezuela." *Nueva Sociedad* 274.

López Maya, M., and L. E. Lander. 2004. "The Struggle for Hegemony in Venezuela: Poverty, Popular Protest, and the Future of Democracy." In *Politics in the Andes: Identity, Conflict and Reform*, edited by J.-M. Burt and P. Mauceri. University of Pittsburgh Press.

Lowenthal, A. F. 2021. "Venezuela's Elusive Transition: Toward a New Path." Woodrow Wilson Center, Latin America Program.

Loxton, J. 2021. "Authoritarian Vestiges in Democracies." *Journal of Democracy* 32: 145–58.

Luciani, G. 1987. "Allocation vs. Production States: A Theoretical Framework." In *The Rentier State*, edited by H. Beblawi and G. Luciani, 63–82. Routledge.

Lührmann, A., and S. I. Lindberg. 2019. "A Third Wave of Autocratization Is Here: What Is New about It?" *Democratization* 26 (7): 1095–113.

Lupu, N. 2016. *Party Brands in Crisis: Partisanship, Brand Dilution, and the Breakdown of Political Parties in Latin America*. Cambridge University Press.

Lust, E., and D. Waldner. 2015. "Unwelcome Change: Understanding, Evaluating, and Extending Theories of Democratic Backsliding." USAID Research Report, June 11.

Maag, S. 2017. "Ecuador's Ruling Party Headed for a Split." Atlantic Council, August 17. www.atlanticcouncil.org/blogs/new-atlanticist/ecuador-s-ruling -party-headed-for-a-split/.

Magaloni, B. 2006. *Voting for Autocracy: Hegemonic Party Survival and Its Demise in Mexico*. Cambridge University Press.

Mahoney, J., and K. Thelen. 2010. "A Theory of Gradual Institutional Change." In *Explaining Institutional Change*, edited by J. Mahoney and K. Thelen, 1–37. Cambridge University Press.

Maingon, T. 2016. "Política social y régimen de bienestar: Venezuela 1999– 2014." *Estudios Latinoamericanos* 38: 115–43.

Mainwaring, S. 2012. "From Representative Democracy to Participatory

Competitive Authoritarianism: Hugo Chávez and Venezuelan Politics." *Perspectives on Politics* 10 (4): 955–67.

Mainwaring, S., and M. S. Shugart (eds.). 1997. *Presidentialism and Democracy in Latin America.* Cambridge University Press.

Mainwaring, S. M., C. Gervasoni, and A. España-Najera. 2017. "Extra- and Within-System Electoral Volatility." *Party Politics* 23 (6): 623–35.

Mance, H. 2009. "Third Term for Uribe Threatens Colombian Democracy." *World Politics Review,* February 5.

Marcella, G. 2003. *The United States and Colombia: The Journey from Ambiguity to Strategic Clarity.* U.S. Army War College Press.

Marczak, J. 2019. "Juan Guaidó's Operation Freedom Gives Venezuela a Shot at Democracy." Atlantic Council. www.atlanticcouncil.org/blogs/new-atlanticist /juan-guaido-s-operation-freedom-gives-Venezuela-a-shot-at-democracy/.

Marks, T. A. 2005. "Sustainability of Colombian Military/Strategic Support for 'Democratic Security.'" Strategic Studies Institute, U.S. Army War College, July. www.files.ethz.ch/isn/14326/Sustainability%20of%20Colombian%20 Military.pdf.

Marsteintredet, L. 2014. "Explaining Variation of Executive Instability in Presidential Regimes: Presidential Interruptions in Latin America." *International Political Science Review* 35 (2): 173–94.

Marsteintredet, L. 2020. "With the Cards Stacked against You. Challenges to a Negotiated Transition to Democracy in Venezuela." *European Review of Latin American and Caribbean Studies* 109: 87–106.

Marthoz, J.-P. 2014. "Venezuela's Foreign Policy: A Mirage Based on a Curse." NOREF Reports. Norwegian Peacebuilding Resource Centre (NOREF), November 14. www.files.ethz.ch/isn/186054/5ac5220191adf69475fb57f9e 303479c.pdf.

Martí i Puig, S. 2009. "Nicaragua 2008: Polarización y Pactos." *Revista de Ciencia Política* 29 (2): 515–31.

Martí i Puig, S. 2016. "Nicaragua: Desdemocratización y Caudilllismo." *Revista de Ciencia Política* 36 (1): 239–58.

Martí i Puig, S., and M. Jarquín. 2021. "El precio de la perpetuación de Daniel Ortega." *Nueva Sociedad* (June 25).

Martín, K. 2016. "Despite Government Obstacles, Over a Million Venezuelans March on Caracas." *PanAm Post,* September 4.

Martínez-Barahona, E. 2010. "Las Cortes Supremas como mecanismo de distribución de poder: el caso de la reelección presidencial en Costa Rica y Nicaragua." *Revista de Ciencia Política* 30 (3): 723–50.

Martínez-Fernández, A. 2019a. "The Illegal Gold Rush Enriching Maduro's Regime." American Enterprise Institute, August 13. www.aei.org/articles/the -illegal-gold-rush-enriching-maduros-regime/.

Martínez-Fernández, A. 2019b. "The National Liberation Army in Colombia and

Venezuela: Illicit Finance Challenges Stemming from Illegal Mining." American Enterprise Institute, July 9. www.aei.org/research-products/report/the-national-liberation-army-in-colombia-and-venezuela-illicit-finance-challenges-stemming-from-illegal-mining/.

Martínez-Gugerli, K. 2020. "Venezuela's Gendered Crisis, Parts 1–3." Venezuelan Politics and Human Rights, Washington Office on Latin America. www.venezuelablog.org/venezuelas-gendered-crisis-differential-impact-humanitarian-emergency/.

Martínez-Gugerli, K. 2020b. "Interactive Map: Degrees of Diplomatic Recognition of Guaidó and Maduro." Venezuelan Politics and Human Rights, Washington Office on Latin America, October 15. www.Venezuelablog.org/interactive-map-degrees-of-diplomatic-recognition-of-guaido-and-Maduro/.

Martínez-Gugerli, K., and G. Ramsey 2020. "Q&A: Demystifying the Failed Silvercorp Operation." Venezuelan Politics and Human Rights, Washington Office on Latin America, July 3. www.Venezuelablog.org/demystifying-failed-silvercorp-operation/.

Martínez, E. G. 2018. "Sobre la ilegalización de partidos en Venezuela." Prodavinci, February 3.

Martínez, I. 2020. "Venezuela: La peste militar." *El País*, March 30.

Mazzuca, S. 2013. "Natural Resources Boom and Institutional Curses in the New Political Economy of South America. In *Constructing Democratic Governance in Latin America*, edited by J. I. Domínguez and M. Shifter, 102–26. Johns Hopkins University Press.

McConnell, S. 1997. "Institutional Development." In *Nicaragua without Illusions: Regime Transition and Structural Adjustment in the 1990s*, edited by T. W. Walker, 45–63. SR Books.

McCoy, J. L. 2004. "From Representative to Participatory Democracy? Regime Transformation in Venezuela." In *The Unraveling of Representative Democracy in Venezuela*, edited by J. L. McCoy and D. J. Myers. Johns Hopkins University Press.

McCoy, J., T. Rahman, and M. Somer. 2018. "Polarization and the Global Crisis of Democracy: Common Patterns, Dynamics, and Pernicious Consequences for Democratic Polities." *American Behavioral Scientist* 62 (1): 16–42.

McDermott, J. 2018. "Venezuela, the New Regional Crime Hub." *New York Times*, July 15.

McKinley, J. C. 2008. "Nicaraguan Councils Stir Fear of Dictatorship." *New York Times*, May 4.

Medrano, M. 2021. "Juramentan a nuevos magistrados del Consejo Supremo Electoral de Nicaragua." CNN en español, May 6.

Mejía, A. 2008. "Colombia's National Security Strategy, A New 'Coin' Approach." U.S. Army War College.

Mejía Acosta, A. and V. Albornoz. 2020. "The Political Management of the Oil Bonanza During Correa's Government." In *Assessing the Left Turn in*

Ecuador. Studies of the Americas, edited by F. Sánchez and S. Pachano. Palgrave Macmillan.

Melimopoulos, E. 2017. "Venezuela: What Is a National Constituent Assembly?" Al Jazeera, July 31.

Melimopoulos, E. 2020. "A Year On, Guaido's Image in Trouble as Opposition Faces Cracks." Al Jazeera, January 24.

Meredith, S. 2019. "What's Next for Venezuela? Anti-Maduro Allies Regroup after the Fight for Humanitarian Aid." CNBC, March 1.

Mijares, V. M. 2017. "Soft Balancing the Titans: Venezuelan Foreign-Policy Strategy toward the United States, China, and Russia." *Latin American Policy* 8 (2): 201–31.

Milanes, J. P., and L. Gamboa. 2015. "Desde dos flancos: hacia una reconfiguración de la oposición en Colombia." In *Elecciones en Colombia 2014 ¿Representaciones fragmentadas?*, edited by F. Barrero and M. Batlle, 233–56. Konrad Adenauer Stiftung.

Millan Lombrana, L. 2019. "In Maduro's Venezuela, Even Gold Bars Is a Challenge." Bloomberg, January 30.

Miller, G. J. 2018. "Of Fear & Hope: Embracing the Carnet de la Patria." Caracas Chronicles, January 11.

Milliken, M., Gregorio, D., E. Chinea, and D. Ore. 2017. "Poll Finds 85 Percent of Venezuelans Oppose Constitution Revision." Reuters, June 10.

Ministerio [del Poder Popular] para la Salud. 2016. "Informe nacional de la declaración política sobre VIH y el sida de 2011." Gobierno Bolivariano de Venezuela. www.unaids.org/sites/default/files/country/documents/VEN_narrative_report_2016.pdf.

Molina, J. E. 2004. "The Unraveling of Venezuela's Party System: From Party Rule to Personalistic Politics and Deinstitutionalization." In *The Unraveling of Representative Democracy in Venezuela*, edited by J. L. McCoy and D. J. Myers. Johns Hopkins University Press.

Monaldi, F. 2013. "Oil and Politics: Hugo Chávez and Beyond." David Rockefeller Center for Latin American Studies, Robert F. Kennedy Professorship Lecture Spring 2013, Harvard University.

Monaldi, F. 2015. "The Impact of the Decline in Oil Prices on the Economics, Politics and Oil Industry of Venezuela." Columbia Center on Global Energy Policy. https://energypolicy.columbia.edu/sites/default/files/Impact%20of%20the%20Decline%20in%20Oil%20Prices%20on%20Venezuela_September%202015.pdf.

Monaldi, F., and M. Penfold. 2014. "Institutional Collapse: The Rise and Decline of Democratic Governance in Venezuela." In *Venezuela before Chávez: Anatomy of an Economic Collapse*, edited by R. Hausmann and F. Rodríguez, 386–417. Penn State University Press.

Montaner, C. A. 1999. "Anatomía del terror." *La Ilustración Liberal* 4: 9–15.

Moraes, J. A. 2015. "The Electoral Basis of Ideological Polarization in Latin

America." Working Paper 403. Kellogg Institute for International Studies, University of Notre Dame.

Morgan, J. K. 2007. "Partisanship during the Collapse of Venezuelan Party System." *Latin American Research Review* 42 (1): 78–98.

Morgan, J. K. 2011. *Bankrupt Representation and Party System Collapse.* Penn State University Press.

Morgan, J. K., and C. Meléndez. 2016. "Parties under Stress: Using a Linkage Decay Framework to Analyze the Chilean Party System." *Journal of Politics in Latin America* 8 (3): 25–59.

Morgenstern, S., J. J. Negri, and A. Pérez-Liñán. 2008. "Parliamentary Opposition in Non-Parliamentary Regimes: Latin America." *Journal of Legislative Studies* 14 (1/2): 160–89.

Morgenstern, S., and J. Vázquez-D'Elía. 2007. "Electoral Laws, Parties, and Party Systems in Latin America." *American Review of Political Science* 10: 143–68.

Morris, C. D. 2018. "Unexpected Uprising: The Crisis of Democracy in Nicaragua." NACLA, May 14.

Moses, J. W., and B. Letnes. 2017. *Managing Resource Abundance and Wealth: The Norwegian Experience.* Oxford University Press.

Mounk, Y. 2018. *The People vs. Democracy: Why Our Freedom Is in Danger and How to Save It.* Harvard University Press.

Mudde, C., and C. Rovira Kaltwasser. 2017. *Populism: A Very Short Introduction.* Oxford University Press.

Müller, J.-W. 2016. *What Is Populism?* University of Pennsylvania Press.

Muñoz, J. A. 2014. "Gobierno de Venezuela revoca las credenciales a periodistas de CNN en Español." CNN, February 28.

Murphy, H., and E. Garcia. 2013. "Colombian Prosecutor's Court Challenge Threatens Peace Talks." Reuters, April 5.

Myers, D. D. 2004. "The Normalization of Punto Fijo Democracy." In *The Unraveling of Representative Democracy in Venezuela*, edited by J. L. McCoy and D. D. Myers, 11–32. Johns Hopkins University Press.

Myers, D. J. 2007. "From Thaw to Deluge: Party System Collapse in Venezuela and Peru." *Latin American Politics and Society* 49 (2): 59–86.

Naím, M. 1993. *Paper Tigers and Minotaurs: The Politics of Venezuela's Economic Reforms.* Carnegie Endowment for International Peace.

Naím, M. 2009. "What Is a GONGO?" *Foreign Policy*, October 13. https://for eignpolicy.com/2009/10/13/what-is-a-gongo/.

Naím, M., and R. Piñango (eds.). 1984. "El Caso Venezuela: Una Ilusión de Armonía." IESA.

Nakamura, D., and R. Barnes. 2020. "With Time Running Out, Trump and GOP Allies Turn Up Pressure on Supreme Court in Election Assault." *Washington Post*, December 10.

Nasi, C., and M. Hurtado. 2018. "Las elecciones presidenciales del 2014 y las negociaciones de paz con las FARC cuando la estrategia de polarizar no basta para ganar." In *Polarización y posconflicto*, edited by F. Botero, M. G. Sánchez, and L. Wills-Otero, 229–68. Universidad de los Andes, Colombia.

Nathan, A. J. 2003. "China's Changing of the Guard: Authoritarian Resilience." *Journal of Democracy* 14 (1): 6–17.

Negretto, G. 2006. "Minority Presidents and Democratic Performance in Latin America." *Latin American Politics and Society* 48 (3): 63–92.

Neuman, W. 2014a. "Slum Dwellers in Caracas Ask, What Protests?" *New York Times*, February 28.

Neuman, W. 2014b. "Support from the Left Helps Keep a Right-Wing President in Power in Colombia." *New York Times*, June 19.

Noboa, A. 2015. "La historia del CNE desde sus inicios en 2008." *El Comercio*, January 20. www.elcomercio.com/actualidad/politica/historia-cne-funcion-electoral.html.

Norden, D. L. 2021. "Venezuela: Coup-Proofing from Pérez Jiménez to Maduro." *Oxford Research Encyclopedia*, Oxford University Press.

North, D. C., W. Summerhill, and B. R. Weingast. 2000. "Order, Disorder, and Economic Change: Latin America versus North America." In *Governing for Prosperity*, edited by B. B. de Mesquita and H. L. Root, 23–29. Yale University Press.

Norwich University Online. 2020. "Do Economic Sanctions Work?" https://online.norwich.edu/academic-programs/resources/do-economic-sanctions-work.

O'Boyle, B. 2017. "On the Front Lines of Venezuela's Worsening HIV/AIDS Crisis." *Americas Quarterly*, October 25.

O'Donnell, G., and P. Schmitter. 1986. *Transitions from Authoritarian Rule: Tentative Conclusions about Uncertain Democracies*. Johns Hopkins University Press.

O'Hagan, E. M. 2014. "Why Colombia's Left and the West Welcome a Right-wing President." *The Guardian*, June 17.

Obert, J. 2018. *The Six-Shooter State: Public and Private Violence in American Politics*. Cambridge University Press.

Observatorio Venezolano de Conflictividad Social. (Various Years). Conflictividad Social en Venezuela. Annual Reports.

Obuchi, R., A. Abadí, and B. Lira. 2011. *Gestión en rojo: Evaluación de desempeño de 16 empresas estatales y resultados generales del modelo productivo socialista*. Ediciones IESA.

OEA. 2006. "Informe de la Misión de Observación Electoral en la República Bolivariana de Venezuela Elecciones Parlamentarias 2005." Organización de los Estados Americanos, April 27. www.oas.org/documents/Venezuela/informe_mision_2005.pdf.

Office of the United Nations High Commissioner for Human Rights. 2017. "Human Rights Violations and Abuses in the Context of Protests in the

Bolivarian Republic of Venezuela from 1 April to 31 July 2017." www.ohchr
.org/Documents/Countries/VE/HCReportVenezuela_1April-31July2017_
EN.pdf.

Office of the United Nations High Commissioner for Human Rights. 2018.
"Violaciones de los Derechos Humanos en la Rep blica Bolivariana de Ven-
ezuela: una espiral descendente que no parece tener fin." www.ohchr.org/
Documents/Countries/VE/VenezuelaReport2018_SP.pdf.

Office of the United Nations High Commissioner for Human Rights. 2020.
"Independence of the Justice System and Access to Justice in the Bolivar-
ian Republic of Venezuela, including for Violations of Economic and Social
Rights, and the Situation of Human Rights in the Arco Minero del Orinoco
Region." https://reliefweb.int/sites/reliefweb.int/files/resources/A_HRC_44
_54.pdf.

Olivar, J. A. 2020. "Las Fuerzas Armadas, su concepción y desarrollo a lo largo
del siglo XX." Prodavinci, November 29.

Ordóñez, A., E. Samman, C. Mariotti, and I. M. Borja Borja. 2015. "Sharing the
Fruits of Progress: Poverty Reduction in Ecuador. Development Progress."
Overseas Development Institute, October.

Osborne, S. 2017. "Venezuela Presidential Election: Nicolas Maduro's Government Blocks Opposition Candidates from Competing." *The Independent*, December 21.

Pachano, S. 2018. "Ecuador: fin de ciclo y elecciones." In *Elecciones y partidos en
América Latina en el cambio de ciclo*, edited by M. Alcántara, D. Buquet, and
M. L. Tagina. Centro de Investigaciones Sociológicas (CIS).

Pachón, M. 2009. "Colombia 2008: Éxitos, peligros y desaciertos de la política de
seguridad democrática de la administración Uribe." *Revista de Ciencia Política*
29 (2): 327–53.

Pape, R. A. 1997. "Why Economic Sanctions Do Not Work." *International Security* 22 (2): 90–136.

Pappas, T. S. 2019. *Populism and Liberal Democracy: A Comparative and Theoretical Analysis*. Oxford University Press.

Pardo, D. 2017. "¿Fraude en la Constituyente? Los argumentos de la oposición
para desconocer los 8 millones de las elecciones del domingo (y qué dice el
chavismo)." BBC Mundo, July 13.

Párraga, M. 2018. "Presidente Maduro designa nuevamente a Iris Varela como
ministra para el Servicio Penitenciario." Ministerio del Poder Popular para
el Servicio Penitenciario (MPPSP), January 8. www.mppsp.gob.ve/index.php
/noticias/2796-presidente-Maduro-designa-iris-varela-como-ministra-para
-servicio-penitenciario.

Partlow, J., and R. Krygier. 2017. "How a New Kind of Protest Movement Has
Risen in Venezuela." *Washington Post*, June 3.

Paton Walsh, N., N. Gallón, and D. Castrillon. 2019. "Corruption in Venezuela
Has Created a Cocaine Superhighway to the U.S." CNN, April 17.

PBS (Public Broadcasting Service). 2020. "Threatened with Violence, Venezuela's Juan Guaido on Finding 'Urgent Solution' to Crisis," January 17.

Penfold, M. 2017. "Clientelism and Social Funds: Evidence from Chávez's Misiones." *Latin American Politics and Society* 49 (4): 63–84.

Penfold, M. 2016. "El país que espera la lluvia." Prodavinci, April 9.

Penfold, M. 2021. "Democratization in Venezuela: Thoughts on a New Path." Woodrow Wilson Center, November. www.wilsoncenter.org/publication/democratization-venezuela-thoughts-new-path.

Penfold-Becerra, M. 2004. "Federalism and Institutional Change in Venezuela." In *Federalism and Democracy in Latin America*, edited by E. L. Gibson. Johns Hopkins University Press.

Pérez-Liñán, A. 2005. "Democratization and Constitutional Crises in Presidential Regimes: Toward Congressional Supremacy?" *Comparative Political Studies* 38 (1): 51–74.

Pérez-Liñán, A. 2007. *Presidential Impeachment and the New Political Instability in Latin America*. Cambridge University Press.

Pérez-Liñán, A., N. Schmidt, and D. Vairo. 2019. "Presidential Hegemony and Democratic Backsliding in Latin America, 1925–2016." *Democratization* 26 (4): 606–25.

Pérez Vivas, C. 2019. "Las minas de Nicolás." *El Nacional*, October 23.

Pestana, R., and B. Latell. 2017. "Nicaraguan Military Culture." Military Culture Series. Jack D. Gordon Institute for Public Policy, Florida International University. https://gordoninstitute.fiu.edu/research/military-culture-series/randy-pestana-and-brian-latell-2017-nicaraguan-military-culture1.pdf.

Pestano, A. V. 2016. "Recall of Venezuela's Nicolas Maduro May Not Happen This Year." United Press International, September 22.

Philip, G. 1984. "Military-Authoritarianism in South America: Brazil, Chile, Uruguay and Argentina." *Political Studies* 32 (1): 1–20.

Phippen, J. W. 2017. "Violence and Claims of Fraud in Venezuelan Vote." *The Atlantic*, July 31.

Pierson, B. 2017. "Nephews of Venezuela's First Lady Sentenced to 18 years in U.S. Drug Case." Reuters, December 14.

Pion-Berlin, D. 1992. "Military Autonomy and Emerging Democracies in South America." *Comparative Politics* 25 (1): 83–102.

Polga-Hecimovich, J. 2015. "How Did Venezuela's MUD Get Its Supermajority?" *Global Americans*, December 14.

Polga-Hecimovich, J. 2019. "Ecuadorian Military Culture." Military Culture Series. Miami: Jack D. Gordon Institute for Public Policy, Florida International University. https://gordoninstitute.fiu.edu/research/military-culture-series/john-polga-hecimovich-2019-ecuadorian-military-culture1.pdf.

Polga-Hecimovich, J. 2020. "Reshaping the State: The Unitary Executive Presidency of Rafael Correa." In *Assessing the Left Turn in Ecuador*, edited by F. Sánchez and S. Pachano, 15–39. Palgrave Macmillan.

Poliszuk, J., and P. Marcano. 2019. "Los jueces de Venezuela asfaltan calles y firman sentencias." ArmandoInfo, February 17. https://armando.info/los-jueces -de-Venezuela-asfaltan-calles-y-firman-sentencias/.

Politika UCAB (Universidad Católica Andrés Bello). 2020. "Mercedes De Freitas: 'Desde hace 17 años en Venezuela existe un patrón sostenido e indolente de corrupción.'" July 2. https://politikaucab.net/2020/07/02/mercedes-de-frei tas-desde-hace-17-anos-en-Venezuela-existe-un-patron-sostenido-e-indolente -de-corrupcion/.

Portafolio. 2019. "La crisis del agua seguirá en una Venezuela sedienta." April 11. www.portafolio.co/internacional/las-causas-de-la-falta-de-agua-en-Venezuela -528475.

Posada-Carbó, E. 2011. "Latin America: Colombia after Uribe." *Journal of Democracy* 22 (1): 137–51.

Pozzebon, S. 2020. "Venezuela Is Quietly Quitting Socialism." CNN, December 18.

Pozzebon, S., and H. A. Alam. 2019. "Venezuelan Government Quashes Military Uprising." CNN, January 21. https://edition.cnn.com/2019/01/21/americas/ Venezuelan-government-military-uprising/index.html.

Przeworski, A. 1991. *Democracy and the Market: Political and Economic Reforms in Eastern Europe and Latin America.* Cambridge University Press.

Puente, J. M., and J. R. Rodríguez. 2015. "Venezuela en crisis: La economía en 2014 y 2015." *Debates IESA* 20 (3): 62–66.

Quintero, Luisa. 2018. "Nombraron a Freddy Bernal Como 'Protector Del Táchira.'" *TalCual*, January 31.

Ragas, J. 2017. "A Starving Revolution: ID Cards and Food Rationing in Bolivarian Venezuela." *Surveillance & Society* 15 (3/4): 590–95.

Ramsey, G., and D. Smilde. 2020. "Beyond the Narcostate Narrative: What U.S. Drug Monitoring Data Says about Venezuela." Washington Office of Latin America (WOLA), March. www.wola.org/wp-content/uploads/2020/ 03/Narcostate-Venezuela-Drug-Trafficking-Ramsey-Smilde.pdf.

Redondo, R. 2020. "Concern in Venezuela and Turkey over the Arrest of Alex Saab." Atalayar, June 16. https://atalayar.com/en/content/concern-Venezuela -and-turkey-over-arrest-alex-saab.

Remmer, K. L. 1991. "The Political Impact of Economic Crisis in Latin America in the 1980s." *American Political Science Review* 85 (3): 777–800.

Rettberg, A. 2010. "Colombia 2009, Progress and Uncertainty." *Revista de Ciencia Política* 30 (2): 249–73.

Reuters. 2017a. "Leftist Vies with Ex-Banker in Nail-Biter Ecuador Presidency Vote." Reuters, February 19.

Reuters. 2017b. "Venezuela Elections: Opposition Calls for Protests after Socialist Party Claims Win." Reuters, October 16.

Rey, J. C. 1991. "La democracia venezolana y la crisis del sistema populista de conciliación. *Revista de Estudios Políticos (Nueva Época)* 74 (October–December): 533–79.

Rice, R. 2021. "Two Different Visions of the Left Divide Ecuador in the 2021 Presidential Election." NACLA, February 13.

Roberts, K. M. 1995. "Neoliberalism and the Transformation of Populism in Latin America: The Peruvian Case." *World Politics* 48 (1): 82–116.

Roberts, K. M. 1998. *Deepening Democracy? The Modern Left and Social Movements in Chile and Peru.* Stanford University Press.

Robles, F. 2016. "Wife and Running Mate: A Real-Life 'House of Cards' in Nicaragua." *New York Times,* October 30.

Robles, F. 2019. "Nicaraguan Supreme Court Justice Slams His Former Ally, President Ortega." *New York Times,* January 12.

Rodiles, A. G. 2014. "Los 'Colectivos' y las 'Brigadas de Respuesta Rápida', cómo funcionan." Estado de Sats, February 22. www.estadodesats.com/los-colectivos-y-las-brigadas-de-respuesta-rapida-como-funcionan/.

Rodríguez, F. 2008. "An Empty Revolution: The Unfulfilled Promises of Hugo Chávez." *Foreign Affairs* 87 (2): 49–62.

Rodríguez, F. 2021. "Toxic Conflict: Understanding Venezuela's Economic Collapse, Kellog Institute for International Studies, Working Paper 446 (November), University of Notre Dame.

Rodríguez, F. 2021. *Toxic Conflict: Understanding Venezuela's Economic Collapse.* Kellogg Institute for International Studies, University of Notre Dame.

Rodríguez, Francisco and Jorge Alejandro Rodríguez. 2019. Venezuela's Powerless Revolution. *The New York Times* (March 26).

Rodríguez, R. E. 2018. "Elecciones en Venezuela: ¿Qué puede hacer la oposición?" *Razón Pública,* January 29. https://razonpublica.com/elecciones-en-Venezuela-que-puede-hacer-la-oposicion/.

Rodríguez, R. E. 2020. "The Venezuelan Economy between the Dollar and the Bolivar." *Global Comment,* February 6. https://globalcomment.com/the-Venezuelan-economy-between-the-dollar-and-the-bolivar/.

Romero, C. A. 2012. "Petróleo y rentismo entre Cuba y Venezuela." Association for the Study of the Cuban Economy (ASCE) Annual Conference.

Romero, C. A., and S. Pedraza. 2013. "Cuba and Venezuela: Revolution and Reform." Association for the Study of the Cuban Economy (ASCE) Annual Conference.

Rosales, A. 2019. "Statization and denationalization dynamics in Venezuela's artisanal and small scale-large-scale mining interface." *Resources Policy* 63: 101422.

Ross, M. L. 2012. *The Oil Curse: How Petroleum Wealth Shapes the Development of Nations.* Princeton University Press.

Reuters. 2020. "Venezuela Appoints Alleged Drug Trafficker El Aissami as Oil Minister." Reuters, April 27.

Sachs, J. D., and A. M. Warner. 1995. "Natural Resource Abundance and Economic Growth." Working Paper 5398, National Bureau of Economics Research (NBER).

Sagarzazu, I., and C. G. Thies. 2019. "The Foreign Policy Rhetoric of Populism: Chávez, Oil, and Anti-Imperialism." *Political Research Quarterly* 72 (1): 205–14.

Salamanca, L. 2004. "Civil Society: Late Bloomers." In *The Unraveling of Representative Democracy in Venezuela*, edited by J. L. McCoy and D. Myers. Johns Hopkins University Press, 93–114.

Salmerón, V. 2013. *Petróleo y desmadre: de la Gran Venezuela a la Revolución Bolivariana*. Editorial Alfa.

Sanchez-Sibony, O. 2017. "Classifying Ecuador's Regime under Correa: A Procedural Approach." *Journal of Politics in Latin America* 9 (3): 121–40.

Sanchez-Sibony, O. 2018. "Competitive Authoritarianism in Ecuador under Correa." *Taiwan Journal of Democracy* 14 (2): 97–120.

Sanchez, F. 2019. "Venezuela's Government Puts Down Mutiny by National Guard Unit in Poor Neighborhood." *Chicago Tribune*, January 21.

Santistevan Gastelú, B. 2019. "Designan a Carlos Osorio Presidente De Corporación Minera." *El Universal*, July 2.

Santos, M. A. 2021. "La Venezuela del día después (y la del día antes)." In *Comunidad Venezuela. Una agenda de investigación y acción local*, edited by A. Fajardo and A. Vargas, 44–65. Bogotá, Centro de los Objetivos de Desarrollo Sostenible para América Latina y el Caribe (CODS) and International Development Research Centre (IDRC).

Schedler, A. (ed.). 2006. *Electoral Authoritarianism: The Dynamics of Unfree Competition*. Lynne Rienner.

Scheppele, K. L. 2018. "Autocratic Legalism." *The University of Chicago Law Review* 85: 545–83.

Schmitter, P., and T. L. Karl. 1991. "What Democracy Is . . . and Is Not" *Journal of Democracy* 2: 75–88.

Seawright, J. 2012. *Party-System Collapse: The Roots of Crisis in Peru and Venezuela*. Stanford University Press.

Secretaría de Comunicación de la Presidencia. 2014. "Rafael Correa, entre los 3 mandatarios con mayor aprobación en Latinoamérica." www.comunicacion .gob.ec/rafael-correa-entre-los-3-mandatarios-con-mayor-aprobacion-en-lati noamerica/.

Seijas Rodríguez, F. 2020. "How to Explain Maduro's Radical Move against Guaidó." *Americas Quarterly*, January 4.

Semana. 2018. "Cuando César Gaviria le hacía campaña a Juan Manuel Santos." *Semana*, January 23.

Sen, A. 1983. *Poverty and Famines: An Essay on Entitlement and Deprivation Reprint Edition*. Oxford University Press.

Sen, A. 2000. *Development as Freedom*. Anchor.

Sequera, V. 2014. "Did Attempted Rape Ignite Venezuela's National Protests?" *Christian Science Monitor*, February 22.

Serbin, A., and A. Serbin Pont. 2017. "The Foreign Policy of the Bolivarian Republic of Venezuela: The Role and Legacy of Hugo Chávez." *Latin American Policy* 8 (2): 232–48.

Sheridan, M. B., and M. Zúñiga. 2019. "Maduro's Muscle: Politically Backed Motorcycle Gangs Known as 'Colectivos' Are the Enforcers for Venezuela's Authoritarion Leader." *Washington Post*, March14.

Shifter, M. 2016. "Civil-Military Relations Sour as Correa Amasses Power in Ecuador." *World Politics Review*, March 3.

Shugart, M. S., and J. M. Carey. 1992. *Presidents and Assemblies: Constitutional Design and Electoral Dynamics*. Cambridge University Press.

Sinergia. 2018. "Agenda 2030 y emergencia humanitaria: Venezuela, un país en franca involución," July 17. www.scribd.com/document/384036259/Agenda -2030-y-Emergencia-Humanitaria-Venezuela-Un-Pais-en-Franca-Involucion #from_embed.

Sinnot, E., J. N. Sinnot, and A. de la Torre. 2010. *Natural Resources in Latin America and the Caribbean: Beyond Booms and Busts?* World Bank.

Smilde, D. 2017. "Q & A on Venezuela's HIV Treatment Crisis." Venezuelan Politics and Human Rights, Washington Office on Latin America, December 12.

Smilde, D. 2021. "Trump's Bluster Failed Venezuela. Biden Must Use Diplomatic and Economic Levers to Address the Crisis." *Washington Post*, January 19.

Smilde, D., and G. Ramsey. 2020. "International Peacemaking in Venezuela's Intractable Conflict." *European Review of Latin American and Caribbean Studies* 109: 157–79.

Smilde, David. 2021. "From Populist to Socialist to Authoritarian Chavismo: Obstacles and Opportunities for Democratic Change." Washington, D.C.: Woodrow Wilson Center, Latin America Program.

Smith, A. E. 2019. "What Does Authoritarianism Have to Do with Venezuela's Food Fight? Everything." Vox, February 25.

Smith, S. 2017. "Ecuador's Accomplishments under the 10 Years of Rafael Correa's Citizen's Revolution." Council on Hemispheric Affairs, April 17. www .coha.org/ecuadors-accomplishments-under-the-10-years-of-rafael-correas -citizens-revolution/.

Soto, N. 2019. "A Vast Corruption Network." Caracas Chronicles, July 26.

Soto, N. 2020. "Access to Gas Will Be Controlled with the Carnet de la Patria." Caracas Chronicles, June 1.

Soto, N., and P. Laya. 2018. "Venezuela's Constituent Assembly Names Cabello as President." Bloomberg, July 18.

Southwick, N., and J. Otis. 2018. "The U-Turn: Moreno Steers Ecuador Away from Correa's Media Repression." Committee to Protect Journalists, July 12. https://cpj.org/reports/2018/07/u-turn-moreno-steers-ecuador-away-correa-media-communication-law/.

Spencer, D. 2012. "Lessons from Colombia's Road to Recovery, 1982–2010." CHDS Occasional Paper. Center for Hemispheric Defense Studies, May. https://williamjperrycenter.org/content/lessons-colombia%E2%80%99s-road-recovery-1982-2010.

Spetalnick, M. 2019. "U.S. Readies Sanctions, Charges over Venezuela Food Program: Sources." Reuters, May 21.

Stasavage, D. 2020. *The Decline and Rise of Democracy: A Global History from Antiquity to Today.* Princeton University Press.

Stefanoni, P. 2017. "Venezuela: Why Don't the Popular Sectors Revolt? An Interview with Alejandro Velasco." NACLA, July 3.

Stokes, S. 2001. *Mandates and Democracy: Neoliberalism by Surprise.* Cambridge University Press.

Stolk, R. 2015. "Dark Days Ahead." Caracas Chronicles, July 16.

Strønen, I. Å. 2016. "A Civil-Military Alliance: The Venezuelan Armed Forces before and during the Chávez Era." CMI Working Paper 2016: 4. Chr. Michelsen Institute.

Stuenkel, O. 2019. "After Correa, Ecuador's Moreno Is Struggling to Offer His Own Vision." *Americas Quarterly,* February 27.

Sucre, F., and H. Briceño. 2016. "Venezuela 2016: Alliances on Trial." The Inter-American Dialogue, February 18. www.thedialogue.org/blogs/2016/02/Venezuela-2016-alliances-on-trial/.

Sudduth, J. K. 2017. "Coup Risk, Coup-Proofing and Leader Survival." *Journal of Peace Research* 54 (1): 3–15.

Sullivan, J. P. 2013. "How Illicit Networks Impact Sovereignty." In *Convergence: Illicit Networks and National Security Organization,* edited by M. Miklaucic and J. Brewer. National Defense University Press.

Svolik, M. W. 2012. *The Politics of Authoritarian Rule.* Cambridge University Press.

Svolik, M. W. 2019. "Polarization versus Democracy." *Journal of Democracy* 30 (3): 20–32.

Taylor, M. M. 2014. "The Limits of Judicial Independence: A Model with Illustration from Venezuela under Chávez." *Journal of Latin American Studies* 46 (2): 229–59.

TeleSUR. 2016. "Ecuador, el primero en reducir la inequidad en Latinoamérica." TeleSUR, October 19.

TeleSUR. 2017. "Venezuela to Install Truth, Justice and Reparations Commission." TeleSUR, August 6.

TeleSUR. 2019. "Venezuela's Constituent Assembly Removes Guaido's Immunity." TeleSUR, April 2.

Thaler, K. M. 2017. "Nicaragua: A Return to Caudillismo." *Journal of Democracy* 28 (2): 157–69.

Thurow, L. C. 1996. *The Future of Capitalism: How Today's Economic Forces Shape Tomorrow's World*. Penguin Books.

Thyne, C. L., and J. M. Powell. 2016. "Coup d'Etat or Coup d'Autocracy? How Coups Impact Democratization, 1950–2008 1." *Foreign Policy Analysis* 12 (2): 192–213.

Tian, N., and D. Lopes da Silva. 2019. "The Crucial Role of the Military in the Venezuelan Crisis." Stockholm International Peace Research Institute (SIPRI), April 2. www.sipri.org/commentary/topical-backgrounder/2019/crucial-role-military-venezuelan-crisis.

Tilly, C. 1985. "Warmaking and State Making as Organized Crime." In *Bringing the State Back In*, edited by P. P. Evans, D. Rueschemeyer, and T. Skocpol. Cambridge University Press.

Tomini, L. 2017. *When Democracies Collapse: Assessing Transitions to Non-Democratic Regimes in the Contemporary World*. Taylor & Francis.

Torres, C. 2020. "Venezuelan Government Denounces Attempted Invasion from Colombia on La Guaira Coast." Ministerio Del Poder Popular Para Relaciones Exteriores (MPPRE), May 3. www.mppre.gob.ve/en/2020/05/03/Venezuelan-government-denounces-attempted-invasion-from-colombia-on-la-guaira-coast/.

Torres, P., and N. Casey. 2017. "Armed Civilian Bands in Venezuela Prop Up Unpopular President." *New York Times*, April 22.

Transparencia Venezuela. 2015. "Parlamentarias: Venezuela 2015." August 20. https://transparencia.org.ve/wp-content/uploads/2016/07/Boleti%CC%81n-1-parlamentarias-2015.pdf.

Transparencia Venezuela. 2019. "Manual contra la corrupción: 12 acciones y un mandato." January 21. https://transparencia.org.ve/transparencia-Venezuela-guia-a-los-venezolanos-en-la-lucha-contra-la-corrupcion/.

Transparencia Venezuela. 2020. "Un conglomerado marcado por la ineficiencia y la opacidad." October. https://transparencia.org.ve/project/un-conglomerado-marcado-por-la-ineficiencia-y-la-opacidad/.

Trinkunas, H. 2005. *Crafting Civilian Control of the Military in Venezuela: A Comparative Perspective*. University of North Carolina Press.

Trinkunas, H. 2019. "The Venezuelan Opposition's High-Stakes Assault on Maduro." *Foreign Affairs*, January 25.

Trivella, A. 2021. "The Communal State: Maduro's Inherited Social Control Machine." Caracas Chronicles, April 13.

U.S. Department of Justice. 2020. "Nicolás Maduro Moros and 14 Current and Former Venezuelan Officials Charged with Narco-Terrorism, Corruption, Drug Trafficking and Other Criminal Charges." March 26. www.justice.gov/opa/pr/nicol-s-Maduro-moros-and-14-current-and-former-Venezuelan-officials-charged-narco-terrorism.

U.S. Department of State. 2020. "The United States Condemns Detention of Interim President Guaido's Family Member." February 15. www.state.gov/the-united-states-condemns-detention-of-interim-president-guaidos-family-member/.

U.S. Department of State. 2021. "Trafficking in Persons Report." July 1. www.state.gov/wp-content/uploads/2021/07/TIP_Report_Final_20210701.pdf.

U.S. Department of the Treasury. 2019. "Treasury Disrupts Corruption Network Stealing from Venezuela's Food Distribution Program, CLAP." July 25. https://home.treasury.gov/news/press-releases/sm741.

Ulmer, A. 2017. "Venezuela's Maduro Is Destructive King Herod, Warns Ex-Oil Czar." Reuters, December 31.

United Nations Human Rights Council. 2020. "Independence of the Justice System and Access to Justice in the Bolivarian Republic of Venezuela, including for Violations of Economic and Social Rights, and the Situation of Human Rights in the Arco Minero del Orinoco Region." https://reliefweb.int/sites/reliefweb.int/files/resources/A_HRC_44_54.pdf.

United States Department of Justice. 2020. "Manhattan U.S. Attorney Announces Narco-Terrorism Charges against Nicolas Maduro, Current and Former Venezuelan Officials, and Farc Leadership." March 26. www.justice.gov/usao-sdny/pr/manhattan-us-attorney-announces-narco-terrorism-charges-against-nicolas-Maduro-current.

United Nations Human Rights Council. 2021. "Report of the independent international fact-finding mission on the Bolivarian Republic of Venezuela," United Nations, September 16. https://reliefweb.int/report/venezuela-bolivarian-republic/report-independent-international-fact-finding-mission-0.

Urdaneta, S., A. Kurmanaev, and I. Herrera. 2020. "Venezuela, Once an Oil Giant, Reaches the End of an Era." *New York Times*, October 7 (updated November 26).

Vachudova, M. A. 2019. "From Competition to Polarization in Central Europe: How Populists Change Party Systems and the European Union." *Polity* 51 (4): 689–706.

Valenzuela, A. 2004. "Latin American Presidencies Interrupted." *Journal of Democracy* 15 (4): 5–19.

Vallejo, V. 2019. "Maduro Released Prisoners to Massacre Pemon Indians." *PanAm Post*, February 24.

van de Walle, N. 2006. "Tipping Games? When Do Opposition Parties Coalesce?" In *Electoral Authoritarianism: The Dynamics of Unfree Competition*, edited by A. Schedler. Lynne Rienner, 77–92.

Varela, C. 2018. "Conindustria asegura que el sector industrial está produciendo solo a 10% de su capacidad." *El Universal*, July 15.

V-Dem (Varieties of Democracy). 2021. Online Graphing Tools. www.v-dem.net/en/online-graphing/.

Velasco, A. 2015. *Barrio Rising: Urban Popular Politics and the Making of Modern Venezuela*. University of California Press.

Venezuela Investigative Unit. 2018a. "Colombia's ELN Reportedly Distributing Venezuela Government Food on the Border." InSight Crime, February 9. www.insightcrime.org/news/analysis/colombia-eln-reportedly-distributing-Venezuela-government-food-border/.

Venezuela Investigative Unit. 2018b. "The Devolution of State Power: The 'Colectivos.'" InSight Crime, May 18. www.insightcrime.org/investigations/devolution-state-power-colectivos/.

Venezuela Investigative Unit. 2018c. "Drug Trafficking within the Venezuelan Regime: The 'Cartel of the Suns.'" InSight Crime, May 17. https://insightcrime.org/investigations/drug-trafficking-Venezuelan-regime-cartel-of-the-sun/.

Venezuela Investigative Unit. 2018d. "7 Reasons for Describing Venezuela as a 'Mafia State.'" InSight Crime, May 16. www.insightcrime.org/investigations/seven-reasons-Venezuela-mafia-state/.

Vera Rojas, S., and S. Llanos Escobar. 2016. "Ecuador: La Democracia después de nueve años de la 'Revolución Ciudadana' de Rafael Correa." *Revista de Ciencia Política* 36 (1): 145–75.

Vincent, I. 2019. "Meet Maduro's Most Corrupt Crony: His Party Boy Son." *New York Post*, July 6.

Vollmer Burelli, C. 2020. "Venezuela's Ecocide Needs International Attention." Center for Strategic and International Studies (CSIS), July 30. www.csis.org/analysis/Venezuelas-ecocide-needs-international-attention.

von Bergen Granell, F. M. 2015. "¿Cuán efectiva fue la campaña de Nicolás Maduro?" Prodavinci, December 16.

von Bergen Granell, F. M. 2017. *Auge y declive de la hegemonía chavista*. Universidad Católica Andrés Bello.

Vyas, K., and J. Forero. 2020. "Venezuelan Opposition Guru Led Planning to Topple Maduro." *Wall Street Journal*, June 26.

Waddell, B. 2019. "One Year after Nicaraguan Uprising, Ortega Is Back in Control." *The Conversation*, April 17.

Wallis, D. 2014. "Venezuela Violence Puts Focus on Militant 'colectivo' Groups." Reuters, February 13.

Way, L. 2011. "Comparing the Arab Revolts: The Lessons of 1989." *Journal of Democracy* 22 (4): 13–23.

Weaver, J., and A. M. Delgado. 2018. "Ring Plundered $1.2 billion of Venezuelan Oil Money, Laundered it in South Florida, Feds Charge." *Miami Herald*, July 25.

Weegels, J. 2018. "Inside Out: Confinement, Revolt and Repression in Nicaragua." Part of the series Speaking Justice to Power: Authoritarianism and Confinement in the Americas. Association for Political and Legal Anthropology.

https://pure.uva.nl/ws/files/34422824/Inside_Out_Confinement_Revolt_and_Repression_in_Nicaragua_Association_for_Pol.pdf.

Weisbrot, M., and J. Sachs. 2019. "Economic Sanctions as Collective Punishment: The Case of Venezuela." Center for Economic and Policy Research, April. https://cepr.net/images/stories/reports/venezuela-sanctions-2019-04.pdf.

Werner, A. 2020. "Outlook for Latin America and the Caribbean: New Challenges to Growth." *IMFBlog*, January 29. https://blogs.imf.org/2020/01/29/outlook-for-latin-america-and-the-caribbean-new-challenges-to-growth/.

Weyland, K. 2001. "Clarifying a Contested Concept." *Comparative Politics* 34 (1): 1–22.

Weyland, K. 2002. *The Politics of Market Reforms in Fragile Democracies*. Princeton University Press.

Weyland, K., and R. L. Madrid. 2018. "Introduction: Donald Trump's Populism: What Are the Prospects for US Democracy." In *When Democracy Trumps Populism: European and Latin American Lessons for the United States*, edited by K. Weyland and R. L. Madrid. Cambridge University Press.

Wills-Otero, L. 2020. "Party Systems in Latin America." In *Oxford Research Encyclopedia of Politics*. Oxford University Press.

Wills-Otero, L., and C. I. Benito. 2012. "De Uribe a Santos: cambios y continuidades en la política colombiana 2011." *Revista de Ciencia Política* 32 (1): 87–107.

Wilpert, G. 2007. *Changing Venezuela: The History and Policies of the Chavez Government*. Verso.

Wolff, J. 2018. "Ecuador after Correa: The Struggle over the 'Citizens' Revolution." *Revista de Ciencia Política* 38 (2): 281–302.

World Bank. 2021. World Development Indicators. https://data.worldbank.org/.

Wyss, J. 2017. "Venezuelan Government Controls More Than 500 Businesses—and Most Are Losing Money." *Miami Herald*, March 14.

Index

Page numbers followed by f or t represent figures or tables, respectively.